Literary Hoaxes

Literary Hoaxes

AN EYE-OPENING HISTORY
OF FAMOUS FRAUDS

by

MELISSA KATSOULIS

A Herman Graf Book
Skyhorse Publishing

For Rosalind Adams: mother, friend, investor

Skyhorse Publishing books may be purchased in bulk at special discounts for sales promotion, corporate gifts, fund-raising, or educational purposes. Special editions can also be created to specifications. For details, contact the Special Sales Department, Skyhorse Publishing, 307 West 36th Street, 11th Floor, New York, NY 10018 or info@skyhorsepublishing.com.

Skyhorse® and Skyhorse Publishing® are registered trademarks of Skyhorse Publishing, Inc.®, a Delaware corporation.

Visit our website at www.skyhorsepublishing.com.

10 9 8 7 6 5 4 3

Library of Congress Cataloging-in-Publication Data

Katsoulis, Melissa.
Literary hoaxes : an eye-opening history of famous frauds / Melissa Katsoulis.
p. cm.
ISBN 978-1-60239-794-1
1. Literary forgeries and mystifications--History. I. Title.
PN171.F6K37 2009
098'.3--dc22
2009030421

Cover design by Adam Bozarth

Paperback ISBN: 978-1-63450-269-6
Hardcover ISBN: 978-1-60239-794-1

Printed and bound in Great Britain by Clays Ltd, St Ives plc

Contents

Contents

Acknowledgments

Special thanks to Gina Rozner, without whom this book would not exist, and also to Andreas Campomar and everyone at Constable. I am grateful to Margaret Body, Giles Coren, Alison Flood, Chaz Folkes, Ivan Helmer, Nicolas Madelaine, Angela Martin, Neel Mukherjee, Michael Prodger, Pete Rozycki, Jerry Sokol, Guy Stevenson, Erica Wagner, Carl Wilkinson. And to Peter Stevenson: the greatest living Greek Scotsman and the love of my life.

INTRODUCTION

*F*ROM DISGRUNTLED MORMONS and fake Native Americans to bored students and lustful aristocrats, the bizarre history of literary hoaxers is every bit as revealing as the orthodox roll-call of Western writers, as is their acute appreciation of what inspires, frightens and resonates with their generation. And their stories are often incredibly funny, too.

This history of the most notable literary hoaxes does not claim to be comprehensive: some well-loved tricksters such as Henry Root and Rochester Sneath have been left out because they seem, on reflection, to be more practical jokers than true hoaxers. Others, like Thomas J. Wise and James Collier, are not included because their rather pedestrian projects must be called forgeries rather than hoaxes. And although it begins in the eighteenth century – the age of the novel and the era when being a publisher or author offered, for the first time, a real chance at what Samuel Johnson called 'the fever of renown' – cases of writers playing games with authorship and authenticity can be traced as far back as the fourth century BC.

Some were hoaxing for their own amusement, as was the case with the philosopher known as Dionysius the Renegade, the earliest hoaxer literary history records. He was the spirited rebel Stoic who, after breaking away from the school which had raised him to believe in the nobility of pain and suffering, manufactured a fake Sophocles play called *Parthenopaeus* and inserted into it a number of insulting acrostics including 'HERACLIDES IS IGNORANT OF LETTERS AND IS NOT ASHAMED OF HIS IGNORANCE'.

Others, such as the unknown author of the famous *Donation of Constantine*, hoaxed for political gain: that two-part document comprising the *Confessio* and *Donatio* which was inserted into a twelfth-century book of canonical law purported to confirm the Emperor Constantine's gift of European dominion to the church in return for Pope Sylvester curing him of leprosy and revealing to him Christ's love.

To understand the significance of the stories collected here (most of which can and should be read as much for sheer amusement at the amazing lengths to which people will go to practise a deception, and the sheer nonsense gullible readers are willing to swallow, as for literary-historical edification) it is useful to consider the three main types of hoax, and the thorny subject of truth-telling in literature more generally.

Not all hoaxes are equal and although the ones chosen for inclusion in this book are arranged chronologically within chapters, they might just as easily have been broken down into the three distinct groups that most hoaxes can be said to fall into. The American academic Brian McHale, one of the surprisingly few literary theorists to attempt a comprehensive taxonomy of the written hoax, has identified these groups as: the genuine hoax, the entrapment hoax and the mock hoax.

Into the first group fall the majority of examples, and nearly all of the very famous ones. The Hitler Diaries, the Ossian poems, William Ireland's Shakespeare papers and the *Donation of Constantine* can all be given McHale's playfully oxymoronic label 'genuine hoax' because they are dishonest literary creations which are intended never to be exposed. They might be done for reasons of financial, ideological or emotional gain, but they are neither self-conscious works of art nor are they intended to poke fun at specific individuals or institutions. The perpetrators of these hoaxes tend to be unfortunate creatures who have been unable to find success with their legitimate works and who are desperate either for the money or recognition that literary success can bring. The eighteenth century's William Ireland is a prime example: he was a boy growing up in London amidst the 1790s frenzy for collecting and classifying European cultural artefacts. Studiously ignored by his bibliophile father, he was considered dim and hopeless and forced into a humble clerking job which he hated. Yet on the day he first presented his Shakespeare-obsessed parent with a piece of paper purporting to bear the bard's signature, all his life's problems began to evaporate. Overnight, he became the focus of his father's undivided attention, praised for his brilliance in sourcing and negotiating deals for the series of Shakespearean papers he was secretly producing using antique paper and specially mixed ink.

The main reason for Ireland's eventual undoing was that he was not a skilled enough writer to convince critics that his 'discovered' works were genuine. Other pliers of 'genuine hoaxes', however, were such skilled stylists that their work has continued to be held in high regard even after debunking and death. Thomas Chatterton's Rowley poems and the bardic verses by Macpherson are both cases in point, and continue to be read and studied today as worthwhile creations in their own right; and particularly in the case of Chatterton, the ill-fated young medievalist from Bristol who came to London to seek his fortune but fell victim to poverty and desperation before his talents could out, the high romance of the hoaxer's real-life story has proved irresistible to future generations. Of all the hoaxers who have caught the imagination of later writers (Ern Malley and Anthony Godby Johnson's appearance in novels by Peter Carey and Armistead Maupin being other examples) the life of Chatterton has continued to inspire great secondary works of art by authors from John Keats to Peter Ackroyd.

Perhaps the boldest 'genuine hoax' is one of the least known, and dates from fifteenth-century Italy. It involves a monk called Annius from Viterbo, near Rome, who so loved his hometown that he stopped at nothing to prove his patriotism – not at planting faked Etruscan fragments of pottery in his neighbour's earth, not at claiming to have discovered hugely significant lost writings by the early religious writer Berosus which claimed that Viterbo was where Noah's offspring first repopulated the world with Aryans after the flood. Nearly a century later his hoaxes were debunked, using the same new forensic critical techniques which exposed the *Donation of Constantine*: careful line-by-line analysis of vocabulary, orthography and parallel texts. And no small amount of common sense.

Chatterton and his ilk might be tragic figures, but the second group of hoaxers has left a body of work more likely to inspire glee than sympathy. These are the people whose intention is to lure a particular academic, publisher or literary community with a prank text and then reveal (often through clues planted in the manuscript itself) how stupid its readers were to believe it – and, by extension, how clever the hoaxer was to trick them. The most famous hoax in Australia – and indeed in twentieth-century English-language poetry in general – was the invented oeuvre of Ern Malley, secretly written by a pair of disgruntled young traditional poets, James McAuley and Harold Stewart, who claimed at the time to have dashed off the ultra-modernist poems in an afternoon. (They almost certainly did not, and ironically are now considered to have produced some of their best work under the Malley name.) They were neither the first nor last group of twentieth-century writers to create bogus texts to make a dismissive point about the cultural fads of their day, and all of their ilk reveal as much about their target audience as they do about themselves. Particularly the Spectra poetry hoax in 1916 (the motivation behind which was similar to McAuley and Stewart's) and the superbly awful erotic novel *Naked Came the Stranger* in 1969, which set out to prove that as long as a book was full of sex it need have no literary merit to succeed. And it is not only lovers of fashionable fiction who get pricked by the hoaxer's barb: when the physicist Alan Sokal successfully submitted a paper composed of pseudo-sociological gibberish to a leading cultural studies journal in the mid-1990s, he proved spectacularly that the entrapment hoax was alive and well. Then, in 2006, the official biographer of

John Betjeman hid the immortal words 'A N WILSON IS A SHIT' in a fake Betjeman love-letter which he submitted to his rival biographer under the anagrammatic name 'Eve de Harben', which was blithely included in the first edition of Wilson's work on the poet. The entrapment hoaxes, although deliberately bringing disrepute to fellow professionals, are certainly some of the most fun to read, and constitute an un-sobering reminder of the value of play and theatre in the often self-important business of publishing and academia.

The final group is also the smallest, but that may not be the case forever. 'Mock hoaxes' are those in which a genuinely experimental writer plays conscious tricks with the very notion of authorship to create a voice which is neither quite theirs nor someone else's. It is the kind of literary ventriloquism we see in the work of Fern Gravel, the ten-year-old girl-poet who gained a cult following in mid-twentieth-century America but was, in truth, an ageing, male writer of adventure stories; the Canadian poet who could only cure his writer's block by adopting the persona of a grizzled Greek fisherman called Karavis; and the eccentric academic almost certainly behind the controversial Hiroshima witness poetry submitted to literary journals under the name Yasusada.

'Mock hoaxes' are often highly literary because they are executed by experienced writers with a genuine artistic end in mind. James Norman Hall, the creator of Fern Gravel, for example, was intent on finding a new, softer outlet for a narrative voice honed on adventure stories and wartime memoir. He believed passionately in the value of the work that his alter-ego was producing and, although it was childish and unsophisticated, critics agree that there is something more substantial than mere charm to Fern's melancholic coming-of-age poems. Of course, not every hoax fits neatly into only one of McHale's three categories, but his groupings do help to identify the main reasons why the peculiar and often underrated writers whose stories are told in these pages did what they did.

From the aristocratic sex addict who wrote outrageous things about the empress Cixi in *fin de siècle* Shanghai to the lonely middle-aged lady who invented for herself a dying, memoir-writing son, all human life is here, and the one thing they nearly all have in common is that they are writing from the margins. Even if they have had a materially privileged start in life or are possessed of a sharp intelligence, at some point each hoaxer has been made to feel excluded from the world they would be part of. An astonishing number of them were missing a parent. Most had once been praised for their literary abilities, but had failed to find success by conventional means. And almost all have a community – real or imagined – whose ways and boundaries they are seeking to protect in their writings. The 'entrapment hoaxers' try to safeguard what they see as the authentic values of their social or academic kin against attacks from new-fangled trends. The 'genuine hoaxers' seek a way to make an imagined world seem real enough for the reading public to buy into. And for those post-modern experimentalists who produce 'mock hoaxes', even their hyper-identity as a writer is meant to be included in the 'reality' of their text.

Reality itself becomes a problem, however, the further one looks into these texts and the more one asks of literature as a gate-keeper of truth. The assumption that some kinds of writing are truer than others is not as straightforward as it might sound. Can it categorically be said that novels are untrue and memoirs are true? Surely not, as anyone who has basked in the wisdom of a great work of art (written, painted or played) will know that the only way to convey what it is like to be alive is to conjure something aesthetically complex enough to approximate to our experience of reality. Because reality, after all, is nothing if not a mystery. Writers of memoir, biography and straight non-fiction have a more tenuous claim on the faithful transmission of truth than might at first be supposed because stories about people, places and events can only ever be passed down through the imperfect, partial minds of others.

A recent example of the memoirist's art coming under theoretical and popular scrutiny is the infamous American author James Frey, whose bestselling book *A Million Little Pieces* claimed to tell the true, harrowing tale of his descent into drug and alcohol abuse and his remarkable self-guided recovery. The book was a huge success on publication in the US in 2003, and the author was held up by Oprah Winfrey as a beacon for others on the road to recovery. Frey's writing style was spare, seemingly immensely candid and instantly readable, and he told stories of extreme physical and mental hardship. Much of what he wrote seemed almost too intense to be true, and indeed it was. But when he was had up for fabricating portions of the book, he argued that the essence of the thing was absolutely real and he had merely changed certain details to better convey the truth of what happened, and to protect the other people involved. There were also rumours of Frey first submitting his manuscript as fiction but being advised that a 'misery memoir' would sell better . . .

The rise and rise of the late-twentieth-century genre known as 'misery memoir' is a peculiarity of contemporary publishing which deserves a closer look, not least because the popularity of books with titles like *Please, Daddy, No!* say a great deal about who we are as readers and what makes us so susceptible to hoaxing. Uplifting stories of personal hardship are clearly very appealing to us and always have been. The defining story of the Christian age gives a clue as to how much we need to witness the pain of others, and as well as the Bible's cast of auxiliary sufferers (Job, Noah et al) most other religions have their own fables about people or gods enduring trials and difficult journeys. Classical tragedians responded to this, understanding the value of catharsis in such tales, and in English literature from Chaucer, Shakespeare and Milton to Bunyan, Defoe and Dickens, there has been a steady stream of popular fiction about men whose physical and mental realities are defined by punishment or abuse. It was not until the twentieth century and the emergence of modern publishing, however, that the idea of actually faking 'real' bad experiences took hold.

The now-forgotten hoaxer Joan Lowell in 1920s New York fooled the publishers Simon & Schuster into believing she had been the sole female on a years-long merchant seamen's voyage and as a result engaged in all manner of unladylike acts. Other phoney memoirists, like the pseudonymous Cleone Knox with her faux-eighteenth century *Diary of a Young Lady of Fashion* or the 'Anonymous' author of the cult drug-diary *Go Ask Alice* who turned out to be a middle-aged Mormon with an axe to grind, hid behind their lurid creations until they could no longer sustain the deceit.

Pretending to have been involved in illicit escapades as a teenage girl hardly compares to the most shocking subsection of fake memoirists, the Holocaust pretenders: Binjamin Wilkomirski, Misha Defonseca, Herman Rosenblat and Helen Demidenko each had different reason for pretending to have been a victim – or in Demidenko's case, supporter – of Hitler's regime. Surprisingly, what can be pieced together of their 'real' true stories often reveals biographies which were every bit as full of adventure, sacrifice and passion as their assumed selves, only without the massively emotive signifier of Nazism.

The second most fascinating question after 'Why lie about the Holocaust?' is 'Why are there so many hoaxers from Australia?' It is true that given the young age and small literary community of that country, a wholly disproportionate number of writers have made their name there on the basis of dishonest claims about authorship. Just as hoaxing says something about what writing is for, so Australia tells us an important truth about hoaxing. In the literary trickery of writers like Marlo Morgan, Nino Culotta and Wanda Koolmatrie we see the bare ambition of the hoaxer writ large and simple. For Wanda, an unpublished white man writing as an indigenous Australian woman, it was an anxiety about nationhood and immigration that made him submit his phoney manuscript. Nino Culotta's motivation was similar but less angry: he, another white Australian writing as a foreigner (this time an Italian builder) wanted to tell some quirky truths about the closed world of the working-class Australian male and saw that his best way of doing so was in the guise of an outsider looking in. Marlo Morgan and Norma Khouri are interesting cases because both are American but have used their belief that Australia is in some way cut off from the rest of the global cultural community to forge a career in illicit memoir writing. Morgan's bestselling *Mutant Message Down Under* was based on her alleged experiences with a lost group of wandering Aborigines who cured her sickness and made her an honorary member of their tribe. She never dared publish her far-fetched story in Australia but when some Indigenous readers got hold of it and balked at her lack of knowledge and offensive claims about their people she was forced publicly to apologize. Khouri wrote about experiencing the honour killing of her best friend in the Middle East and claimed she had moved to rural Australia to escape the threats of the Jordanians who were seeking revenge on her for speaking out about their crimes.

Of course, the fact that both these women's hoaxes were exposed by Australian investigations proves that that country is nothing like the intellectual black hole they narrow-mindedly assumed it to be; but it does suggest that the Antipodean creative scene allows things to happen that other countries might not. One important reason for that is that racism and far-right politics is less taboo there than it is in other parts of the English-speaking world (a fact that the outspoken comments of the Nazi-hoaxer Helen Darville/ Demidenko prove beyond doubt). Another is perhaps that in a young culture where identities are still in flux and anxieties about racial integration abound, there is a desperation to prove – and believe – certain emotive points about how to live, and literature is the best way to do it.

In the future, technological developments will undoubtedly change the way hoaxes are perpetrated and received. The internet has played a vital role in the debunking of all the hoaxes of the last ten years, but it will also enable writers of far less ingenuity and skill to pull off increasingly audacious deceptions. Fake blogs, such as the long-running one by an American girl supposedly suffering from a terminal illness who turned out to be the fantasy of an unhappy middle-aged woman, may become more widespread. And in the 'mock hoax' category, the UK novelist is not alone who recently set up a detailed fake internet profile for his pseudonymous memoir's 'author' to throw readers off the scent of the fact that the real writer was not the dissolute, wine-loving littérateur described on the book jacket but a rather unassuming writer of genre fiction: increasingly, publishers encourage authors to use the internet as a tool for making their artful voices seem real, thus blurring the line between truth and fiction even more.

The way we use literature to communicate will change in unimaginable ways, but it will also stay the same. Books – whatever form they take – will always ask us to enter into a contract of trust with them. For as long as there are publishers to bestow upon an author the incredible power of seeing their work in print, there will be writers who abuse, pervert and wilfully misconstruct the printed word. But you only have to read the stories of fantastic literary hoaxers like Grey Owl or Romain Gary to know that the world would be a much duller place without them.

I

THE EIGHTEENTH CENTURY

WILLIAM LAUDER

*N*OT MUCH IS known of the early life of the angry young Scotsman William Lauder, least of all his date or place of birth. What is known is that ever since meeting with an unfortunate golfing accident on the Bruntsfield Links just outside Edinburgh, which led to the amputation of one of his legs in the early 1730s, he became a bitter and resentful man with 'a sallow complexion and rolling, fiery eyes', hell-bent on stirring up trouble and knocking down literary icons. The accident (in which he took a rogue ball to the knee, causing an injury which, due to lack of proper care, went septic) was only the first of a series of disappointments which led him to turn his talents to a most audacious hoax, and one which, if it had succeeded, would have ruined the reputation of the finest religious poet in the world, John Milton.

Lauder's talents were undeniable. Always a keen scholar, he had been taken on after graduating from Edinburgh University as an assistant teacher to his ailing master, Professor Adam Watt, in 1734. Trusted to teach Latin to Watt's students, he assumed he would take over his position after the old man died, but in fact was passed over after his superiors decided he was too inexperienced for the job. He also seems to have been someone whom it was difficult to get on with, judging by the total lack of kind words from his contemporaries. Accounts of his difficult personality abound in the conscientiously kept diaries and correspondences of mid-eighteenth-century Edinburghians, including his colleague, the well-known classicist Thomas Ruddiman, who recalled being 'so sensible of the weakness and folly of that man, that I shunned his company, as far as decently I could'.

Reduced to applying for non-academic positions, he sought a job at the University Library but this too was unsuccessful, so instead he decided on a career in the publishing and translating of holy Latin texts. In 1739 he worked on a book of religious poetry with Ruddiman which not only got published but was recommended for use in schools, and buoyed by this success he managed to amass enough references to support an application to the faculty of religious history at the university, but it was, alas, turned down. On receiving this bad news, he flew into an indignant rage and fled, as did so many others before and since, to London, where he felt sure his talents would be recognized.

Perhaps, even with his awkward personality, he could have made it as a littérateur if he had not become gripped by what was, according to his peers, an un-quenchable obsession with doing down Milton. Although universally praised as a poet of genius, there was at that time a strong vein of antipathy to Milton's republican politics, and one of the chief proponents of this was Samuel Johnson, who would become awkwardly entangled in Lauder's hoax. Lauder's theory was this: that Milton had drawn so closely on other contemporary religious sources for his great work *Paradise Lost* that it was time he were outed as a fake. As evidence for this claim he cited a series of passages, which he had translated (badly) to seem almost identical to verses of Milton's, from a range of not very well known Latin works such as *Adamus Exul* by Hugo Grotius, *Sarcotis* by Jacob Masen and even the Scottish writers Andrew Ramsay and Alexander Ross.

All this evidence was described by Lauder in a submission to the *Gentleman's Magazine* and initially, at least, it was accepted by his readers, including Johnson, who was happy to be associated with the young Milton sceptic. However, on closer inspection the passages Lauder had cited as lifted from others' works were found either to be such bad translations as to be effectively made-up, or copied from a Latin version of the very Milton text it was supposed to be exposing.

One reader of the *Gentleman's Magazine*, Reverend Richard Richardson, wrote a letter to the editor in January 1749 pointing out that some of the passages Lauder claimed to be from Grotius were in fact from William Hog's Latin translation of *Paradise Lost*, and others were nowhere to be found at all. But it was Dr John Douglas, later Bishop of Bath (although at that time a not very committed churchman) who spent the season in London hob-nobbing with fashionable bookmen, who ultimately confirmed the hoax. Johnson immediately reneged on his support of the thesis, admitting he had been duped, but claiming that it only happened because of his 'thinking the man too frantic to be fraudulent'.

However, Lauder was unwilling to go quietly and immediately set about publishing a rebuttal of the accusations made against him, producing, in 1750, his essay 'On Milton's use and imitation of the moderns, in his *Paradise Lost*'. But with the whole of literary London on his tail, and his excitable and increasingly bizarre accusations against Milton beginning to make him look quite mad, he wrote a letter of apology to Douglas (on Johnson's instruction, and some say with Johnson's help) explaining the peculiar psychological circumstances leading up to the hoax.

He was, he said, a man made miserable and ground down by repeated rejections and dismissals from a literary and scholastic establishment which would never give him a fair trial. He had, he lamented, seen no other way to gain the respect he longed for than to massage Milton's texts to his own ends. He hoped, of course, for forgiveness and understanding.

So poor was the quality of the faked material he created, so unlikeable was he and so rude were his suggestions about Milton, that he in fact found very little support at all after the exposure of his hoax. He decided to flee Europe altogether and ended up working as a schoolmaster in Barbados where, his neighbours recorded, he was as ill-tempered, hot-headed and badly behaved as he ever was at home. When he died in 1771 fewer people will have mourned him even than poor Thomas Chatterton, who had died the year before.

JAMES MACPHERSON

*T*HERE CAN BE nothing so conducive to planning a grand literary hoax than waking up one morning and realizing you're a supply teacher in rural Scotland instead of the cutting-edge poet your university chums had had you down for. So it is perhaps not surprising that James Macpherson, who had published a few verses when he was at Edinburgh and made no secret of his high literary ambitions, suddenly 'found' some miraculously on-trend manuscripts which he knew would have all the critics in the country jumping up and down with excitement.

This eighteenth-century Scottish ne'er-do-well is one of the most famous of all literary hoaxers. Of course, he did do well in one sense – well enough to fool a continent of burgeoning Romantics and make himself a tidy sum while he was about it. But the famed Highland 'translator' of the Ossian poems never really succeeded at his game, because even though his work is still studied and even read for pleasure by some, there is a general agreement that he was never a good enough writer to achieve the immortality he craved. Like William Lauder, he was also said by almost all who knew him to be a thoroughly unpleasant man. But, unlike Lauder, his work has been the subject of a storm of controversy that has only recently died down.

His personal story is the first in the history of hoaxers to be available to us in full detail, thanks to his being taken up by all of Scotland's and much of Europe's intelligentsia which, in the mid-eighteenth century, consisted of such trustworthy and prolific writers as Hume, Carlyle, Johnson and, perhaps most famously, Goethe.

Born in 1738 in the Scottish Highlands to an old and influential family, James Macpherson was, it seemed, destined for the priesthood. But this clever little boy, educated first at Inverness and then at Aberdeen and Edinburgh, had a passion for old Gaelic folk tales and a love of language which did not go unobserved by his family, who began to realize that something a little more creative than the kirk might be his destiny.

At Edinburgh University he wrote and published a few poems which were generally considered to be quite terrible, including one called 'The Highlander', an ambitious and interminable heroic poem which appeared in 1758 and which he later tried to suppress. The pattern of attempting to publish something as fiction which you later bring out as objective fact (or at least a literary *object trouvée*) is typical of the literary hoaxer, and its implication of a last-ditch attempt of a would-be writer to make his name is as pertinent to Macpherson as it is to the twenty-first-century's James Frey.

After graduating, the only gainful employment Macpherson could find was a post as a tutor for the staid and isolated Balgowan family. He hated it. Spending long dark evenings cloistered with the offspring of a family of uninspiring dullards and no prospect of the literary success he still longed for, it is perhaps no wonder that he resolved to make his mark on Scottish letters by any means necessary. So, in 1760, still resident at Balgowan, he produced the first of the manuscripts which would make him famous.

These *Fragments of Ancient Poetry collected in the Highlands of Scotland* were, he said, great Gaelic poems by a bard called Ossian which he had collected and translated on his lonely travels around the Highlands. The hero was Fingal (*Fionnghall* meaning 'white stranger') and they told:

A TALE of the times of old! The deeds of days of other years.

The murmur of thy streams, O Lora! brings back the memory of the past. The sound of thy woods, Garmaller, is lovely in mine ear. Dost thou not behold Malvina, a rock with its head of heath! Three aged pines bend from its face; green is the narrow plain at its feet; there the flower of the mountain grows, and shakes its white head in the breeze. The thistle is there alone, shedding its aged beard. Two stones, half sunk in the ground, show their heads of moss. The deer of the mountain avoids the place, for he beholds a dim ghost standing there. The mighty lie, O Malvina! in the narrow plain of the rock.

A tale of the times of old! The deeds of days of other years!

Who comes from the land of strangers, with his thousands around him? The sunbeam pours its bright stream before him; his hair meets the wind of his hills. His face is settled from war. He is calm as the evening beam that looks from the cloud of the west, on Cona's silent vale. Who is it but Comhal's son, the king of mighty deeds! He beholds the hills with joy, he bids a thousand voices rise. 'Ye have fled over your fields, ye sons of the distant land! The king of the world sits in his hall, and hears of his people's flight. He lifts his red eye

of pride; he takes his father's sword. Ye have fled over
your fields, sons of the distant land!'

What might seem like a fairly trite piece of pseudo-
mythological arcana to our cynical modern ears appeared
just at the right moment to be taken seriously. It was a
time when all Europe's young countries were madly
trying to clothe their cultural identities with any tattered
bits of history they could find, so the idea of an ancient
Scottish Homer was too good to be true. This was
Rousseau's moment, and alongside his 'noble savage'
stood Macpherson's hero of the Highlands, a creature
of windswept splendour imbued with an innate sense of
chivalry and order. Here was an earthy soldier, schooled by
mother nature, who would fight for the reputation of rural
Scottish culture and give readers a good many thrills besides.

And if a side-effect of Macpherson's fortuitous discovery
was great riches, glory and, eventually, a seat in the House of
Commons, well, those were crosses he was willing to bear.

When *Fragments of Ancient Poetry collected in the Highlands of Scotland* was an instant success for its publisher,
earning its 'translator' the ultimate accolade – a letter of
recommendation from the philosopher David Hume –
Macpherson did what all literary wunderkinds must do: he
quit his job and set off to find more inspiration. Luckily for
him, it took no more than a few sallies forth into the heathery
countryside to miraculously come upon enough material to
fill two more books of Erse verse, *Fingal* (1762) and *Temora*
(1763).

It was around this time, however, that eyebrows began
to be raised over the authenticity of Ossian's work. Samuel

Johnson, never a man to mince his words, claimed that not only could any man have written this doggerel, but many children could have done so too. Yet the books had been translated into several European languages and, as with so many hoaxers, the juggernaut must have seemed to Macpherson to be impossible to stop now. And anyway, why would he want to? His attitude to his doubters was relaxed, even when all the major names in publishing and criticism were at war over the veracity of his poems. He claimed to have the original manuscripts of much of the work, but declined to share them with his readers. (Years later, one of his supporters did publish the 'originals' but they were Gaelic poems written in Macpherson's hand, and only sparked off a new controversy over whether they hadn't been translated from English to Gaelic in the first place.)

Now hideously pompous and ill-humoured, Macpherson was nobody's favourite. Even Hume, not known for his bitching, said he had 'scarce ever known a man more perverse and unamiable'. Macpherson disingenuously conceded in his preface to the 1765 edition of *The Poems of Ossian*, that his overnight renown 'might flatter the vanity of one fond of fame'. He further wrote that 'The eagerness with which these Poems have been received abroad, is a recompense for the coldness with which a few have affected to treat them at home'. But given that within a few years he would have abandoned poetry for a life in colonial politics, it seems that the plaudits of foreigners were not recompense enough.

By 1764, he was preparing to leave the British Isles for the colony of Pensacola, now Florida (a suitable retirement place for a wealthy old cross-patch even now) where he had been offered an official post.

For the next part of his relatively short life, he kept out of the literary scene which had built him up and knocked him down, but on returning to London in 1766 he misguidedly decided to take up the pen again, producing his version of the history of Britain. If this got laughed out of the critics' circle (which it did) nothing could compare to the monumental pasting his translation of Homer's *Iliad* received in 1773. It takes an author of supreme confidence to undertake a work of this magnitude, especially when one of the greatest versions of all time – Alexander Pope's – had been published a generation before. What bedraggled laurels Macpherson had to rest on as an interpreter of ancient heroic myth were not enough to shield him from the merciless kicking he now received. But perhaps by this time he was genuinely unbothered by the scorn poured on him from all corners. Perhaps he was happy just to be rich, well-travelled and talked about. Considering what we know of his insatiable desire for fame, surely he would have been rather pleased to know that long after his death he would continue to ignite passionate debate about the authorship of his most famous work.

Critics and historians have now proved conclusively that Macpherson did some admirable and interesting things. He did love the poetic folklore of his native lands, and did indeed travel there extensively, recording songs and poems told to him by locals. He probably even used his not very brilliant knowledge of the Gaelic language to translate snatches of what he heard into English prose. And he inspired such important figures as Sir Walter Scott in their grand literary projects. But he had neither the linguistic skills nor the imaginative ones to do what he claimed to have done: to translate a great lost work of folk literature into the English language. All he wanted was fame enough to have his name echo down the corridors of future libraries. Which it still does, albeit for all the wrong reasons.

THOMAS CHATTERTON

*T*HE MOST FAMOUS image of England's most romantic hoaxer is of him lying dead in his Holborn garret, flame-haired and pale-faced, surrounded by torn-up pieces of manuscript. Outside the little window London's grey rooftops stretch into the distance. The scene in the bare room is pitiful. But the real locus of the story is in Bristol, in the muniments room of the beautiful parish church at St Mary Redcliffe.

Sextons of this church had been members of the Chatterton family for generations, and at the time of Thomas's birth in 1752 it was in the hands of the poet's uncle. Thomas was born after his father had died, and his impecunious mother, with a daughter to raise as well as her son, had to take in sewing to make ends meet. Finding a way to put food on the table was therefore of greater concern than giving her son a literary education, but Thomas, the quality of whose literary output would lead many to call him a genius, was drawn to letters as if by fate. Specifically, he was drawn to some fragments of illuminated manuscript which fell into his hands one day as he played in the vicarage. His mother had been tearing the pages up for scraps, but when she saw the child's wonder at their content she set about teaching him to read.

Before long, despite being constantly undermined and teased at his tough school for the poor boys of Bristol, Chatterton was composing verses of his own and borrowing from the library book after book of medieval poetry and history. His school, Colston's Charity, was a brutish place, and although many considered the quiet and melancholy Chatterton to be soft in the head, one master, Mr Philips, was a writer of poems himself and so encouraged his boys to experiment with writing. At twelve, Chatterton showed him 'Elinoure and Juga', a poem he claimed to be by a little-known fifteenth-century author. Philips was impressed. Chatterton began to work on more such compositions, forming in his mind the apocryphal story of how he had found the manuscripts in an old stone chest in the church's store room. In fact he probably did take the bare materials for his forgeries from there, just as he took the imaginative ones from his excursions into the works of Spenser, Chaucer and John Kersey's *Dictionarium Anglo-Britannicum*.

The story he would tell was that the poems he found were by a young man called Rowley, also of Bristol, who several hundred years before had written under the patronage of real-life local burgher Master William Canynge. Chatterton inhabited this fantasy quite fully, even imagining a vision of the young Canynge as a boy genius like himself, as these lines from 'The Storie of William Canynge' illustrate:

When the fate-marked babe acome to sight, I saw him eager gasping after light. In all his sheepen gambols and child's play, In every merrymaking, fair, or wake, I kenn'd a perpled light of wisdom's ray; He ate down learning with the wastel-cake; As wise as any of the aldermen, He'd wit enow to make a mayor at ten.

But even before he started composing the poems in earnest, he submitted another *object trouvée* to a local newspaper, and had it not only accepted but roundly praised by all who saw it. This was the supposed account of a twelfth-century mayor crossing a new bridge over the Avon in Bristol, which would have been of interest to local historians because the new bridge which had just been built in that one's place was currently the talk of the town.

He also tried his hand at creating a pedigree for a local pewter-maker who had high hopes for his genealogy, taking payment for 'discovering' a document which said that the man, Henry Burgum, was descended from one Syrr Johan de Berghamme.

Now aged fifteen and apprenticed to a lawyer, a job he hated but had little choice in taking, Chatterton began devoting all his spare time to the Rowley hoax. All his life he had mooned around the church and its environs, its effigies and manuscripts his only friends, but now there was a purpose to his being 'alone and palely loitering' as Keats, who would dedicate his 'Endymion' to him, might have seen it.

Chatterton was by now a poet of considerable powers and it is hard to believe he was only a teenager when he wrote works such as the great dramatic poem 'Aella'. He showed the Rowley poems not only to his former teacher but to a local historian, Mr Barrett, his supporter and patron, Henry Burgum, and the collector, George Catcott. Then he decided to move things up a level, approaching the

London publisher Robert Dodsley and asking him whether he might submit to him some 'ancient poems, and an interlude, perhaps the oldest dramatic piece extant, wrote by one Rowley, a priest in Bristol, who lived in the reigns of Henry VI and Edward IV'.

Dodsley was a key figure in eighteenth-century letters and a man whose rags to riches story was well known. He was the publisher of almost every famous writer of the late 1700s, from Defoe and Richardson to David Garrick and Edmund Burke. He himself had started life as a weaver and then a footman but, having been discovered by the great poet Alexander Pope and set up as a publisher, playwright and poet, he went on to define the literary canon of his generation with his famous anthology, *A Collection of Poems By Several Hands*. It must have seemed to an ambitious young Chatterton that he might look kindly on a boy from a similarly lowly background with equally grand literary aspirations.

When his submissions received no reply, he felt the bite of the first of many professional disappointments, but resolved to try someone else. Horace Walpole looked like the right candidate, and this time he appeared to have some success: Walpole, of course, had perpetrated his own literary hoax in the shape of *The Castle of Otranto* (which he confessed to having written quite soon after its first publication) but this did not at first seem to lend him any special powers of detection, for he replied that he should like to see more of Rowley's 'wonderful' work and quite possibly publish it. But in the time it took for Chatterton to write back detailing his tall tale of the discovery of the papers in a church chest and outlining his life story as one who is poor but who wishes to better himself, Walpole had shown the manuscripts to his friend, the poet Thomas Gray, who had pronounced it a fake. So poor Chatterton received a brusque brush-off and was advised to seek his fortune elsewhere. Years later, and too late for it to do any good, Walpole would admit he thought there never 'existed so masterly a genius'.

At this stage Chatterton was still optimistic and believed that he would soon be able to make a living from writing rather than clerking in a dreary law firm. He also dearly wished to help and reward his mother who was now hard at work teaching as well as sewing and carrying on the business of keeping an impecunious young family together. He decided to try his hand at writing satire for some of the many political magazines that were in vogue at the time, and it is to his credit that his abilities were elastic enough to earn him professional work in the *Middlesex Journal, Town and Country Magazine* and the *Freeholder's Magazine*. He lampooned the leading figures of the day and just before Easter 1770 pulled off his journalistic *coup de grâce*: the bold, semi-satirical 'Last Will and Testament' in which he expressed his intention to take his life the following day due to his dissatisfaction with the modern world and his hopeless place in it. Reading this impassioned piece, his formerly hard-nosed master, Mr Lambert, released him from his employ on the spot and sent him off to London to seek his literary fortune.

By the end of April that year he was in the capital, living in Shoreditch and determined to earn money from his writing. He did manage to get work for various periodicals, and sat up all night writing endlessly in poetry and prose, satirical and straight, even parodying Macpherson's Ossian poems in one piece. But although he had the flattery of editors he was hardly being paid enough to eat. Despite having spent his first wages on presents for his mother and sister back home in Bristol, he somehow found the money to move into a room in Brooke Street, just off Chancery Lane. It was here, little more than a couple of months after arriving in London, that he must have realized what little luck he had was running out. Neighbours reported that he wandered around looking half-starved, but always too proud to take the meals and charity they offered. Determined to make his own way but disillusioned by the difficulty of earning money in London's overcrowded literary world, he reverted to the comfort of the Rowley poems, producing a new work, the 'Excelente Balade of Charitie'.

No longer having access to the piles of forgotten old books and papers of St Mary Redcliffe, he could come by no parchment to write on so made what he said was a transcription from a medieval manuscript found in Bristol. He sent it off to the *Town and Country Magazine* in high hopes but it was rejected. Chatterton, still less than twenty years old, would not live to see another summer. When his body was found in the little room in Brooke Street, dead from self-administered arsenic, it was thought he hadn't eaten for several days. The room was strewn with scraps of hand-written manuscript which he had torn into tiny bits in the hours before his death. It is hard to imagine a more pathetic scene, except perhaps for the pauper's burial he had the next day in a municipal ground round the corner.

Hoaxing, for Thomas Chatterton, was more an outlet for his immense creative powers than a ruse to gain fame.

Although he needed money, and desperately, and no doubt realized he was owed not only payment but respect for the work he was creating, the circumstances of his dishonest project were so urgent, passionate and – crucially – tinged with the satirical humour of one who liked, despite all his life's hardships, to laugh, that he must surely be considered the noblest of the English hoaxers. His legacy reflects this: not only was he posthumously taken up by the Romantic poets – Keats and Wordsworth both lauding him in verse and holding him up as an inspirational figure and even a martyr to the cause of poesy – but even in the twentieth century his story is still being retold and plumbed for new meaning. Recent examples of his afterlife can be found in the work of the novelist Peter Ackroyd, the opera composer Ruggiero Leoncavallo and the Australian vocal artist Matthew Dewey.

However for one young man – also a melancholy lawyer's apprentice with a troubled home life – the story of Chatterton would become an obsession, and one which, less than two decades after the Bristol poet's demise and about half a mile down the road from where he died, would replay itself in much more daring, if less glorious, terms. That young man was William Henry Ireland.

WILLIAM HENRY IRELAND

*W*ILLIAM HENRY IRELAND was only a teenager when he pulled off one of the most daring hoaxes ever to dupe literary London. In 1775 he was born into a world and a family in thrall to the notion of literary and historical relics, which would pay a high price to own an object or book touched by the hand of one of Europe's great minds. Before the century was out, William and his father Samuel would pay a far higher price than either could have imagined when the plan first took hold in the younger man's mind. The gusto with which William produced the faked Shakespeare documents that made him famous before he had reached adulthood was incredible: he executed all the documents in his bulging dossier in little under two months in 1795. And the spur which endowed him with this extraordinary energy for composition was neither money nor fame but the peculiar circumstances of his unfortunate upbringing.

William Henry was brought up by Samuel Ireland, a socially and intellectually ambitious man from East London who may or may not have been his real father, and Samuel's 'housekeeper' Mrs Freeman, who may well have been his mother. Raised to believe his birth mother had died, the naturally weedy and shy William fought a constant battle for attention at home. At school, his main aim was to avoid the attentions of his masters, so impossible did he find it to excel or even keep up in any of his classes. Also sharing the family house at Norfolk Street, just off the Strand, were Mrs Freeman's two delightful and intelligent daughters; and if they weren't enough to take attention away from poor William, at the centre of it all was Samuel's beloved collection of books and antiquities which he protected and nurtured with the single-minded obsession of a new mother. He made a living by selling books of engravings and historical relics to the aristocrats and intellectuals whose company he craved, and the house had become something of a museum by the time the likes of Boswell came to view the priceless Shakespeare papers he claimed to own. Mrs Freeman herself was an occasional writer of satire, the girls were keen artists, and most evenings the family would sit amongst Samuel's treasures disporting and bettering themselves by reading aloud from Shakespeare.

William himself did not seem to have inherited any of the talents of his family, his only passion being to sit in his bedroom making pretend suits of armour. However, the family had connections in the Drury Lane Theatre and it was here that William seemed most at home, revelling in the make-believe world of the back-stage scene-builders and costume designers, and even getting the odd walk-on part in a play. But most of the time he found himself centre of attention for all the wrong reasons: rarely able to get his family's attention, never the recipient of anyone's praise and always wondering about the true nature of his parentage, he must have cut a forlorn figure as he sloped around the city on errands for his father. When he was eventually allowed to leave school he was apprenticed to a law firm in one of the nearby Inns of Court, a job he hated. He had already read about Chatterton (who had the same job and also lacked paternal love) and, he wrote in his confession years later, was already wondering what other similarities there might be between them.

At nineteen years old, William was plugging away at his dreary job and coming home to a family who had little time for him. Yet outside this little world, as he must have known from his father's doings, England and Europe were in the grip of an obsession with literary and historical relics which would ultimately enable him to make his mark. The fall of the great French families in the Revolution meant the international market in *objets d'art* was suddenly flooded with the flotsam of their grand existences. Collectors were going wild for paintings, furniture and books with impressive pedigrees and grand connections. At the same time, as a reaction to this, some ingenious Englishmen were trying to create a market in home-grown arts and artefacts which celebrated the landscape, history and culture of their own land. Samuel Ireland, engraver, artist and inveterate collector was one such man, and the success of his collections of sketches of places such as the Avon valley were what enabled him to buy the house in Norfolk Street.

The chief obsession of the day, however, was Shakespeare. The emerging cult of bardolatory was sweeping the land, thanks largely to the irrepressible actor-manager David Garrick. In 1769 this famous Shakespeare-lover had staged an exuberant jubilee celebration at his hero's birthplace in the Midlands. Statues were erected, encomia were written, celebrities were invited to attend balls in remembrance of the playwright and, as an offshoot of this grand affair, a crooked industry sprang up selling spurious bits of tat to tourists. The Irelands themselves were duped by one such tradesman when they made a trip to Stratford and came away with a chair said to have been sat in by Shakespeare as he wooed his wife.

Unsurprisingly, then, the one thing that William's father lusted after but could never get his hands on was something written in Shakespeare's hand. A whole play would be too much to hope for, of course, but even a single signature or scribbled note, he was fond of saying, would be worth exchanging his whole library for. His son was listening. And some time between the family holiday to Stratford in 1793 and the autumn of 1794, he came up with a perfect way to win the respect of the bardolatrous Samuel.

William had sense enough to begin with a dry run. From one of the many local booksellers near his house he bought an old book of prayers, written by a member of Lincoln's Inn, which bore the stamp of Queen Elizabeth. By faking a note from the author to the queen, he would be able to say it was a rare presentation copy rather than merely one which had been bought for the royal library. He did so, trying his best to imitate the spidery handwriting of the sixteenth century, and took the results to a bookbinder in New Inn Passage for approval. To this man, a Mr Laurie, he quipped that he was planning to play a trick on his father and wanted to know if his creation looked authentic enough to pass muster. Laurie and his assistant agreed that it did, but recommended he rewrite it using a special ink preparation, well known to scribes of the day, which would make it look more genuinely aged. The solution was sold to him in a vial and he was instructed to hold the written sheet up to the fire to make the antique-looking writing come up a satisfyingly dark mottled brown. He did as he was told, and his father was fooled and delighted.

William swiftly followed this with another mini-hoax, a forged letter pertaining to a bust of Cromwell. Typically of his lack of thoroughness, he had not bothered to find out that the correspondent claiming to be giving this fine portrait-sculpture to Cromwell was in fact one of the man's arch rivals and so very unlikely to be wishing him anything but ill luck. Fortunately, Ireland Senior was also oblivious to the fact and accepted the new addition to his collection with glee.

Now the stage was set for William's hoaxing operation to launch in earnest. He stocked up on old paper by buying the unused end-pages of folios from a bookseller in St Martin's Lane. He bought a collection of antique seals and doctored them according to his limited knowledge of Elizabethan heraldry. He even tore a piece of cloth from a wall-hanging in the House of Lords, when he visited to hear the king speak, and pulled it apart to make the string with which he had heard old documents were customarily tied together. Finally, he laid in a good supply of the magic ink from the man in New Inn Passage and set about practising the signature he had seen in facsimile in his father's copy of Dr Johnson's *Shakespeare*. Then he went back to Norfolk Street and told an astonished Samuel that he had found the bard's signature on a mortgage deed.

At that moment, after nearly twenty years of effective parental abandonment, William had the full and rapt attention of his father. Overjoyed with his son's discovery, Samuel immediately wanted more. He begged to know where the boy had found this incredible relic and William, thinking on his feet, began to spin the unlikely tale of Mr H.

Mr H, who wished to remain anonymous, had, he said, encountered William by chance one day when he was on an errand and discovered that the boy had an interest in antiquities. He happened to mention that he had a chest full of old papers at his grand house across town and, having little interest in such things, invited William to come and rifle through it and take away anything that caught his eye.

Blinded by ambition to the absurdity of this story, Samuel implored his son to return to Mr H's house and bring him back more treasures, even hinting at the specific sort of things it would be most pleasing to have him unearth. Fuelled by his father's enthusiasm, William threw himself into a frenzy of activity which must have been something of a shock to the system for such an idle youth. Happily, his employer was rarely in his chambers, so he kept his forging materials in a locked cabinet there and continued his work undisturbed.

The next Shakespeare document he produced was a receipt pertaining to the business of the Globe Theatre. Claiming to be a rare promissory note from the bard to his colleague John Hemynge, it contained both a mistake in the year the theatre was built and a misspelling of Stratford. This was passed off as a mere sign that, in Shakespeare's time, orthography was less standard, and scribes were more careless. William appeared to be on a roll. Another note regarding a play performed before the Earl of Leicester was dated after Leicester's death and also misspelled his name, but, astonishingly, no one seemed to mind. William even created a letter claiming to be from Shakespeare to an ancestor of the Irelands (also called, coincidentally, William) thanking him for saving him from drowning.

Of course Samuel, not wishing to compromise his carefully built reputation as a serious book-collector, sought to have all these papers authenticated. Poor William had to sit by half-terrified and half-amused as the city's foremost handwriting, bookselling and heraldry experts scrutinized everything from seal to letter-formation. The fact that these great men would sit in what William now realized was a bogus Shakespeare courting chair only served to increase the sense of superiority the young hoaxer felt when they all deemed the documents bona fide.

Before long, William was using his phoney papers to paint the great man in colours which he thought would especially please his father. Unbelievably boldly, these included a lengthy profession of Shakespeare's Protestant faith, written in his own hand, which was designed to put paid once and for all to rumours of his Catholicism. Then came a love-letter to Anne Hathaway, complete with lock of hair and romantic verses. In his later *Confession*, William would admit he composed these things 'just as the thoughts arose in [his] head' and, as for the actual writing, a spidery scrawl with weird orthography and nothing recognizably Shakespearean, he merely used as many '*double-yous* and *esses* as possible'.

How could so many people have been fooled? How could even Boswell be blind to the truth? To a large extent the lack of special forensic techniques must be to blame, and also the paucity of examples of Shakespeare's real writing. But in the main, as with all successful literary hoaxes, it was simply because people wanted it so much to be true. Like the perpetrators of the Sophocles hoax and the Hitler Diaries, William Henry had tapped into a vein of cultural enthusiasm so rich that it obscured the rational minds of any number of intelligent men.

If the imaginations of the victims were willing, so was that of William himself, albeit to a different, more private end. He was never so unhinged as to trick himself into believing his output was real, but as he began to see that his actions might actually be discrediting his father rather than helping him, he began to enter into a most bizarre correspondence with him – writing as Mr H.

Samuel had wanted to apply in writing to Mr H to ask him about the provenance of the papers, and William encouraged him to do so. In his replies he used his imagined relationship with the son to tell the father how much he liked and admired the boy, and how clever and soulful he thought he was. In one letter, which reads very much like a schoolboy's made-up games note, he even opined that he thought Samuel ought to stop making William powder his wig, because it was unnecessary and expensive. In this imagined voice, over a series of increasingly emotional letters, he says to his father all the things he could not say in real life. This is about as far from hoaxing for financial gain as you can get.

Still using the story of Mr H, still responding to the excitable desires of Samuel who was now becoming quite famous in London for his burgeoning collection of Shakespeare papers, William set about the *coup de grâce* that would ultimately bring the whole edifice of his deception crashing down around him: the creation of an entire new Shakespeare play.

The story of Vortigern and Rowena is one Shakespeare might well have told. It can be found in Holinshed's *Chronicles*, one of his favourite sources, and tells a *Lear*-ish, *Macbeth*-ish tale of an ancient British king who would give away half his crown. But in Ireland's clumsy hands it is about as un-Shakespearean as it is possible to imagine. At the very worst, it reads like a silly pastiche, or so thought the various dissenters, growing in number and led by the renowned Shakespeare critic Malone, who were beginning to question the papers' authenticity. And so thought the cast and audience at Drury Lane when, amazingly, in April 1796, Samuel persuaded his contacts in the theatre to put on a performance of it.

By this time, even before the night of the ill-fated play (which surely rates as one of the most disastrous events in English theatre), William knew he was in too deep. Journalists were writing unforgiving editorials about the Shakespeare papers, cruel satires on William's crazy spelling abounded in magazines and more and more experts were joining Malone in opposing the Irelands' version of events. Despite the initial support of the Prince of Wales, Pitt the Younger, Edmund Burke and Boswell, William was making too many mistakes for his hoax to last for long. He had just produced an 'original' text of *King Lear*. Its spelling was a sight to behold ('Unfriended, new adopted' becoming 'Unnefreynnededde newee adoppetedde') but even if that did nothing to alert any remaining doubters, the fact that he prefaced the text with an address to 'mye gentle Readerres' ought to have rung alarm bells with anyone conversant enough with Shakespeare to know that he had viewers, not readers.

Malone, referring to the mythical chest in which William claimed Mr H kept the papers, said that after the imaginary chest in which Chatterton had 'found' his poems, he 'did not expect to have heard again, for some time at least, of such a repository for ancient manuscripts'. A satirical poem was written about Ireland, positioning him alongside Macpherson, Chatterton and Lauder as one of the famous 'four forgers' of the day. And when the cartoonist James Gillray illustrated the verse with an unkind caricature, the Irelands' fate never to be taken seriously was surely sealed.

Finally, William decided to confess his crime to his family. First he told Mrs Freeman and his sisters, then his father. All of them flatly refused to believe him. It was beyond their comprehension that the intellectually puny black sheep of their family could pull off such a stunt, and it would take months of persuasion for them even to start to believe that maybe this Mr H was the hoaxer. As long as he lived, which was not to be very long, Samuel never accepted his son had perpetrated the scam.

William would go on to marry, travel, set up a private lending library in Kensington and write many books and poems, not all bad, of his own. But his most fascinating work is his *Confession*, published some time after the event, in which he describes his duplicitous acts as those of a foolish boy who only wanted to please his father. And in 1832 he would publish *Vortigern* as his own work of fiction – a final publicity-hungry move which prefigures the twentieth-century literary hoaxer's vogue for selling as fiction what he was once vilified for trying to ply as fact.

2

THE NINETEENTH CENTURY

MARIA MONK

*R*IGHT-WING AMERICA in the 1830s was in the grip of a religious hatred far greater than that felt by some for Islam or Judaism today. It was the conviction of Protestant groups that the increasing numbers of Irish Catholics who were arriving on the East Coast had been instructed by their pope to eradicate America's precious Protestantism by overrunning the population with their people. So serious was this perceived threat, and the notion that the Democratic party was in cahoots with it due to its many Irish supporters, that new political groups were being founded on anti-Catholic principles which would eventually combine to become the Republican party.

But the Grand Old Protestants who would eventually take control of the States were, at the time of the great hoax of Maria Monk, only getting started. Monk – her real name – was born to Scottish–English parents in Canada in 1816 or 1817. By the time she was grown up (and she grew up before her time) North America would be rife with propaganda and even riots and arson attacks against Catholic institutions, and the seeds of this unrest were already sown when the young Maria was sent to the Magdalen Asylum for Wayward Girls in Quebec. Maria was barely educated and entirely despaired of by her parents by the time she was sent away from home: her unpredictable behaviour, lack of academic ability and refusal to adhere to rules was, it seems, brought on by a childhood head injury in which a pencil got stuck in her ear. It cannot have been an easy decision for her family to send her into the arms of Papists, but they were convinced no other charitable institution could help their uncontrollable daughter, especially as one aspect of her shameful behaviour seems to have been sexual, and there is some evidence that she earned money from prostitution while she was at the asylum, which also functioned as a school.

By the time she was eighteen and had been there for seven years the nuns had her expelled for just about the worst crime a Catholic or pseudo-Catholic can commit: unmarried pregnancy. Destitute and outcast, wandering the streets of Quebec, she sought help at the Canadian Benevolent Society and somehow managed to become acquainted with its director, a man called William K. Hoyte. Hoyte's Protestant missionary work was fuelled by a passionate hatred of Catholicism, and clearly he saw poor, pregnant Maria as an example of just how damaging a spell living in a convent could be. He also fell in love with her. He took her as his live-in mistress and promptly moved her to New York to assist him in the various Catholic-bating projects which would result in the most explosive autobiographical book of the decade.

In New York he and Maria gathered round them a group of educated friends who shared Hoyte's religious and political views. Among them were the Reverend John Slocum, Reverend George Bourne and Theodore Wight, all members of the nativist movement which campaigned for new laws to halt immigration by Irish Catholics. Slocum fancied himself as a writer and, as it turned out, he rather fancied Maria too.

It was decided that the group would collaborate on a book based on Maria's experiences in the Magdalen Asylum which would bring their cause the attention and money it required if it was to rid America of the Irish scourge. Mostly written by Slocum, with Hoyte and Bourne as advisors, *The Awful Disclosures* began to take shape as the story of an innocent girl who was plucked from her God-fearing Protestant home and flung into a den of terrible sin masquerading as a religious order. Clearly, Maria had told some tall tales to her lover-rescuer, Hoyte, and given her likely history of brain damage it may have been unclear even to her which aspects of her story were true and which were made-up. But she – and they – had nous enough to know that the more lurid the revelations about sex and violence behind the closed doors of the Hôtel Dieu, the more successful the book would be.

The Hôtel Dieu was a real institution and in the aftermath of publication it maintained a dignified silence on the subject of Maria's supposed revelations. And what revelations they were: the book reads like the spiciest kind of gothic novel. Beginning with the arrival of the optimistic young Maria as a novice, she is surprised to find that when she goes to her first confession, which is taken by priests from the monastery next door, the man on the other side of the wooden grille 'put questions to me, which were often of the most improper and even revolting nature, naming crimes both unthought of and inhuman' and using any number of 'corrupt and licentious expressions'.

She is further surprised to hear from another inmate a story about a young Indian girl who used to visit a particular priest and whose dead body was found soon after, along with a knife bearing that priest's name. The violent punishments inflicted by the nuns – including the use of archaic instruments such as leather gags – become commonplace, and other than needlework, it seems that the academic side of life is completely ignored. But it is when she finally takes holy orders herself, moving from the state of novice to Sister of the Hôtel Dieu, that the full horror of the institution is matter-of-factly revealed to her. After a ceremony involving her lying half-smothered in an incense-scented coffin bearing her name (a detail likely to appeal to Protestant readers), the mother superior makes it clear to her that as well as serving God she will now be expected to service the priests next door. And should she become pregnant from one of these liaisons, her offspring will go the way of all the convents' illegitimate children: 'baptized and immediately strangled'.

So, aside from the fact that these Catholics talked rude in the confessional and gagged or murdered their wayward charges, they were fornicating baby-killers to boot. Just as the authors suspected, the public lapped it up.

Coming hot on the heels of two similar bestselling exposés, *The Nun* by Mrs Sherwood and *Six Months in a Convent* by Rebecca Reed, the first print run in 1836 sold out immediately, bringing exactly the combination of revenue and scandal that Maria's keepers had hoped for. Despite the book not containing any sexually explicit language, its content was considered so inflammatory that the publishing house Harper Bros went so far as to set up an imprint especially for it in the name of two of its workers, Howe and Bates.

The 1836 Howe & Bates edition – which would be followed by several others that year alone and dozens more for well over a century afterwards – was well received not only by readers but by the anti-Catholic periodicals popular in New England at the time: *The American Protestant Vindicator* welcomed the book, as did the even more powerfully named periodical *The Downfall of Babylon*.

But as with all such extreme literary hoaxes, there were one or two people clear-sighted enough to question the content of the book from the outset. One such man was William Leete Stone, a Protestant and indeed an adherent to Hoyte's nativist ideology, but one who happened to be staying amongst Catholics in Canada in the year of the book's publication and who heard and saw evidence that no such salacious horrors had ever existed in the region's religious communities. He proposed to visit the Hôtel Dieu and investigate whether there were indeed mass graves of murdered babies, underground prison cells containing recalcitrant novices and a secret passage connecting the priests' house next door with the women's quarters. At first the nuns admitted him only into the public areas of the convent, but he saw enough of life there to feel sure that Maria's testimony was made-up. He returned to New York to interview her and then took the trouble of journeying back to Montreal for one last decisive tour of the nunnery. This time the nuns – seeing that he was in serious pursuit of the truth and not a mere scandal-obsessed tourist – let him see everything. It was abundantly clear that *The Awful Disclosures* bore no relation to reality.

If Maria was undone by these revelations, her male handlers undid themselves by becoming embroiled in a series of angry legal disputes over who owned the rights to the book they had created. The fact that Maria had recently ceased being the mistress of Hoyte and gone over to the charms of Slocum only made their wrangling more bitter. Amidst the legal furore over authorship, money and romantic affiliation, Maria did what she had done last time things got tricky: she ran off with a new man to a new city. She arrived in Philadelphia the year after publication and when the brief liaison that had taken her there ended, she found lodgings with a local physician called William Sleigh. At first her charms worked on him sufficiently well that he believed her story that she had been kidnapped by a group of priests who were trying to cart her back to Montreal to be punished by the evil inmates of Hôtel Dieu. If he felt let down by her eventual admission that this story was not entirely true, he was at least able to cash in on the Monk mania sweeping the American media by publishing his account of his time with the now infamous woman, *An exposure of Maria Monk's pretended abduction and conveyance to the Catholic asylum, Philadelphia by six priests on the night of August 15, 1837: with numerous extraordinary incidents during her residence of six days in this city.*

The hoax now having reached that point where irrespective of its veracity it had taken on a life of its own, Maria was able to publish a follow-up to the original book, despite the fact that she had been discredited quite comprehensively as a reliable memoirist and that this second book, *Further Disclosures by Maria Monk concerning the Hôtel Dieu nunnery of Montreal*, contained little new information. It did not net her much money.

Maria was a chaotic, restless and psychologically if not neurologically damaged young woman. She was itinerant. She was excluded from her family. And she was never to find peace or enough of an income to thrive for the rest of her short life. Publishing rights having being wrested from her by greedy ideologues and her name having been tarnished irrevocably by whichever religious group she moved among, she bore another illegitimate child in 1838 and lived out the remaining decade of her life on the edge of destitution. In 1849 she was arrested for stealing money from one of her lovers and that same year she died, aged only thirty-three.

In a telling postscript to Maria Monk's life as a character in someone else's story, a woman came forward decades later claiming to be her daughter, and auctioning a tell-all book about Maria's final years to the highest bidder. But by that time few people had any interest in the putative author herself. Her story – with its rampant padres, sadistic nuns and gothic *mise en scène* – had a life of its own by now, and well into the twentieth century it was still being published and peddled to feed the flames of anti-Catholic sentiment across the English-speaking world. After all, how much more exciting it is than the tale of yet another subjugated woman, fighting against men, money and religious morality to escape from the margins of history; than the real story of Maria Monk.

THE PROTOCOLS OF THE ELDERS OF ZION

*A*RE YOU A raging anti-Semite obsessed with the idea of a Jewish conspiracy to take over the world by infiltrating its media and financial institutions? Hopefully not. But if you are, you'll know all about *The Protocols of the Elders of Zion* already. If not, you may well have heard of this infamous *fin de siècle* literary hoax anyway, because not only did it spread across its author's native Russia like wildfire, but it served as one of the founding documents of Hitler's plan. And it is a sobering example of how, even after a hoax has been given an incontrovertible debunking, those who really want to believe in its truth will stubbornly continue to do so.

The Russian word 'protocols' might literally be translated as 'minutes', as in the minutes of a meeting, and that is exactly what this spurious text proposes to be. It is the imaginary proceedings of a summit of Jewish leaders in which they hatch a plan for world domination, focusing on such wily corrupting tactics as banning alcohol, propagating pornography and encouraging anarchism. There are twenty-five items on this ambitious list of Things To Do, and aside from advice to the would-be King of the Jews (not, critics point out, a phrase which real Jewish elders are particularly keen on) guidance is given on such matters as the destruction of Christianity and Islam, the promulgation of Darwinism, arranging for terrible things to happen to Jews and using this as an excuse for their unreasonable acts, creating a system which appears to be free and fair but is in fact secretly oppressive, and promising adherents a wonderful new-age of liberty and riches.

Although summarized here, the full-length *Protocols* is hardly discursive. In fact it extends only to enough pages to form a slim pamphlet, and has traditionally been fleshed out with similarly extreme anti-Semitic literature and commentary in order to fill up a respectable-sized paperback book. Its tone is general and its style is quasi-official-sounding, as in this extract from Protocol 16, in which the role of a Jewish president is delineated:

> The president will, at our discretion, interpret the sense of such of the existing laws as admit of various interpretation; he will further annual them when we indicate to him the necessity to do so, besides this, he will have the right to propose temporary laws, and even new departures in the government constitutional working, the pretext both for the one and the other being the requirements for the supreme welfare of the State.

Typically, this entry is light on specifics and heavy on pseudo-legalese, and this of course is one of the reasons that *The Protocols* lends itself so easily to the ideologies of so many racist leaders the world over, from the Arab states to Africa and America.

The story of the origins of *The Protocols* is still shrouded in some mystery, and may never be known in full, but it is now generally agreed that the author was a Russian secret police officer known for his forging abilities. His name was Pytor Ivanovich Rachovsky and he was part of the movement whose aim was to quell the troublesome revolutionary uprisings in a Russia beginning to outgrow its old aristocratic leadership, and for whom the prospect of a Jewish rebellion was regarded as a real possibility. One of the specific targets of Rachovsky and his cronies was the national finance minister, Sergei Witte, whose reforms seemed to play into the hands of the modernizers so feared by the old guard. This was in the very first days of the twentieth century, but the story of how the text came to take the form it did begins several years earlier: for Rachovsky was not just a hoaxer, he was a plagiarist too.

There were two works of fiction from which the author drew to create his bogus historical tract. The first was a little-known piece of satirical writing by the Frenchman Maurice Joly, published in 1864 under the title *Dialogue aux enfers entre Machiavel et Montesquieu*. This imagined dialogue in hell between Machiavelli and the Enlightenment theorist Montesquieu was intended as a veiled attack on the political aims of Napoleon III (represented by the Italian) whose methods were set against the liberal thesis of Montesquieu. An example of the popular dialectical style of rhetoric, the satire has each speaker make increasingly drastic claims for their preferred style of ruling. At one point, Joly's Machiavel boasts of how he would seize power through control of the press, employing an image unusual in nineteenth-century France to illustrate his point: ' "Like the god Vishnu, my press will have a hundred arms, and these arms will give their hands to all the different shades of opinion throughout the country." '

Invoking the Hindu god Vishnu would have been equally unexpected to readers in turn-of-the-century Russia when, in *The Protocols*, we find the intention that: ' "These newspapers, like the Indian god Vishnu, will be possessed of hundreds of hands, each of which will be feeling the pulse of varying public opinion." '

The second literary precedent for the hoax was a novel called *Biarritz* written by a particularly shady Prussian called, variously, Hermann Goedesche, Sir John Retcliffe or John Readcliffe. By day he worked as an openly anti-Semitic journalist and post office employee, but by night he was a romantic novelist – a sort of Prussian Walter Scott. And all this time he was actually a spy for the secret police as well. Just like Rachovsky, he used his literary skills to fake papers and letters which exposed left-wing politicians as dangerous democrats. And just like Rachovsky, he was a plagiarist. In *Biarritz* he borrows heavily from the satires of Maurice Joly as well, but appends to his story a section of his own creation that would directly prefigure the setting of *The Protocols*: the chapter entitled 'In the Jewish Cemetery, Prague' features an evil rabbi detailing a plot to overtake Europe with his bloodthirsty, Christian-hating ways.

This passage caught the attention of impressionable readers and publishers so readily that it would go on to be published as an essay in its own right, independent of the rest of the book. It would be seized upon for its consolidation of a Jewish threat that was felt by many, in the turbulent Eastern Europe of that time, to be all too real. Quite quickly, it seems, the fictional origins of Goedesche's writings were forgotten and by 1872 it was being circulated as reportage. So by the time *The Protocols* were first published in St Petersburg in 1903, in the newspaper called the *Banner*, the ideological framework of them would have been familiar to many readers. And the Jewish menace, as it was perceived by many of them, was tied up with the mystical threat of the Masons, with whom the evil Zionist Elders were supposed to be in league.

A couple of years later there was another craze for the pamphlet, as an anti-Semitic group who opposed Russia's progressive new parliament used it to garner support for their cause. At this time, in 1905, a publisher and dabbler in the occult called Sergei Nilus included the full text of

The Protocols in his book *The Great Within the Small: The Coming of the Anti Christ and the Rule of Satan on Earth*. Nilus was known to be slightly mad, but his book became a success and the idea of the secret Jewish summit was kept alive.

Then, throughout the time of the Russian Revolution and the rise of Nazism in Germany, the text was used over and over again to authenticate the rising tide of anti-Semitism in Eastern and Central Europe. Hitler quoted it in *Mein Kampf*. In 1920 it was published in Britain by one George Shanks, whose father, a businessman in Moscow, had been ruined by the Russian Revolution and so had a vengeful axe to grind.

Finally, in 1921, *The Times* published a detailed exposé of what many had long suspected, and what the British-Jewish journalist Lucien Wolf had already outlined in a ground-breaking article of his own: that this inflammatory piece of writing was a work of pure fiction, engineered to sow hatred and fear among its readers. The lengthy piece in *The Times* describing the literary and political origins of *The Protocols* was written by the paper's stringer in Constantinople, Philip Graves (half-brother of the more famous Robert), and it was he who set passages from the Frenchman Joly's text side by side with those of Rachovsky.

That, you might think, was that. But the allure of this particular hoax will not die. Consistently, since that detailed and incontrovertible 1921 debunking, anti-Semites the world over have used Rachovsky's text to support their far-fetched claims. In 2009 the student who searches for 'The Protocols of the Elders of Zion text' on the internet will be offered, at the top of the list, the online proceedings of a group called Jew Watch. Leaders and mainstream thinkers in countries such as Syria (where it is apparently a bestseller), Iran (where a popular 2004 television series promoted it as a historical document) and Saudi Arabia (where extracts from it are used in educational textbooks), as well as Africa and Asia, all advise their people to take seriously the message of a Jewish conspiracy as it is outlined in this phoney text. Pytor Rachovsky was no doubt an unpleasant man working for a desperate secret service in the last days of the old Russia. But would he regret the end result of his hoax if he could have lived to see it acted upon so terribly by Hitler and others? Or would he look upon the afterlife of his hoax with pride? Hopefully there will never be a comparable literary hoaxer to provide a model for answering that question.

VRAIN-DENIS LUCAS

ONE DAY IN Paris in 1867 the eminent mathematician Michel Chasles approached the French Academy of Science with a most extraordinary discovery. He had in his possession a number of letters which could change the course of the history of science, proving that it was a Frenchman, not an Englishman, who discovered gravity; and not a Dutchman but an Italian who first saw Saturn's moons. Chasles, then in his seventies but still producing ground-breaking work at the Sorbonne, was one of the most respected academics of his generation: unmarried, doggedly focused on his subject and never known to be swayed by the many social diversions of mid-nineteenth-century Paris, he had worked solidly all his life to prove new mathematical truths and correct the theoretical mistakes of his forebears. He was known to be a man of absolute honesty, professional integrity and perfect good manners, as well as one possessed of a tremendous intelligence. In short, he was not the type to fool or be fooled.

Yet the letters he presented to his peers at the Academy seemed almost too good to be true, especially the folder of notes from the seventeenth-century academic Blaise Pascal, which contained letters he wrote to fellow scientists Boyle and Galileo, as well as Newton himself, claiming in no uncertain terms that he had discovered the forces of gravitational attraction long before Newton did. Many of these letters were in a chatty style, but contained fairly detailed accounts of experiments and observations which would indeed alter the course of scientific history, placing France at the centre of the great discoveries of Enlightenment Europe. And that of course was a circumstance greatly desired by the Parisian establishment.

At first, the Academicians were overjoyed. And more so when they learnt of the existence of other letters by other Frenchmen, all purporting to support the notion of France as an ages-old centre of learning and culture. Before long, however, some members began to wonder about the origins of the papers that had fallen into their laps. When the Pascal letters were inspected more closely, questions began to be asked. Was that really his writing style? Did those dates quite add up? And as for the Galileo letters, in which he claimed the astronomical discoveries of Huygens for his own, they seemed to be dated after the year when the great Italian famously went blind.

Old Chasles assured his colleagues there must be a perfectly rational explanation for this, and when he went back to the source of these documents he was able to purchase more letters explaining away these apparent inaccuracies, including an extraordinary missive from Galileo confiding that he was not really blind, as he had been making out, but in fact just pretending, and would be grateful if his correspondent would keep this fact to himself. The fellows of the Academy found themselves in a terrible quandary. Here was one of the greatest, most revered brains in Paris presenting them with documentary evidence of things that in their nationalistic hearts they longed to believe, but which could not by any stretch of the imagination be deemed to be genuine. And they hadn't even seen the letters from Cleopatra, Mary Magdalene and Alexander the Great, yet. All written in idiomatic French and all praising that country to high heaven, these were tucked away in Chasles's library alongside the 27,000 others he had paid over 100,000 francs for over the previous twenty years.

What, the Academy finally dared to ask, was the source of these letters? According to Chasles's supplier, they came originally from a Revolution-era collector named Boisjourdain, who had acquired part of the famous antique Charnage Library and taken it to show academics in America, but had thankfully brought it back to France intact, albeit slightly water-stained after a shipwreck that interrupted his passage home. He had, Chasles said, been forced to sell off his priceless papers after falling on hard times and had sold them on to an intermediary for whom Chasles's supplier was working. This supplier was a young man called Vrain-Denis Lucas. He was the most prolific and daring literary hoaxer France has ever known.

Lucas was born to a poor family in the humble village of Lanneray, near Chateaudun, about a hundred miles south-west of Paris, in 1818. His father was a labourer and for some time the young Lucas worked alongside him to help earn enough to keep their family fed and clothed. But in his early teens he heard about a position vacant at the house of a local gentleman, and went into service. It was here that his intelligence and interest in history was first noted and here too, it is safe to assume, that he first got a taste for things slightly finer than those he had known growing up. The clothes, books, good food and witty conversation in even a relatively unremarkable provincial French manor house would have seemed dazzling to a young peasant brought up in the squalor of rural poverty, and Lucas resolved to better himself at all costs. Before long, his master recommended him for a lowly job in a lawyer's office, and Lucas transferred his skills from the domestic environment to a professional one, working as a clerk and messenger by day and, in any spare time he had, holing himself up in the local library to improve his knowledge of history, literature, science and classics. There is even a note left by a Chateaudun librarian observing that this hard-working little autodidact ought to go far.

In 1851 he got as far as Paris, where he arrived with no money and no possessions apart from a folder of his own poems, which were fairly uninspired verses imitated from the old poets he had been studying in the library back home. Paris in 1851, although the best place in the world for a young man to be if he were rich, was no fun for the homeless unemployed, and the fact that Lucas threw himself into life there and landed on his feet so quickly shows he possessed that combination of ambition and audacity so typical of the successful hoaxer. Somehow he managed to get a job with a company that would both help him earn money in the short term and provide him with the technical and psychological skills that would enable and sustain him in his career as a phoney letter-writer.

The place was a '*cabinet généalogique*' – a service for researching the pedigrees of any Frenchman with money and social ambition enough to seek proof that he was, indeed, related to whichever noble old lord he had in mind. Much of this work was genuine historical research, and the great boon for Lucas was that the firm's employees were granted access to the Imperial Library, the splendidly beautiful and complete bibliographic collection that was the predecessor to today's ugly Bibliothèque National on the left bank. When a client came to the atelier whose ancestry could not be traced satisfactorily, however, it was common practice for Lucas and his colleagues to use their knowledge of antique styles and forms to invent the kind of pedigree that they might have hoped to find. The place was a school for mendacious scribes.

So, like William Henry Ireland before him, Lucas was able to combine his experience of the pomp and technical language of lawyers with an acquaintance with the practical deceptions undertaken by calligraphers and printers. And like Ireland, he struck just at the right moment to fool an enthusiastic old man into believing he had the one thing he most wanted.

Exactly how Lucas met Chasles is not clear, but in 1861 they made their first transaction. The letters supposedly from Pascal were the first to be produced, which suggests Lucas had done his research and targeted his subject quite carefully. Perhaps he thought – or had heard – that the old professor was losing his grip on reality as he approached his seventh decade? Certainly, Chasles's failing mind is the explanation some choose to give for his being fooled so spectacularly. Yet he was still doing important work in mathematics throughout these years, so it is more likely that Lucas was playing on his inflamed sense of intellectual nationalism, a fervent vein of which was running through France at that great time of nation-building in Europe.

Whatever the reasons behind the old man's uncharacteristic credulousness (and after a career of questioning and analysing everything before him, it really is perplexing), an alternative explanation, that he might have been in league with Lucas, is impossible to believe, because he had all the money and prestige a man could hope for. But he had the desire and the capital for more and more of Lucas's forged documents, and this meant that the hoaxer was working flat out in the library to create texts which not only sounded, to his mind, convincing in their style, but looked the part too. To this end, he employed the techniques of many hoaxers before and since, toasting the leaves in front of the fire to achieve a sepia tint and submerging some in water – which technique he was overzealous at, and therefore invented the story of Boisjourdain's shipwreck. The precise means by which Lucas claimed to be obtaining the documents are even more reminiscent of William Henry Ireland, the Shakespeare hoaxer: he said he went to collect them from an old man who wished to remain nameless, and whom he would never betray by naming.

This *'vieux monsieur'*, it seemed, could not only come up with more of the exact type of document Chasles most wanted at the drop of a hat, but had in store a series of increasingly unbelievable letters from antiquity. And while the sad story of the old professor being duped into thinking the French were the greatest scientists in the world can just about be explained, the tale of his spending thousands of francs on letters like the one below is nothing short of incredible:

> Queen Cleopatra
>   to her dearly beloved Emperor Julius Caesar
>   [. . .] Our son Caesarian is doing well. I hope that soon he will . . . voyage from here to Marseilles, where I intend to have him instructed both because of the good air that one breathes there and the fine things that are taught there . . .
>   Cleopatra

Next, another famous woman of antiquity – Mary Magdalene – sends a postcard home from a trip to la Belle France:

> Magdalene to her dearly beloved Lazarus.
>   [. . .] we are very fond of . . . these provinces of Gaul . . . these Gauls, who we were told are barbarous peoples are not at all that way . . . it must be from there that the light of learning must come
>   Magdalene

Charlamagne is another important figure given the opportunity to speak up for the Gauls, and in a letter dated 20 August 802, and executed in a bizarre faux-medieval script purporting to be the hand of the great man himself, he thanks the scholar Alcuin of York for sending him:

proof . . . of the stay of Hercules among the Gauls and that he married Galatea . . . What reason could anyone have not to believe in this union? . . . why must we have less regard for the Gauls . . . than the nations that are foreign to us?

The letters from Joan of Arc to the Parisians, Rabelais to Martin Luther and of course the scientists Pascal and Galileo are less surprising to find written in French, but although their handwriting looks vaguely of the right period, it is impossible to comprehend, now, how a man of Chasles's stature would be willing to pay for their bogus autographs. If we are charitable to him, we can assume he knew full well they were bogus but, believing Lucas to have access to genuine manuscripts as well as these, decided to keep him sweet by buying everything he offered. Or perhaps Chasles, buying into what was, after all, a fairly well-designed story of traceability, believed them to be copies made in the time of Boisjourdain of letters which had really existed? Or, despite being a mathematical genius and a gentleman, he simply had a terribly blind and soft spot for ancient history.

Either way, Chasles parted with enough money over the years to make Lucas a rich man. However, such was the demand for more and more manuscripts that he hardly had time to spend it. Little is known about his personal life, but at the investigation over the Pascal letters during which he was finally hauled before the Academy, it was attested that he spent all day every day in the library, taking brief, solitary meals in a nearby café but otherwise keeping himself to himself. Whatever his private proclivities or spending habits were, or whether he was sending the money home to Lanneray, may never be discovered. Yet he did not give the impression of being a rich man, and when, finally, the Academicians and a humiliated Chasles called his bluff and had him arrested, he wrote in a letter of confession that mere financial gain had not been his only motivation. This letter may be the only truthful text France's master hoaxer ever wrote, and it accounts in some way for why he did what he did and, considering he disappears completely from the public record after being sentenced to two years in prison in February 1870, it serves as a typically odd epitaph for this most peculiar of literary hoaxers.

> Maison Centrale de Poissy, 13 August 1871.
> To my most respected Sir, . . . Michel Chasles,
> . . . I address you with the hope that you will find it in your heart to pardon me . . .
> I alone had penned the letters . . . widely believed to be from the hands of Pascal, Newton . . . and others – letters that you took to be the authentic voices of the past . . . I have at all times acted with patriotism . . . and in the service of science . . .

MARK TWAIN

THE EXUBERANT MARK Twain, the English-speaking world's best-loved chronicler of the madness of the late nineteenth-century America, was something of a hoaxer all his life. He flitted between careers, names and personae, leaving many in doubt as to who he really was; and for his readers this innate ventriloquism is surely part of his appeal.

If you have never had the pleasure of reading any of Mark Twain's journalism, here is an example of the kind of writing his devoted band of followers in 1860s Nevada grew to love. It tells of an accident which befell his editor and friend, Dan DeQuille:

Our time-honored confrere, Dan, met with a disastrous accident, yesterday, while returning from American City on a vicious Spanish horse, the result of which accident is that at the present writing he is confined to his bed and suffering great bodily pain. He was coming down the road at the rate of a hundred miles an hour (as stated in his will, which he made shortly after the accident), and on turning a sharp corner, he suddenly hove in sight of a horse standing square across the channel; he signalled for the starboard, and put his helm down instantly, but too late . . . Dan was wrenched from his saddle and thrown some three hundred yards (according to his own statement, made in his will, above mentioned), alighting upon solid ground, and bursting himself open from the chin to the pit of the stomach. His head was also caved in out of sight, and his hat was afterwards extracted in a bloody and damaged condition from between his lungs; he must have bounced end-for-end after he struck first, because it is evident he received a concussion from the rear that broke his heart; one of his legs was jammed up in his body nearly to his throat, and the other so torn and mutilated that it pulled out when they attempted to lift him into the hearse which we had sent to the scene of the disaster, under the general impression that he might need it; both arms were indiscriminately broken up until they were jointed like a bamboo; the back was considerably fractured and bent into the shape of a rail fence. Aside from these injuries, however, he sustained no other damage. They brought some of him home in the hearse and the balance on a dray. His first remark showed that the powers of his great mind had not been impaired by the accident, nor his profound judgment destroyed – he said he wouldn't have cared a d–n if it had been anybody but himself . . . Dan may have exaggerated the above details in some respects, but he charged us to report them thus, and it is a source of genuine pleasure to us to have the opportunity of doing it. Our noble old friend is recovering fast, and what is left of him will be around the Brewery again to-day, just as usual.

In the early days of his career, before he had started writing in earnest and when he still went under his given name, Samuel Langhorne Clemens, Twain had travelled to Nevada as assistant to his brother Orion, whom Abraham Lincoln had made territorial secretary. The role of assistant was, however, decidedly nominal, and provided him with little to do. Worse still, it was presenting him no obvious way to raise enough money to pay off the considerable debts he was accruing, so he began to search for some more rewarding outlet for his profusely creative intelligence than taking notes and filing documents for his older brother.

Being a young, energetic man in Carson City in 1861 must have been exciting. The city itself, full of prospectors and schemers, investors and get-rich-quick merchants, was the epitome of the optimistic young American town. Twain describes life there in his wonderful book, *Roughing It*:

> Joy sat on every countenance, and there was a glad, almost fierce, intensity in every eye, that told of the money-getting schemes that were seething in every brain and the high hope that held sway in every heart. Money was as plenty as dust; every individual considered himself wealthy, and a melancholy countenance was nowhere to be seen. There were military companies, fire companies, brass bands, banks, hotels, theatres, 'hurdy-gurdy houses,' wide-open gambling palaces, political pow wows, civic processions, street fights, murders, inquests, riots, a whisky mill every fifteen steps . . .

This piece of writing was no hoax – times were flush, and Samuel was determined to enjoy himself as much as possible. But in the back of his mind was the thought of his mother and sister back home, wondering if he would make something of himself like his brother had. Their expectations, coupled with his desire for beer money, led him to hatch a plan which would not only start him off on his writing career but give birth to the man called Mark Twain.

The two main local newspapers at that time, the *Territorial Enterprise* in Virginia City and the *Evening Bulletin*, were locked in competitive rivalry, each seeking the best stories and the best writers with which to lure a reading public hungry for gossip. In the summer of 1862 Samuel – initially under the pen-name Josh – began writing to the letters page of the *Enterprise*. These letters were amusingly told tales of the doings of local businessmen, socialites, animals and policeman, and it was not long before the paper's editor saw in him a talent that would enchant his readers and possibly steal a few from the *Bulletin*. 'Josh' was duly offered the job of local reporter, and charged with running around town talking to people, drinking with them (not hard for the liquor-loving, sociable younger brother of the more serious Clemens) and writing up what they told him. For this he was to be paid no less than $25 a week which seemed to him a 'sinful and lavish' amount.

After a respectful period of time reporting on the genuine doings of the local community, Twain realized that his colleagues in the newsroom, not least his friend and mentor William Wright (who wrote under the name Dan DeQuille) took a peculiarly relaxed approach to journalistic integrity. The reporting of hard facts, especially on a slow news day, would always come second place to giving the readers what they wanted, which was blood, guts and scandal. Years later, in an autobiographical piece for that very same newspaper, he would unashamedly recall the 'feats and calamities that we never hesitated about devising when the public needed matters of thrilling slaughter, mutilation and general destruction'.

Twain would always claim astonishment at the gullibility of his readership, whom he never expected to swallow his tall stories without a pinch of salt. But his naturally playful, anecdotal style, even when reporting something that really happened, probably coaxed his readers into thinking he was just one of those people to whom extraordinary stories seemed to gravitate.

Perhaps the most famous of his invented news stories, and the one which, knowing the author's mischievous sense of humour, seems almost impossible to take seriously, was nonetheless taken as gospel by most who opened their paper on the morning of 4 October 1862 to read this report, now under the byline Mark Twain:

A petrified shah was found some time ago in the mountains south of Gravelly Ford. Every limb and feature of the stone mummy was perfect, not even excepting the left leg, which had evidently been a wooden one during the lifetime of the owner – which lifetime, by the way, came to a close about a century ago, in the opinion of a savant who has examined the defunct.

The body was in a sitting position, and leaning against a huge mass of droppings; the attitude was pensive, the right thumb rested against the side of the nose; the left thumb partially supported the chin, the forefinger pressing the inner corner of the left eye, and drawing it partly open; the right eye closed, and the fingers of the right hand spread out. This strange freak of nature created a profound sensation in the vicinity, and our informant states that, by request, Judge Sewell at once proceeded to the spot and held an inquest on the body. The verdict was that 'deceased came to his death from protracted exposure'.

Can you see what it is yet? This was far from the only story in which Twain slyly thumbed his nose at his readers. Another, under the compelling headline 'HORRIBLE AFFAIR', was also entirely fictional, and includes teasing allegations of a hoax-within-a-hoax in the opening paragraph on 16 April 1863:

For a day or two a rumor has been floating around, that five Indians had been smothered to death in a tunnel back of Gold Hill, but no one seemed to regard it in any other light than as a sensation hoax gotten up for the edification of strangers sojourning within our gates. However, we asked a Gold Hill man about it yesterday, and he said there was no shadow of a jest in it – that it was a dark and terrible reality. He gave us the following story as being the version generally accepted in Gold Hill: That town was electrified on Sunday morning with the intelligence that a noted desperado had just murdered two Virginia policemen, and had fled in the general direction of Gold Hill. Shortly afterwards, some one arrived with the exciting news that a man had been seen to run and hide in a tunnel a mile or a mile and a half west of Gold Hill. Of course it was Campbell – who else would do such a thing, on that particular morning, of all others? So a party of citizens repaired to this spot, but each felt a natural delicacy about approaching an armed and desperate man in the dark, and especially in such confined quarters; wherefore they stopped up the mouth of the tunnel, calculating to hold on to their prisoner until some one could be found whose duty would oblige him to undertake the disagreeable task of bringing forth the captive. The next day a strong posse went up, rolled away the stones from the mouth of the sepulchre, went in and found five dead Indians! – three men, one squaw and one child, who had gone in there to sleep, perhaps, and been smothered by the foul atmosphere after the tunnel had been closed up. We still hope the story may prove a fabrication, notwithstanding the positive assurances we have received that it is entirely true. The intention of the citizens was good, but the result was most unfortunate. To shut up a murderer in a tunnel was well enough, but to leave him there all night was calculated to impair his chances for a fair trial – the principle was good, but the application was unnecessarily 'hefty.' We have given the above story for truth – we shall continue to regard it as such until it is disproven.

The hesitant disclaimer in the last line was never going to put off readers who wanted to believe in the dangers of underground suffocation, murder and Indians. Another hoax article that played on the bloodthirstiness of the *Enterprise*'s fans was his piece 'BLOODY MASSACRE' of 28 October 1863:

It seems that during the past six months a man named P. Hopkins, or Philip Hopkins, has been residing with his family in the old log house just at the edge of the great pine forest which lies between Empire City and Dutch Nick's. The family consisted of nine children – five girls and four boys – the oldest of the group, Mary, being nineteen years old, and the youngest, Tommy, about a year and a half. Twice in the past two months Mrs. Hopkins, while visiting in Carson, expressed fears concerning the sanity of her husband, remarking that of late he had been subject to fits of violence, and that during the prevalence of one of these he had threatened to take her life. It was Mrs. Hopkins' misfortune to be given to exaggeration, however, and but little attention was paid to what she said. About ten o'clock on Monday evening Hopkins dashed into Carson on horseback, with his throat cut from ear to ear, and bearing in his hand a reeking scalp from which the warm, smoking blood was still dripping, and fell in a dying condition in front of the Magnolia saloon. Hopkins expired in the course of five minutes, without speaking. The long red hair of the scalp he bore marked it as that of Mrs. Hopkins. A number of citizens, headed by Sheriff Gasherie, mounted at once and rode down to Hopkins' house, where a ghastly scene met their gaze. The scalpless corpse of Mrs. Hopkins lay across the threshold, with her head split open and her right hand almost severed from the wrist. Near her lay the ax with which the murderous deed had been committed. In one of the bedrooms six of the children were found, one in bed and the others scattered about the floor. They were all dead. Their brains had evidently been dashed out with a club, and every mark about them seemed to have been made with a blunt instrument. The children must have struggled hard for their lives, as articles of clothing and broken furniture were strewn about the room in the utmost confusion. Julia and Emma, aged respectively fourteen and seventeen, were found in the kitchen, bruised and insensible, but it is thought their recovery is possible. The eldest girl, Mary, must have taken refuge, in her terror, in the garret, as her body was found there, frightfully mutilated, and the knife with which her wounds had been inflicted still sticking in her side. The two girls, Julia and Emma, who had recovered sufficiently to be able to talk yesterday morning, state that their father knocked them down with a billet of wood and stamped on them. They think they were the first attacked. They further state that

Hopkins had shown evidence of derangement all day, but had exhibited no violence. He flew into a passion and attempted to murder them because they advised him to go to bed and compose his mind.

The sheer unbridled naughtiness of Twain's prose, and the fact that he readily admits to being drunk while writing much of his journalism of this period, makes it hard to judge him as we might judge a mendacious journalist today. The mitigating circumstances of the crazy times in the crazy town in which he and his readers were living make his hoaxes far less serious than others of their ilk. Moreover there is the absence of a formal debunking in which the caught-out author was forced either to admit his crime or foolishly protest his innocence; rather, Twain cheerfully admitted when asked years later that *of course* these tall tales were made-up. Indeed, putting the responsibility on the intelligent reader to determine the truth of a text is a canny trick that many subsequent hoaxers would have done well to learn from Twain. It might have saved them, and their readers and publishers, a great deal of trouble if they had.

SIR EDMUND BACKHOUSE

*T*O BE AN Englishman in turn-of-the-century Peking (today's Beijing) was to have unbridled access to a range of luxuries, pursuits and services unimaginable to those at home in Victorian Britain. And to be fleeing debt, an aristocratic family you loathed and a boyhood full of homosexual confusion would seem to lay perfect foundations for a life of secrecy, intrigue and devil-may-care carnality. So it was for Sir Edmund Trelawney Backhouse, 2nd Baronet.

Backhouse (pronounced Bacchus, as he liked to remind people) was born in Darlington to a rich Quaker family of long and illustrious standing whose sons had latterly forgone pacifism for military careers (his brother would go on to become the First Sea Lord). At first Backhouse followed the predestined path of St George's, Winchester and Oxford. An unstable and highly emotional child, he always felt he was the black sheep of the family, and was said to nurture a particular resentment towards his mother, over whose corpse he reputedly screamed curses (in several languages). He did however have a fond homosexual uncle who may or may not have introduced him to the voracious love of men which would characterize his later life. Although a brilliant linguist, the young Backhouse never managed to complete his studies in Asiatic languages at Oxford, instead passing his days in a recreational splendour he could ill afford and incurring phenomenal debts of more than £20,000. Still an undergraduate, and not daring to stick around long enough to complete his degree, he fled the country to seek his fortune elsewhere.

That was in 1895. Four years later he arrived in Peking, almost fluent in Russian, Japanese and Mandarin, and found work as a translator for the Australian-born *Times* journalist Dr George Morrison. The city at that time – especially the ex-pat south-eastern district where Backhouse lived when he first arrived – was alive with music, food, art and, most appealingly to Backhouse, flesh. For the wealthy and curious there were brothels full of boys and girls where long, lazy afternoons could be spent not only fornicating but drinking tea, bathing and watching others disport themselves similarly. Out in the open, the business of modernization in imperial politics was rumbling on, with the royal household doing its best to quash the anti-Western feeling that would soon lead to the famous Boxer Rebellion. Journalists and businessmen from Europe had their work cut out in this extraordinary city and, before long, Backhouse, who had more or less decided to remain in this charmed place for the rest of his life, saw that he could capitalize on this period of change. Having cemented his image as a well-bred, well-dressed, well-connected (he arrived in China with a letter of recommendation from the prime minister, Lord Salisbury) linguist and Sinophile, he set about planning the first of a number of daring hoaxes.

Not all his cons would be literary. All his life he exploited his connections with the English establishment for financial and reputational gain, at one point faking long correspondences between Chinese arms dealers and the British government which led to huge sums of money being forwarded to him for deals that would never take place. But his greatest talent was for making up stories and characters of just the sort his less clued-up fellow Englishmen wanted to hear. He was, those who knew him agreed, possessed of a vivid imagination and a wickedly colourful turn of phrase and honed his skills for salacious reportage by feeding questionable stories to British journalists.

His best customer was the reporter John Otway Percy Bland. Bland, who was a minor diplomat and composer of light verse as well as deputy to *The Times'* Dr Morrison, enjoyed a similarly charmed existence to Backhouse, albeit with his wife rather than a bevy of rent-boys. They started working together on pieces of journalism, for which Backhouse would provide the anecdotes which Bland's *Times* style would shape into publishable form. Before long, the two men set about executing two works of fascinating contemporary history about the bizarre world of the Forbidden City and the ways of the irascible Empress Tsu Hsi (better known nowadays as Cixi) which would bring them instant recognition and sell in their thousands.

Their books continue to fascinate historians and general readers today, and much of what is written there about daily life in the corridors of power stands – after all, both Bland and Backhouse did have rare access to some high-ranking players in the Ch'ing court. The first book, *China Under the Empress Dowager: Being the History of the Life and Times of Tsu Hsi* (1910), provides an extensive overview of the country at the turn of the century, and by far the most intriguing chapter of it is that entitled 'The Diary of his Excellency Ching-shan: Being a Chinese Account of the Boxer Troubles'. This is fifty pages of what purports to be the gossipy journal of a Manchu soldier at the heart of the royal household and it was this chapter which sold the book to the English publisher William Heinemann when Backhouse returned to England with a sample, promising as it did a rare peek into the inner sanctum of one of the most mysterious palaces in the world.

With his fantastical imagination running at full throttle, Backhouse told Bland he had stumbled upon the diaries just as a band of Sikh soldiers were looting the recently dead Ching-shan's house during the Boxer Rebellion. He wrote to Bland that the manuscript had been in a 'camphor-wood Chinese escritoire which stood on the k'ang on the old man's inner room. That leaves were all strewed on the k'ang and some had already been used by the Sikh for packing papers and other base purposes.' This was some years previously, in 1900, and Backhouse had, he claimed, spent the best part of the last decade translating it.

It is true that Ching-shan had indeed existed, but in fact he was only an administrative assistant on the periphery of court affairs, and not the confidant of anybody important. And he certainly never kept a diary full of well-informed, perfectly pitched journalistic observations about the rebellion as seen from the empress's side. Still, there was at that time no known record of any private writing from the inside of the empress's court, when half the court was in favour of the Boxer movement, and half against. Any inside information would have been gold dust to contemporary historians. As one leading commentator of the day, Sir Robert Hart, said at the time: 'It would be interesting to get a really reliably account of the Palace doings – and Peking doings – during 1900. As it is, we are all guessing and inferring . . . but we have not got the facts yet.' Backhouse would have heard similar things being said all over Peking and London, and he knew full well that one of the most hotly contested issues surrounding the fall of the Manchu dynasty was whether the empress's grand secretary, Jung-lu, was really as pro-Western as he made out. This became one of the central revelations in the fifty-page Diary. It testified to Jung-lu's consistently moderate ideology and his wholehearted attempts to stop the violence of the rebellion.

This fanciful creation was to be only the beginning of Backhouse's career as a hoaxer. It is now believed that almost all the research he supplied to writers and academics in the form of reportage and interviews was made-up by him, often with the assistance of a calligrapher. He did of course have the language skills and cultural immersion to base his fictions on a keenly observed reality, and this – even now – is enough for many scholars to consider his papers worthwhile historical documents.

It seems remarkable that a man with so profuse an output could have got away with it for so long, but the main reason for his hoax not being debunked sooner than the twentieth century was the linguistic and social exclusivity of his subject. Meeting – let alone speaking to – members of the royal household would have been such a complex undertaking that no sceptical English inquisitor would have been able to saunter up to Cixi's cohorts and ask them what they thought of it all. It is telling that only Dr Morrison – the one Englishman with language skills and personal connections in Peking to rival Backhouse's – accused him of fakery from the outset. To the general English reader and publisher, however, Backhouse was a gentleman and polyglot who had made his life among the upper echelons of Peking society. He also had the trust of several internationally respected foreign correspondents. Why doubt him?

This good faith was made manifest just before the First World War when he was asked to return to England to become Professor of Chinese at King's College, London. This honour was slightly less than he had hoped for, his sights having been set on a position at his *alma mater*, Oxford, and he blamed ill-health for only undertaking the post for a short while before returning to live out the rest of his seventy years in Peking – now living in the west of the city, where few foreigners cared to tread. However, in order to gain the interest of the universities in the first place he had some time previously begun shipping vast quantities of books back to the Bodleian Library as gifts. Thousands of manuscripts were conveyed by him from China, and as he and Bland had now published a second, well-received book, *Annals and Memoirs of the Court of Peking*, his credentials as a serious academic were hardly doubted. But the more he was thanked and lauded for bestowing upon the university these books, the more he became carried away with the idea of donating more, and so furthering his reputation as the English emperor of Chinese studies. He took cash advances for the complicated shipping arrangements, by land and sea, of something he called 'the famous palace library' – some 60,000 manuscripts and journals all said to be pricelessly rare and beautiful. But the palace library, like Ching-shan's diary and the arms contracts, never existed. And the Bodleian was of course never able to trace its money.

Despite incurring the wrath of the educational and governmental institutions whom he tricked out of money, and continual bad-mouthing by Dr Morrison, who grew to loathe Backhouse but still kept him on as an assistant, the slippery baronet was never exposed in his lifetime. And thanks to occasional bail-outs from his family back home in England he was able to continue living the life he loved. Those English diplomats and officials lucky enough to draw him out of his lodgings would describe him as an impeccably polite member of any party, especially delighting in the company of women; but the journalists and other men of lesser orders he encountered spoke of his lascivious tongue and dependence on 'caffeine crystals' and sleeping pills. In all his eccentricity, he became a Peking institution, much talked about but rarely seen. Even when the Japanese invaded Peking in the 1940s he was excused internment, and having refused the passage home offered by his family in England, preferred instead to remain living in a single, humble room in Peking (claiming he had been robbed of his treasures and books by dishonest staff), always dressed in Chinese robes, and attended on by one faithful Chinese servant. In the last few years of his life, although living in near total isolation, he was befriended by a Swiss doctor, Reinhard Hoeppli, who would persuade – and pay – him to complete the last, excessive flourish in his life's work as a hoaxer: his memoirs.

These two books, charting his life as a miserable public-schoolboy, then an oversexed undergraduate and culminating in his arrival in China and the dawn of a new, unbridled age of sexual and political exploits, stretch the reader's credibility almost to breaking point. And after a while, their tolerance of pornography too. Hoeppli says that Backhouse's physical health improved as he wrote these volumes, but whether that was the function of catharsis or sheer self-titillation is unclear. Backhouse claimed that his long career as an active homosexual began when the French poet Verlaine came to teach a term at his school. This might be true, but from there the account spirals off on a tangent of what can only be described as literary-historical sexual fantasy. Travelling Europe with his new friend Verlaine, he becomes intimate with almost every famous writer of the *fin de siècle* cultural scene: Oscar Wilde and Lord Alfred Douglas; the actor Harry Stanford; Aubrey Beardsley;

Ellen Terry; Henry James; Joseph Conrad; Edmund Gosse. The list goes on. Once he is established in Peking, aside from the hundreds of young men he had sex with in brothels and backstreets, he describes being summoned to the inner sanctum of the septuagenarian dowager empress herself and given the honour of engaging in a marathon of love-making, aphrodisiac-taking and general ritualized pleasure-making with her. Pure, adulterated fantasy.

It was not until Hugh Trevor-Roper (who we will encounter again later in connection with some other more famous bogus journals) discovered these later diaries and made their author the subject of one of his brilliant studies in the mid-1970s that the full story of Backhouse's extraordinary, playful powers of illusion were exposed. While the memoir seen by Trevor-Roper contains nothing like an explicit confession, enough of it is the work of a blatant fantasist to warrant calling his entire oeuvre into question. An openly gay Englishman who claims to have had sordid sexual liaisons with the ageing Empress Cixi herself, as well as being an intimate of her Grand Eunuch is, by anybody's standards, something of a loon. But what a successful loon he was. Deluded, greedy, desperate for recognition from the university at which he had failed so conspicuously to shine as a young man, yes, but ultimately one of those inimitable eccentrics without whom the history of English letters – and Englishmen abroad – would be a far less colourful place.

3

NATIVE AMERICANS

WHITE AMERICA'S RELATIONSHIP with her native population is complex and only relatively recently beginning to get away from the stereotypes of cowboys 'n' Injuns. But as with Americans of African origin, the figure of the native American is still bound up with any number of insecurities and simplifications which result in him being seen as either unrealistically strong and capable (the warrior king of the plains, preternaturally skilled in bushcraft and ancient lore) or hopelessly feeble (the unemployable drunk languishing on a reservation). Nowadays many white Americans look for Indian blood in their heritage as keenly as they once delved into their Celtic or northern European provenance, while other more reactionary types rue the positive discrimination they see their native countrymen receiving. All these tensions combine in the literature of First Nation America, but for every fine authentic novelist like Sherman Alexie there is a Nasdijj – the unfortunate white man who decided to hijack the identity of a Navajo and pass it off as his own to capitalize on the vogue for confessional autobiographies and the romance of the

Indian. But long before he put mendacious pen to paper, there were other hoaxers whose immersion in their assumed native identities were even more comprehensive and often done for a far better cause than mere self-promotion. The greatest of them all was Grey Owl.

GREY OWL

*I*N LONDON IN 1937 a weathered-looking Apache Indian stood in long hair, skins and moccasins before the entire royal household in Buckingham Palace and spoke movingly about the urgent need to protect the natural world from greedy developers. He was one of the world's first naturalists (just the sort of man, in fact, that the future heir of the young Princess Elizabeth would adore), and a tireless campaigner, through his books and lectures, for the land he loved best: the Canadian wilderness. Only on his death the following year would questions about his true identity begin to be raised. Who was Grey Owl? And how should the answer to that question affect the way his books are read?

The story begins in Hastings, Sussex, at the turn of the twentieth century, when young Archie Belaney was twelve years old. The child of a dissolute father and under-age mother, he was raised by his maiden aunts, who sent him to grammar school and hoped for a good steady office job for him afterwards. But Archie had only one passion – the Indian warriors of the Wild West. He devoured books about heroes like Buffalo Bill, and soon his obsession with the Aboriginal way of life extended to his eschewing his bed for the hard floorboards (because no good backwoodsman can sleep on a soft bed), camping out overnight in the garden and collecting such specimens from nature as the Sussex countryside would offer up. And just as much as he loved this alternative world, he hated and feared the one marked out for him at home. His terror of ending up an office worker led him to run away to Canada in 1906 at the tender age of sixteen.

Arriving in Ontario, Belaney soon made his way to the beautiful wilderness of Temagami, the home of the Ojibwa nation. Amongst the expansive woods and lakes of this unspoilt territory the boy who had felt so cooped up and misunderstood in the suburban streets of East Sussex finally breathed a sigh relief. He was happy, relaxed and inspired. And, like many a young traveller, in the mood for love. So he swiftly found and married a local girl and began to make it known that he was the son of a Scotsman and an Apache woman from New Mexico who had come north to live off the land and learn more about the way of the Ojibwa. Despite having blue eyes, his tanned skin and increasingly long hair allowed him to pass as mixed-race, and his boundless enthusiasm for bushcraft saw him first employed as a trainee guide then a fire ranger, and eventually he was taken in by the Ojibwa, who taught him their language and customs. They even gave him a ceremonial name.

He and his wife Angele and their children were living a Walden-like dream, but in 1914 his happy life was interrupted by the First World War. Grey Owl, as he was now called, enlisted in the Canadian Army and was shipped out to France to fight. So began a hiatus of several years during which time he was injured by shrapnel and mustard gas and sent to hospital in England to recuperate. Here, he rekindled an old love with a girl from Hastings and even made a brief bigamous marriage, but as soon as he was well enough he returned to Canada and his first love: not Angele, for he was to marry more than once again, but the life of the tepee-dwelling, beaver-trapping, fire-making brave.

Then along came Pony. Her real name was Anahereo but everyone called her by her nickname. She was a charismatic, very beautiful Iroquoi woman who was destined to change him from a trapper to an animal-lover, and from a runaway to a celebrity. She was not yet twenty when she met the tall exotic Grey Owl (by now in his late thirties) but her passion for nurturing animals convinced him to move in with her and a pair of rescued baby beavers, give up trapping and start writing and lecturing about the precious and dying way of life of the Indians, whose lives were already becoming fatally tainted with the greedy unsustainable ways of white men.

Perhaps because he had read so much as a child and an invalid, Grey Owl was able to write engagingly enough about his experiences of life on the reservation for editors to take notice. His first pieces were for magazines such as *Country Life* and the publication of the Canadian Forestry Association (CFA), *Forests and Outdoors*. His pieces were on such subjects (as enthralling to deskbound readers then as now) as 'The Perils of Woods Travel', 'The King of the Beavers' and 'A Day in a Hidden Town'. The CFA took him up as something of a mascot and encouraged his burgeoning media career, even making a film about his life with Pony and their pet beavers. By the time he became the subject of the 1935 bestseller, *Grey Owl and the Beaver* (Thomas Nelson and Sons Ltd), he had started the lecture tours that would make him famous all over the world. First in America then Europe, he would attend societies and educational institutes dressed in full Ojibwa regalia, promoting not only his writings but a general ethos of sustainability and respect for nature. By now an ardent critic of trapping, which had, he felt, become something done more for financial gain than necessary subsistence, he was beloved by women and children (as well as the usual adventure-minded males) as a kind and philosophical noble savage. It would be a long time, of course, until the Native American world would find a critical voice loud enough to speak out against this sort of objectification.

Amazingly, on one of his lecture tours to England Grey Owl gave a talk at a hall in his hometown of Hastings, which was attended by the very aunts who had tolerated his boyish obsession with all things Indian several decades previously. They of course recognized the nephew they had raised from birth, but out of love and respect for a boy who finally seemed to have found happiness and success, kept his secret to themselves. How very English.

When Grey Owl finally died in 1938, his lungs weakened from mustard gas and his constitution not up to the years of travelling and working outdoors, his true identity was quickly revealed to a disbelieving public. He had looked and acted – and, crucially, written – the part so completely, that it was hard to believe this tall, craggy-faced, wise old Indian was in fact no more than a fanciful lad from Hastings.

The pattern of the hoaxer as a fatherless child who retreats into an imaginary world and ends up involving the public in his fantasies is becoming a familiar one. But there is a new significance, in terms of the way we think about authorship, in Grey Owl's story. In a sense, the books and articles he wrote were not hoaxes at all, because although they were the work of Grey Owl and Grey Owl did not exist (in that that was the name given to the imagined Apache character he presented to the Indians he met in Canada), the content of the writings was absolutely true. The author's knowledge of the environment he called home was profound. His passion for the traditional ways of life he advocated was real, and strong. And his radical message, that the whole world should join in protecting faraway wildernesses, was based on an understanding of the deleterious effects of global industrialization that was quite ahead of his time. So when a young Queen Elizabeth and her sister listened to this strange visitor speak his creed in Buckingham Palace in the 1930s, they were in the presence of an inspired man who, despite not having the origins he claimed, came with an important and undeniably true message.

Although easy to see with hindsight, his unmasking in a series of newspaper articles after his death caused considerable problems for those institutions who had been involved with him. His publisher, Lovat Dickson, although initially sceptical of articles such as that in *The Times* which presented the evidence for Belaney and Grey Owl being one and the same, finally had to admit he had been fooled. He immediately halted publication of his work. The Canadian conservation organizations he had worked with were also tarnished by their association with the hoax, and it would be some decades before Canadian, Indian and

British authorities would come to see Belaney's project as one undertaken in good – if peculiarly eccentric – faith.

CHIEF BUFFALO CHILD LONG LANCE

*A*ROUND THE SAME time as Grey Owl was passing himself off as an Apache son, the African-American son of a school janitor from North Carolina was playing a similar game. Long before he wrote his supposed autobiography, Sylvester Clark Long began to create fictions around his origins, telling the world – and the board of the Indian school he wanted to attend – that he was Cherokee. Looking like he might be, and able to speak a few words of the Cherokee language, he easily passed and joined the Carlisle Indian Industrial School in a class he shared with the soon to be legendary Geronimo. After graduating with excellent grades and an impressive sporting record, he went on to join a military academy at which he, as the only 'Indian' in his year, earned the nick-name of Chief. Although an unsuccessful West Point applicant, he joined up with the Canadian Expeditionary Force in 1914 and was sent to France, where he fought – still as a proud Indian – and was wounded.

It was after the war, when he returned to Canada, that his career as a writer – and hoaxer – began in earnest. Claiming not only to be a West Point graduate but a decorated war hero, which he most certainly was not, he secured a job at the *Calgary Herald* reporting on Indian issues. A staunch campaigner for First Nation rights and the maintenance of traditional lifestyles, he touted his pretend Cherokee affiliations until he was blue in the face and eventually was officially welcomed into the nation of the Blackfoot Indians and given his ceremonial name, Buffalo Child.

This was a gift to Long in more ways than one, as it gave him just the credibility he needed to set himself up as a fake memoirist amongst the buzzing literary salons of New York. He moved there in 1927 and spent a year writing *The Autobiography of Chief Buffalo Child Long Lance* about a humble Indian boy born to Blackfoots in Montana and who went on to fight heroically in the Great War.

Almost overnight he became desired and lauded in New York City: sought after as a party guest, after-dinner speaker, celebrity endorser of a brand of shoes and even a movie star, he was able to command $100 for a personal appearance, and enjoyed, for a while at least, about the best kind of life a handsome young man can have.

It was on the set of the silent film in which he had a part that questions were raised about his true identity which led to his eventual undoing. Once it was reported that he could not properly describe his Cherokee lineage, a coterie of suspicious (and racist) minds set about ruining him. People who knew him when he was growing up were found, and testimonies about his true identity were collected. Shamed, Long took work as a bodyguard for a well-known actress. But he was unable to toe the line sufficiently in this submissive type of work, and was let go. Tragically, in 1932 he was found with a self-administered gunshot to the head, unable to bear any longer the real life he had tried so hard to write over.

Considering the trappings of wealth and fame achieved by Long, it would be easy to pass him off as one whose hoax was perpetrated simply for material gain. But aside from the fact that he, like Grey Owl, became a genuinely impassioned spokesman for Native American issues, the prize he sought ought not to be seen in terms of parties, clothes and girls: born into the bitterly segregated community of Winston-Salem, North Carolina, the material wealth he wanted to gain was no more or less than freedom itself. This grandson of slaves capitalized on the traces of Anglo-Saxon and Indian blood in his veins which made him handsome in a way that would appeal to white people and used every resource he could – his charm, his strength and most of all his literary talent – to smart his way out of the South. Which is a good deal more heroic – if less psychologically complex – than a man like Grey Owl, who simply thought being English was boring.

FORREST CARTER

O F ALL THE First Nation writers in America, genuine or fake, there can be none so controversial as Forrest Carter, the bestselling author of *The Education of Little Tree*, a book of gentle back-country musings originally published in 1976 with the subtitle 'A True Story', but now sold as fiction. Carter's real story is one of an audacious deception which tricked a generation of readers into believing they were reading the autobiography of a soulful, Cherokee-raised boy instead of the fantasies of Asa Carter, a former Ku Klux Klan member and professional white supremacist. You couldn't make it up. Although many of Little Tree's fans have tried to prove that Carter's enemies did just that.

That Asa Carter and Forrest Carter were one and the same man is beyond question, even though the man himself, once he had taken on his new persona, tried to deny it. When he appeared on television to promote his book, viewers from his old stomping ground called in to say they recognized this folksy, leather-hatted storyteller as the same man, albeit a thinner, browner version, who had worked for one of the South's most violently racist politicians. The very man, indeed, who wrote the speech in which Governor George Wallace famously screamed: 'Segregation today! Segregation tomorrow! Segregation forever!'

The intermingling of the two Carters and the life of the book itself presents a puzzle for critics and readers, because it is almost impossible to reconcile the hate-filled rhetoric of Asa Carter the Klansman with the down-home New Ageisms of Forrest Carter, who wrote about his life as an orphan raised in the ways of 'Indian thinking' by Cherokee grandparents. Asa was a man who hated African Americans so much that he found the Ku Klux Klan too soft and had to set up his own more hard-line White Citizen's Council and then felt compelled to leave that too after a row over allowing pro-segregationist Jews to join. He even ran for governor of Alabama on the hard-line white supremacist ticket. Yet his famous book seems to preach tolerance and peaceful co-existence, and the twinkly, hippyish persona he assumed for it was a far cry from the slick, hate-filled former boxing champ he was in the Alabama days. It seems that he came round to supporting the Indians because he saw a link between his Confederate heroes (from one of whom he took the name Forrest) and the independent-minded Indians who sometimes supported them in their hatred of 'guv'mint' interference, but this is only half the story.

The reason Asa became Forrest is not because he had a sudden change of political heart, or because he truly believed that the Cherokee wanted the same things as the white supremacists. It was because abysmal failure in his political career forced him out of Alabama to seek a new life, a new audience and a very different kind of writing career in a new state.

Carter had been writing speeches for the segregationalist Governor of Alabama, George Wallace, setting up the white racist magazine *The Southerner* and touting his views on local radio stations. He was the sort of man who never liked to be too far from his bottle of whisky or his gun. When war came, he joined the navy, saying he'd sooner fight the Japanese than the Germans, who he saw as his racial kin. But as Wallace's career took off, Carter was seen as too extreme even for him, and he was let go from the gubernatorial staff. His own political ambitions had never got off the ground, and his heavy drinking and alleged violent tendencies were already getting him in trouble.

In 1973 Carter and his wife left for Florida where he quickly started work on a Western novel called *Gone to Texas*. Soon after, he did just that, re-inventing himself again in the Lone Star State as a kindly Floridian, born of Cherokee parents, who was none other than an official storyteller for his Indian community. This new identity could only help his debut novel, a *Dances-With-Wolves* sort of story (and some say a progenitor of that famous film, as well as the actual film version made by Clint Eastwood with the title *The Outlaw Josey Wales*) in which a former Confederate soldier, Wales, goes native and flees into the hills, using Indian wisdom and folklore to survive. The book was a success, with critics praising it as a cut above mere genre fiction, so he set about writing the book that would finally make him famous.

The Education of Little Tree: A True Story was published by Delacourt Press in 1976 and Carter set about promoting its sweetly simple philosophical message as conscientiously as he had his uncompromising political one a decade earlier. Although ostensibly very different from the blood-and-guts adventure story of *Gone to Texas*, critics soon pointed to a similar ethos of man living free of government control and the conventions of post-war social organization. But with its accessibility to readers of all ages, not to mention its appeal to the burgeoning 1970s back-to-nature movement, it became an instant success amongst readers and school librarians all over the United States.

That same year, however, Carter's cover would be blown, and an increasingly enlightened literary establishment would reject him as an author deserving of nothing but scorn. As well as this kindly old storyteller being recognized by people who had know him in Alabama, he was the subject of two damning articles in the *New York Times*, one of them by a distant cousin of his, Dan Carter. These pieces officially outed him as the man who only six years previously had said that the idea of a black man becoming a policeman was absurd because he would be 'as uncivilized as the day his kind were found eating their kin in a jungle'.

Some would say he got his comeuppance when he died, ignoble and drunk, in shady circumstances after a fight at his son's house in Abilene, Texas. Certainly, the many friends he had made during his incarnation as Forrest were shocked to find, when his death was reported in the media later that week, that he was in fact Asa the Anglo-Saxon tub-thumper, not the eponymous hero of *Little Tree*.

The story of the two Carters was not to end with their

deaths, however. In 1985, with his most famous book still flying off the shelves, the rights were bought by the publishing arm of the University of New Mexico, but the classification of the book – which had already been unofficially changed from non-fiction to fiction by the compilers of the *New York Times* bestseller lists at the time of Dan Carter's piece – was quietly altered. Although the introduction to the new edition mentioned nothing about the furore over Carter's deception, the words 'A True Story' were taken off the front cover.

In 2007 the book became the first hoax publication to be publicly de-recommended by Oprah Winfrey, after she found out that the cutesy spiritual memoir which she had recommended to viewers of her website was in fact the work of a duplicitous bigot. The book has its devotees, however, and not only amongst those for whom the unpalatable racism of the pre-Civil Rights era is still an ideological reality. Look up *Little Tree* on the most famous online encyclopaedia and you will find it touted generously as a 'memoir-style fictional novel written under [a] pseudonym'. Go in to a school library in America and only the words 'Young Adult Fiction' on the book's cover suggest that this literary artefact is anything less than a simple child's memoir.

NASDIJJ

*I*N 1999, *ESQUIRE* magazine received a manuscript from a man calling himself Nasdijj, who claimed to be a Navajo writer, outraged that the magazine had never published a story by a *Native American*.

*   *   *

The story it accompanied was a stark, harrowing but stylishly wrought piece of autobiographical writing about the Navajo author's attempts to help his terminally ill son, Tommy, enjoy his short life and die with dignity at home on the reservation. *Esquire* published the work and almost immediately Nasdijj was hailed as an extraordinary new voice in Native American writing, winning competitions, making personal appearances and giving interviews. He even received a six-figure sum to publish more of his candid autobiographical jottings.

First there came a longer version of *Blood Flows Like a River Through My Dreams*, published by the extremely reputable Houghton Mifflin in 2000, then *The Boy and the Dog Are Sleeping* in 2003 which told the story of another sick child, this time dying of AIDS, who Nasdijj had apparently adopted and cared for. It spoke not only of the love of an adopted parent for his son, but of the problem of disease and access to health-care in his community and the prejudice he, as a Navajo, typically came up against when dealing with 'Anglo' bureaucrats and doctors. Finally, in 2004, he published *Geronimo's Bones*, whose focus is the traumatic upbringing of Nasdijj and his brother Tso. The boys were apparently born to a Navajo father and a white mother into an itinerant migrant-worker household where sexual abuse and alcoholism were the only certainties. Darkly witty as well as painfully sad, the love of two brothers with nothing to live for but each other was a hit with readers and critics alike, and seemed to confirm Nasdijj's place at the heart of the new misery-memoir culture (subset: ethnic).

As a successful author, Nasdijj was invited to appear on panels and speak at bookshops all over America.

Some people noticed that he bore no physical traces of his supposed Navajo blood, looking, if anything, kind of Scandinavian. But when asked to define his racial identity at a PEN forum in 2002, he proclaimed: 'I am Navajo and the European things you relate so closely to often simply seem alien and remote.'

It would be another two years before the author's true identity was revealed, but all this time, while Nasdijj was basking in the recognition and respect of literary America, there was a very scared, very white, writer of gay porn from Michigan wondering where on earth this was all going to end. Should he confess? Should he apologize? Should he simply say that after a series of rejections from mainstream publishers and a spell on an Indian reservation, the character of Nasdijj just came to him, fully formed and ready to write?

Tim Barrus was ill in hospital when that first letter of acceptance came from the editor of *Esquire* in the late nineties. He never thought his work would be taken on, he later admitted, but with a wife and daughter to care for and only the money from his pornographic writings and occasional work as a carer, he wasn't going to turn down the chance of a career which could pay his medical bills and set him up in his old age.

Besides, this wasn't only about money. Although it is hard to know much about the real Barrus because interviewers and friends all agree he has an unusual relationship with reality and identity at the best of times, it is clear that his emotional needs were as pressing as any financial ones. Perhaps the most revealing insight into this strange, many-faced man comes from an extended interview he agreed to give to *Esquire* seven years after that magazine broke him as a new talent.

In it, he apologizes for deceiving people, and claims his years as Nasdijj were 'Awful. It's hard to have to lie to people. It's creepy.' But he also says: 'When you create a character, create someone with an emotional life, you see the stories through his eyes. So to me, he was very real.' He also reveals a trauma that could well have been at the heart of the whole hoax: just like the protagonist of *Blood Flows Like a River Through My Dreams*, he had indeed adopted a sick child, back in the seventies. He and his wife had loved the child to distraction but his behavioural problems – which Barrus claims were a result of undiagnosed foetal alcohol syndrome, like the boy in the story – were so severe that the couple ended up giving him back to the state. The child's name was Tommy, just like the one in the book. The terrible guilt over this act would not only break up Barrus' marriage but propel him on into a lifelong habit of assuming various extreme personae as an alternative to simply living the decidedly un-playful life of a failed writer grieving for his lost son.

Such details of his life that are known support this. There was the article he submitted to a fishing magazine: an invented autobiographical story in which he claimed that as a boy he sailed to Cuba with his father and fished with Hemingway. Jack Fritscher, the founder of one of the adult magazines Barrus wrote for, who claims to know him well, told *Esquire* that Barrus has, in the past, greeted him in the character of a strange Indian man or a naked leather-bound bondage-freak. He had even suspected that the author's second wife, Tina, was merely a figment of the imagination until he saw proof that she was indeed a real woman: 'It's not a question of whether he's lying or not. He's exploring the territory of identity.'

The game was up for Nasdijj when the periodical *LA Weekly* published a story entitled 'Navahoax' in 2006. This was in January, the same month as the big-news revelations about fellow misery memoirist James Frey hit the headlines, and the coincidence of another hoax being revealed at the same time ensured the Nasdijj story would not go away. Critics from the Indian and non-Indian writing communities both weighed in with their censure. Although Barrus must have been relieved, in a way, not to have to keep up the pretence any longer, he must also have been hurt when such Native American literary lions as the great novelist and commentator Sherman Alexie rounded on him for hijacking the real-life pain and cultural identity of his people.

There was a rumour of Barrus writing a tell-all about his years as Nasdijj, but so far this haunted, shadowy figure has turned to blogging and film-making (the rather uncomfortable results of which can be seen on YouTube – if you're not too squeamish about voyeuristic footage of very young men washing themselves). In the period immediately following his exposure he answered back to critics, with the hackneyed but no less true statement: 'What you want to believe you want to believe.' But for the time being the case has been closed on Nasdijj, the heroic Indian survivor who never was. And the origins of that strange name of his? It means 'to become again' in Navajo.

4

CELEBRITY TESTAMENTS

*T*HE CULT OF celebrity is nothing new, but the desire to see all the worst and smallest parts of a big star is emphatically a post-war invention. Seemingly overnight, we went from being a culture devoted to keeping our idols on their pedestals at all costs to bringing them down with a crash. And because the unearthing of sordid details about well-known figures is such a big-money game, it is no surprise that literary hoaxers with dollar signs in their eyes have sprung up in all corners of the media to capitalize on it. The most famous of these hoaxes is surely the Hitler Diaries: those expensive embarrassments which promised readers of the *Sunday Times* intimate details of the Führer's digestive complaints and household pets. The Howard Hughes autobiography comes a close second for an audacious assault on the credulity of a gossip-loving public, but for sheer silliness and cheek it is the phoney love-letters of Abraham Lincoln which take first prize.

THE ABRAHAM LINCOLN LETTERS

*A*BRAHAM LINCOLN IS famous for many things, but being a great and passionate lover is not one of them. The man who quipped that people shouldn't call him two-faced because if he were, he'd hardly choose to be wearing this one, has never exactly been matinée idol material. For a few months in the late 1920s, however, all that was set to change, thanks to a plucky young Californian woman called Wilma and one of the cheekiest hoaxes ever played on literary America.

The *Atlantic* has always been America's most highly respected journal of new writing, famous since its inception in 1857 for publishing Twain, Longfellow and just about every significant US writer since. Its staff has always been knowledgeable, educated and erudite and not at all the sort to be taken in by a beautiful, doe-eyed chick from San Diego with famously irresistible curves and a sparky wit. But when Wilma Frances Minor approached the magazine with a newly unearthed collection of love-letters between the sixteenth president and his first love, Miss Ann Rutledge, the editor, Ellery Sedgwick, was blissfully fooled.

It seems the idea had come to the young journalist in the mid-1920s when she had interviewed an old man called Scott Greene, who told her that his father had known Abraham Lincoln in the 1830s and had often heard the future president talk longingly about Ann, the young woman he had loved and lost. Ann had died before the two could wed and although the romance was not news in itself – historians had been discussing its significance for years – the interview gave Wilma the inspiration for the hoax that would make her infamous. She hatched a plan to 'discover' Lincoln's lost love-letters.

Her accomplice in this project was her mother, one Cora De Boyer, to whom she was unusually close. However, De Boyer was no ordinary supportive parent: she was a clairvoyant, and one with a state-wide reputation for invoking the spirits of the great and the good. Some time later, Wilma would claim that the content of the letters had been taken down verbatim during a séance at which her mother had contacted the spirits of Abraham and Ann, but when she first made contact with the *Atlantic* she proffered the more credible explanation that she had inherited the letters from an older family member and now wished to turn them over to the nation.

Wilma proposed that the magazine publish her discoveries – with attendant contextual articles by her – in three instalments and then bring out a complete study of them in book form. Ellery Sedgwick asked to see proof of the letters and the grainy photostats he received by return of post so impressed him that he decided to waive the magazine's long-standing no illustrations policy to display them in their original form. He also handed over the extremely tidy sum of $6,500 for the exclusive rights.

For several weeks, the offices of the *Atlantic* were abuzz with what they were about to unleash on the world (and the glamorous young Wilma was no doubt doing some serious shopping in light of her windfall). The letters betrayed a yearning, adoring heart and a distinctly soppy turn of phrase which had been hitherto unsuspected in the venerable sixteenth president. He was, at the time of writing, a young man working at menial jobs in New Salem and convinced, as this letter from Ann shows, that semi-literacy was no bar to love:

> my hart runs over with hapynes when I think yore name. I do not beleave I can find time to rite you a leter every day. stil I no as you say it wood surely improve my spelling and all that . . . I dreem of yore . . . words every nite and long for you by day. I mus git super now. all my hart is ever thine.

Not that young Abraham's literary powers were much of a match for his obvious powers of attraction:

> My Beloved Ann . . . I am borrowing Jacks horse to ride over to see you this coming Saturday. cutting my foot prevents my walking. I will be at your pleasure to accompany you to the Sand Ridge taffy-pull. I will be glad to hear your Father's sermon on the Sabbath. I feel unusually lifted with hope of relieving your present worry at an early date and likewise doing myself the best turn of my life. with you my beloved all things are possible. now James kindly promises to deliver into your dear little hands this letter. may the good Lord speed Saturday afternoon.
>
> affectionately A. Lincoln

As well as letters like these, which were all carefully written on old paper (Sedgwick had a chemist test it for age), there were extracts from journals and notes by people who knew the courting couple and could attest to their love. This diary entry from Ann's cousin Matilda, supposedly written after

Ann's untimely death, is typical of their eccentric style: 'the kin ses Abe is luny. I think he is broaken-harted. he wants me to keep his 5 leters from her coz he is perswaded he will soon foler her I expect he will too.'

The Atlantic ran the first of the extracts in December 1928 and no sooner had the issue hit the stands than the magazine was receiving taunting notes from scholars who saw the letters were out-and-out fakes. 'Have you gone insane or have I?' asked W. C. Ford of the Massachusetts Historical Society. But alongside the dissent of critics as esteemed as Paul Angle, the Secretary of the Lincoln Centennial Association, who was the first officially to accuse Minor of trickery, there were enough venerable commentators who believed the letters to be genuine to encourage Sedgwick to bring out the other two instalments as planned. The second one, which appeared in January 1929, attracted even more criticism than the first, and by the time of the trilogy's conclusion in February that year even Sedgwick was beginning to smell a rat. For Minor had made the mistake of so many excitable young hoaxers and not checked her facts properly: one letter, dated twenty years before the state of Kansas was named, had Lincoln referring to 'some place in Kansas'. Another spoke about surveying land in Sangamon County, where Lincoln was working, and referred to 'section 40' of a plot that could only, under federal planning law, have ever had thirty-six sections.

The game was very nearly up for Wilma Minor, and a red-faced *Atlantic* launched an investigation into her claims, resorting to employing a private detective and a handwriting expert to examine the details of the case. But so lax was this careless mother–daughter hoaxing team at covering their tracks that when Mrs De Boyer wrote a stiff letter to the magazine asking them to stop hounding her 'high strung and supersensitive girl who does not seem to understand how to cope with the rebuffs of this crass world', it did not take a graphology expert to see that the handwriting was suspiciously similar to that of the love-struck young Lincoln's.

Finally, towards the end of 1929 the two women started to tell people that the truth was that the voices transcribed in the letters had come to them via the spirit world at one of their regular séances. By this time, however, the reading public and the historical societies of the United States were heartily sick of this pair of time-wasters, and wasted little more attention worrying about their claims.

Poor Ellery Sedgwick had to admit in print that he had been had, and although the *Atlantic* was an august enough organ to reclaim its good name after the affair, Ms Minor was not. She went on to flit through a number of ill-conceived marriages and incarnations as a writer but never made such a name for herself again as she did, briefly, in the roaring twenties. And the truth about Abraham and Mary remains their secret.

THE JFK LETTERS

*A*FTER ABRAHAM LINCOLN, the next most iconic president of the United States is, without a doubt, John Fitzgerald Kennedy. So it is no surprise that he too was the subject of a bold literary hoax involving spurious letters supposedly written at a particularly intense time in his romantic and professional life. But the JFK letters, being 'discovered' in the age of multimillion-dollar media deals, did more than embarrass a venerable literary journal: they netted a fortune not only for the perpetrator but for the Pulitzer Prize-winning journalist who was taken in by them.

It was in the mid-1990s that Lex Cusack, the son of an attorney who had worked for the Catholic archdiocese of New York, came forward with his revelatory stash of papers. Those papers, which he claimed to have found among his late father's belongings, revealed that Lex Cusack Senior had been none other than Kennedy's secret legal advisor and the documents were, without a doubt, absolutely the most inflammatory things anyone with an interest in JFK (i.e. just about everyone) could hope to read. They detailed, both in the form of legal contracts and tear-stained love-letters from a certain 'Happy Birthday'-singing film star, the full extent of the mess the thirty-fifth president had found himself in shortly before his murder in 1963. He was a bigamist. He had been having an affair with Marilyn Monroe and had paid her a large sum of money to keep quiet about his bigamy, their affair and – perhaps worst of all – his connections with the notorious mobster Sam Giancana and various other underworld figures. And he was afraid that J. Edgar Hoover was on to him and his game would very soon be up.

These three scandals had been the stuff of rumour and gossip ever since the mid-sixties but until Lex Cusack came forward with his father's letters there had been no material proof of them whatsoever.

In 1985, Lex's well-known father Lawrence X. Cusack had died, leaving the big names in New York's Catholic community bereft of one of their most trusted legal aides. His funeral mass was attended by every bishop, priest and nun who was anybody, and his career as a scrupulous and discrete attorney was celebrated lovingly in the press. His practice had spanned the most crucial years in twentieth-century American Catholicism: the period during which the Kennedy clan had risen to prominence amidst unprecedented allegations about rigged elections and double-dealings. If America's first Roman Catholic president had, as the papers suggested, had a secret first marriage which was never officially ended but rather informally annulled by understanding bishops, Lawrence would have known about it. And so, according to these letters, he did.

In the immediate aftermath of his death, the Manhattan law firm of which he was a founding partner, Cusack & Stiles, instructed one of their clerks, who also happened to be his son Lex, to sort through the thousands of papers left behind in Lawrence's office. Amongst these papers were, Lex would claim, the 300 or so which revealed the close advisory relationship, hitherto unknown to anyone, between Cusack and Kennedy. Cusack characterized his father as an all-knowing 'Holmes' figure to the troubled president, and this special partnership contained such damning evidence as a trust agreement committing Kennedy to paying for Monroe's mother's healthcare in return for Marilyn keeping quiet about all she knew of the president's underworld connections and illegal marriage.

Just as the impulse to consolidate his father's reputation by linking him with one of the most famous icons of the day is reminiscent of other bygone literary hoaxers such as William Ireland, so too is what Lex – in cahoots with his wife – did next.

According to an investigation by the *New York Times*, the Cusacks decided that if they could get some of the less controversial papers in the collection authenticated by experts, it would make it easier to persuade purchasers that the more shocking documents were also genuine. There was no doubt that the trademark Kennedy scrawl on the notes and cards looked quite genuine to the untrained eye – as did the White House headed paper – but only with the stamp of approval of an expert could they proceed to cash in their treasure trove. They turned to the Connecticut memorabilia dealer John Reznikov, who took a look at the papers and supplied a letter attesting to their authenticity. Then the graphology expert Joseph Maddalena was approached with some equally small-fry letters and was willing to part with a few hundred dollars to buy them for his own collection, but never officially authenticated them. The Cusacks now had credibility enough to start selling the papers to the highest bidder.

It was not long before one of America's best-known investigative journalists, Seymour 'Sy' Hersh sought a piece of the action. He had recently signed a seven-figure contract with Little, Brown to produce the definitive book about JFK's assassination but once he connected with Cusack he turned his attention from the events of 1963 to the years before Kennedy's death and the potentially far more explosive stories to be found there. Of particular interest to Hersh was the suggestion, in some of the letters, that the then FBI boss J. Edgar Hoover knew all about Kennedy's insalubrious dealings with the mob and was using the information to make Kennedy's life a misery.

Even before Hersh lent his good name to the project, however, Cusack had sold several of the letters to private collectors, earning himself enough money to live in far greater comfort than the average paralegal. His touting of a potential book written by himself about his late father had largely fallen on deaf ears, but once Hersh was on board, deals from big television networks and magazines were there for the taking and the money began rolling in in earnest. Letters such as the one in which Kennedy refers to 'MM', with her dangerous knowledge about his private life needing to be sorted out even pointed to the popular conspiracy theory that Marilyn had been murdered by government agents trying to cover up a scandal. And another note, suggesting that just before her demise Marilyn was about to call a news conference and tell-all about the president who had broken her heart, only fuelled the rumours further.

Sy Hersh, who had now used his access to Cusack's papers to increase his book advance by several hundred thousand pounds, was as much of a Kennedy enthusiast as the next American, but he was also a highly professional journalist with a peerless reputation to protect. So, very sensibly, he began to ask friends and associates of the Kennedys to tell him what they knew about Camelot's relationship with Lawrence Cusack (or 'Larry', as he chummily calls him in the notes). Worryingly, he drew a complete blank. Even Kennedy's former secretary, whose name appeared on some of the letters, claimed never to have heard of the lawyer. Another graphologist was brought in to scrutinize the handwriting and although she conceded that it looked like Kennedy's, she was able to discern the tell-tale stops and starts and minute irregularities in pressure that characterize a painstakingly forged script.

By this point, with the finger of suspicion already hovering over Lex Cusack, some fatally damning careless mistakes were found in the letters. On one letter there was a zip code – something that had not yet been invented. Then it was discovered by forensic experts that some of the typewritten papers had been created on a machine which hadn't existed at all in the early 1960s. But the detail which indicates most emphatically that Lex was the type of underachieving, glory-hunting son to make it all up was the discovery by Hersh that he had lied about his army qualifications and academic credentials in a wedding announcement in the *New York Times*.

Hersh knew full well that hoaxers frequently turn out to have left a trail of mis-truths and self-aggrandizing lies, and eventually he had to admit he had been conned. In 1999 Lex was imprisoned for ten years for defrauding his buyers of a total of $7,000,000.

Astonishingly, despite Cusack's conviction, and although scraps of paper were found in his office which appear to show him practising Kennedy's handwriting, some of those buyers were determined to reclaim their property from the government lawyers who seized them in the process of the case. One collector, Mike Stern, who spent $300,000 on forty documents in the mid-nineties, told journalists: 'We paid for them, we're entitled to them. Stamp them with the word "forgery" if you have to, but we want to hang them on our walls even if they are fake.' It seems, then, that the enduring strength of the Kennedy myth is very much above the law, whatever you believe about the man himself.

THE AUTOBIOGRAPHY OF HOWARD HUGHES

*H*OWARD HUGHES IS one of the most enduring symbols of Hollywood's golden age. As a director, he discovered the film stars Jean Harlow and Jane Russell, as a lover he was associated with Katherine Hepburn, Ava Gardner and Ginger Rogers, and as a pilot and racing-plane designer he broke several world speed records. But the side of his life that fascinated the gossip column-reading public more than anything was his self-imposed exile into his own, reputedly very strange, world during the last fifteen years of his life. After suffering a breakdown in the late 1950s, his obsession with germs and an escalating drug problem led him to isolate himself completely from the outside world, living in a series of sealed-off luxury hotel suites and attended only by a few trusted and hygienic glove-wearing intimates.

Although the full details of his later years were not fully known until after his death from heart failure in 1976, stories would occasionally leak out, and he became known as a madman who never cut his nails or wore clothes and sat naked in a white leather chair all day watching old films. It was at the height of speculation about Hughes that the writer Clifford Irving – a New Yorker living in Ibiza who had written several critically acclaimed novels and, interestingly, a biography of an art forger – came up with the idea for an extraordinary literary hoax. Judging by the fact that his commercially unsuccessful novels had never earned him the kind of money he liked to spend, and that his latest effort had not been accepted for publication at all, it is safe to assume that his chief motivation was financial.

According to his own account of the affair, *The Hoax*, which he published in 1981, he had been in Spain, about to cross over to Ibiza, when he bumped into his friend, the writer Richard Suskind. Suskind was a children's author who specialized in historical adventure stories and although he was less of a literary player than Irving, he was used to doing a considerable amount of research to give his books a feel of historical accuracy. During their conversation, talk turned to the reclusive film director and one of the men struck upon the idea that there was a lot of money to be made out of a book about the man – if only the public (and the publisher) would believe it was in some way authorized. It occurred to Irving that if his friend were willing to research everything there was to know about Hughes' life, he himself would write it up and capitalize on his relationship with the respected publishing house McGraw-Hill to get them a book deal.

They decided to tell the publishers that Hughes had granted a series of exclusive interviews to Irving and had also turned over to him a number of letters and sworn statements for use in what would be the only authorized book ever to be written about the man. Irving would, in effect, be ghost-writing Howard Hughes' autobiography. By the time he went to his editors later in 1970 he had put together a proposal which they would be made to turn down. Documents apparently from Hughes (in fact forged by Irving on the basis of a handwriting sample he had seen in a magazine) were produced to verify Irving's claims, and a handsome advance of $100,000 was offered. After some tough bargaining, this was raised to a massive $665,000 for Irving and a further $100,000 for Hughes. Cheques were duly written and paid into Irving's bank account and also a Swiss account opened in the name of H. Hughes by Irving's wife Edith.

Now the job of writing could begin, and drawing on every newspaper and magazine article and official record they could find on the man (plus a few less publicly available sources) enough biographical data was amassed to fill a very authentic-seeming volume of memoir. One of the private sources used by the men was an unpublished ghost-written autobiography of Noah Dietrich, the man who had for years been Hughes' closest confidant. Dietrich had worked as Hughes' general assistant prior to his retirement and, now in his eighties, was seeking help putting his memories down on paper. A writer called James Phelan had been given the job, but it was easy for Irving to get his hands on the manuscript: he let it be known that he – a more accomplished writer – would gladly consider working on the manuscript instead of Phelan (who was not doing a brilliant job), and the editors handed it over.

Odd though it may seem, one worry Irving and Suskind never seem to have had is that Howard Hughes himself would hear about their ruse and try to stop it. They were convinced that the old director would either be insane and detached enough not to know what was going on in the world, or so paranoid about interaction with the public and ashamed of what he had become that he would never dare come out of his luxurious hermit's cave to challenge them.

Assuming these things, Irving blithely presented his

manuscript to McGraw-Hill towards the end of 1971. Alongside the text he presented a number of notes written in Hughes' hand, which he had managed to get authenticated by a graphologist. The publishers must have known that high-profile people who had been close to Hughes were saying that this book could not be for real: that Hughes would never do such a thing. Just to make absolutely certain, they subjected Irving to a polygraph test to make sure he was telling the truth about his meetings and interviews with Hughes. During the test, Irving managed to keep his cool almost perfectly, betraying only signs of 'inconsistencies' not outright lies. Apparently, that was to be expected – after all, there would necessarily be some aspects of the Irving–Hughes relationship that were justifiably private. So, as planned, the imminent publication of the book that would finally lift the lid on the most enigmatic celebrity of the twentieth century was announced via a press release, and a lucrative serialization deal was brokered with *Time* magazine. The preface alone, in which Hughes sets the tone for the confessional mood of the pages to follow, must have been enough to get dollar signs flashing furiously in eyes:

Since 1957, as is well known, I haven't granted an interview or had a photograph taken . . .

The fact that I shunned publicity had a backlash. Just because I was the richest man in the world and wouldn't give interviews . . . Every newspaper and magazine in this country has a reporter whose sole job is to snoop into my private life and the doings of my companies . . .

But now, because I'm nearing the end of my life, I want to set the record straight.

They tried to put me in an asylum. They wrote outright lies about me. The portrayal of me as an aging lunatic – I won't have it.

I want the balance restored. I don't want future generations to remember Howard Hughes only as an obscenely rich and weird man. There's more to me than that . . . intend to be dead honest . . . This is the truth about my life, warts and all.

The veteran television journalist Mike Wallace interviewed Irving about his remarkable coup and, although he believed everything he said, he admitted afterwards that as soon as filming was over, his cameramen and sound technicians had all agreed there was something very suspicious about the writer. As he later recalled 'They understood. I didn't. He got me.'

Then, just as it seemed Irving and his accomplices would get away with it, a strung-out but lucid Howard Hughes broke his silence. In the first week of 1972 he arranged a conference call with a group of journalists he had worked with in the past. By now the news, gossip and entertainment media were baying for blood and even Irving himself must have been longing for a resolution of some kind. Television cameras were set up in the office where the journalists were to receive the call, and at the appointed time, as the world looked on, the phone rang. Hughes, sounding remote but enervated, made it clear that he had never met this Clifford Irving, knew nothing about him, and certainly had not given anyone permission to co-write his autobiography.

A less desperate hoaxer would have given himself up there and then, but Irving, from his own private hideaway in Ibiza, denounced this phone call as a fake, and then suggested that Hughes, who was obviously of unsound mind, had changed his mind and the book was to go ahead. But with McGraw-Hill now starting to worry about where their money had gone, a full investigation was launched. One of the first things it uncovered was the fact that the bank account in Switzerland into which Hughes' portion of the advance money had been paid had only been opened recently, and by a woman calling herself Helga Hughes. This woman was quickly identified by bank staff as exactly resembling Irving's wife, Edith. Even when Swiss police turned up at the Irvings' home, they tried at first to deny any knowledge of a hoax – hinting merely that someone posing as Howard Hughes might perhaps have taken them in. But by the end of the month it was clear even to the eternally optimistic and ambitious Clifford Irving that the game was up, and on 28 January both he and his wife agreed to make a confession.

After the trial for fraud that followed, Irving was incarcerated for fourteen months, his accomplice Suskind for five, but Edith's sentence was suspended. Perhaps unsurprisingly, their marriage was not to last. Hughes would not last much longer either, but he did live long enough to see Irving come out of prison a stronger, fitter man (he had given up his smoking and drinking lifestyle and turned into a gym addict). It must have irked Hughes further to see Irving not only resurrect his novel-writing career but to take it to a greater heights than he ever had before, writing several bestsellers. Finally, in 1981 (once Hughes was no longer around to spoil his fun) Irving wrote his book-length account of the hoax that made his name. And it was this that inspired the 2006 film *The Hoax* starring Richard Gere as Irving and Alfred Molina as Suskind, which ensured that a whole new generation of cinema-goers are fully conversant with the wild man of Hollywood and the daring schemer who believed he could get away with the grandest identity fraud on record.

THE HITLER DIARIES

ASK SOMEONE TO think of a literary hoax and the first one they will come up with is probably the Hitler Diaries. This headline-grabbing affair captured the public imagination not only because the diaries fed into the on-going fascination with the most influential villain in twentieth-century history, but because – despite being very shoddily executed – they hoodwinked some of the most prestigious newspapers and academics in Europe. They were, in the words of the autograph expert Kenneth W. Rendell, 'bad forgeries but a great hoax'.

The story began in the early 1980s when Gerd Heidemann, a journalist for the popular German news magazine *Stern*, came to his editors with the remarkable news that he had found an antiques dealer who had dozens of notebooks in which Adolf Hitler had recorded his innermost thoughts between the years 1932 and 1945. It would be hard to imagine a more significant literary discovery. So much is known of Hitler's public life but so frustratingly little of his inner life that something like this – a genuine insight into his character and his responses to the evils his regime committed – could well change the understanding of history.

Heidemann himself was known to nurture an unhealthy interest in the material leftovers of the Third Reich, and was a keen collector of Nazi memorabilia. His most prized possession was *Carin II*, the yacht once used by the Luftwaffe commander Hermann Goering, which he had bought in the mid-1970s, having saved up the money during his fifteen-year career as a reporter on *Stern*. By the early eighties the repairs on the boat were costing him so much he decided to sell, and one of the first people he approached as a likely buyer was a more wealthy memorabilia collector, Fritz Steifel. During a meeting at his house, Steifel revealed that he had in his possession a most remarkable book: a single bound leather volume of Adolf Hitler's diaries. Heidemann was dumb-struck by this revelation. He had never heard even a rumour that such a thing existed – and quizzed Steifel as to its provenance. He was told the book – and dozens more like it, each covering a six-month period in Hitler's life – had been found in the wreckage of a plane crash in East Germany at the end of the war and fallen into the hands of a high-ranking official who sold it for hard currency to an antique dealer in Stuttgart. That dealer had then sold it on to Steifel.

Heidemann, who was known by his colleagues to be a very enthusiastic if somewhat gullible reporter, sped back to *Stern* with the heady news. But only one of his colleagues paid his unlikely story any credence, the magazine's historical researcher, Thomas Walde. Together, the two men decided to journey to the site of the plane crash and see for themselves what they could find. They managed to locate the crash site and although there were no remaining manuscripts to be found there, the sight of the mangled plane was enough to convince them the story was true and they assumed all the valuable loot had been taken away by local residents.

In fact, that part of the tale was true after a fashion. At the end of the war, a plane load of sensitive documents had indeed been removed from Hitler's bunker in Berlin and flown, for safe keeping, towards Bavaria in a mission called Operation Seraglio. However, the plane had crashed and the papers were lost. After leaving the crash site, Heidemann and Walde then managed to track down the alleged antiques dealer in Stuttgart, who their contacts in the illegal world of Nazi memorabilia-trading had said was called Herr Fischer.

This Fischer turned out to be a low-rent criminal and forger whose real name was Konrad Kujau. Throughout the 1970s he had been selling phoney artefacts to collectors like Steifel, 'authenticating' each one with an official-looking certificate of his own fabrication. He carried on his work untroubled by fears of retribution because he knew full well that if any of his patrons suspected him of fakery, they would hardly go to the police about it. He was not making a fortune, but was doing better than his brother, who was a railway porter in East Germany. One day, on a whim, he had made a single volume of Hitler's diaries out of an old school exercise book and offered it to Steifel, one of his best customers, but had not been planning to create any more until Heidemann came to him with an offer of 2,000,000 marks for the entire set of diaries. Obviously, Kujau was not about to turn this money down, but he knew he would need time to manufacture the other volumes he had spoken of. He decided to tell Heidemann that he would have to get the books smuggled out of East Germany one by one by his brother (who he elevated to the position of army general for the purposes of the ruse), which could of course take some months or even years. He also stipulated that he would deal with nobody apart from Heidemann himself. All this having been swiftly agreed to, the two journalists now had to persuade their bosses at the magazine to come up with the money to pay for them. When it was pointed out how much extra revenue such a scoop could garner for *Stern*, they agreed.

Over the next few years, as the diaries were 'smuggled' out of East Germany (in reality they were hastily put together by Kujau), Heidemann would regularly make the trip to Kujau's office with a suitcase full of cash to pay for each new instalment. But whereas he told the magazine each one cost 200,000 marks, he was actually only paying Kujau 85,000. The huge commission he was dishonestly skimming off Kujau's fee, in addition to the massive new contract he had negotiated with *Stern* in return for his work on the diaries, was making him a very rich man.

By the beginning of 1983 *Stern* had enough of the small black leather-bound volumes to unleash the scoop of the century on its readers. The diaries may not have contained the extended passages of psychological insight into the Führer's mind that they had hoped for, but along with accounts of all the meetings and official engagements that he attended, there were glimpses into his private life with Eva Braun and his personal problems with ill-health which would nonetheless make them highly sought after. The magazine began to negotiate syndication rights to other newspapers and media groups, one of which was

News Corp, who proposed to buy the British rights to the story and splash it across the *Sunday Times*. At this point, *Stern*'s editors also sought independent verification for the manuscripts from a small handful of handwriting experts. Had they been less worried about keeping their scoop a secret, they might have contacted some of the country's many highly regarded war historians and Hitler experts, but instead they only went to graphologists – and what's more, the examples of Hitler's 'real' handwriting they produced to compare the diaries to had themselves been faked. By Kujau. A police forensics officer was casually contacted for advice, but by the time his report (which was inconclusive) came through, they had already gone to press.

Rupert Murdoch's News Corp, the parent company of the *Sunday Times*, however, was going to take no chances if it was going to stake a huge amount of its financial and reputational capital on bringing the documents to a British audience, so on 8 April 1983, just before publication, it sent the world-famous Hitler historian Hugh Trevor-Roper (by now Lord Dacre) to authenticate the diaries. Although initially sceptical, when he saw the sheer mass of information in the collection, Trevor-Roper became convinced it was all genuine, and wrote as much in a sensational article for the Sunday paper, in which he expressed the opinion that while it was easy to fake the odd note or memo, creating thousands of pages of seemingly accurate material and presenting it in a consistent style could not be the work of a petty forger. Readers familiar with his exposé of *The Hermit of Peking*, aka Sir Edmund Backhouse (see p. 70) might have disagreed.

Stern was of course delighted with Trevor-Roper's support, and with that of the American magazine

Newsweek's hired expert who had travelled to Germany at the same time, and on Monday 25 April the magazine ran its first special edition devoted to their amazing discovery. That very day they held a press conference with Trevor-Roper and others to consolidate the magnitude of their discovery and display the diaries for the first time; but unbeknownst to them, the famous English historian had, in the days after first seeing the manuscripts, become increasingly doubtful over them. The press conference proved to be nothing like the triumphant *Stern*-fest the magazine had hoped for, and jaws dropped when a red-faced Trevor-Roper made his uncomfortable announcement: 'As a historian, I regret that the, er, normal method of historical verification, er, has, perhaps necessarily, been to some extent sacrificed to the requirements of a journalistic scoop.'

The conference was brought to a hasty conclusion and panicked *Stern* executives decided they must now – as they should have done before – go to the highest archival authorities in Germany to get the diaries certified one way or the other. The books were duly sent off to Hans Booms of the Bundesarchiv and in the first week of May they were denounced emphatically as fakes. The main clue to their inauthenticity was that the factual content of each entry had been lifted – mistakes and all – from a book (well-thumbed in Kujau's library, as it turned out) called *Hitler's Speeches and Proclamations*. There were other giveaways as well: rudimentary errors, such as Hitler's initials being inscribed wrongly on a title page, as well as the cheeky personal entries which verged on schoolboy larkishness. We have Hitler complaining of his terrible flatulence and bad breath, and Eva Braun giving him hell about it; December

1938's unlikely 'Now a year is nearly over. Have I achieved my goals for the Reich? Save for a few small details, yes!'; and notes to self such as 'Must get tickets for the Olympic games for Eva'.

With the hoax now undeniable, the fall-out for the newspapers who had been taken in was massive. Both *Stern* and the News Corp group had to issue shamefaced apologies to their readers. (Murdoch-haters in the UK had particular fun with the *Sunday Times*, even though they had only run an article by Trevor-Roper and not the extracts themselves by the time of the debunking.) In the midst of this flurry of admissions, recriminations and jibes from rival papers, Konrad Kujau fled his home for Austria, terrified he would be incarcerated for the rest of his life if the police came looking for him. They did, of course, but in the end he gave himself up before they found him, writing out a full confession in Hitler's handwriting as a final flourish to the long saga of his deception. The reason for his sudden admission of guilt? He had learnt from newspaper reports the full amount of money *Stern* had been giving Heidemann to pass on to him, and when he realized how badly he had been fleeced, he decided to incriminate the journalist by telling all.

Heidemann, who continued to protest his innocence of the deception, was put on trial alongside Kujau in the summer of 1984, charged with stealing more than a million marks from his employer, much of which was never able to be traced or repaid. He was convicted of embezzlement and given a custodial sentence. Kujau served a prison sentence of just over three years for his part in the hoax, and on his release set himself up in a gallery selling 'honest fakes' – his copies of art works by famous painters like Van Gogh and Miro (and indeed Adolf Hitler), signed both with his own signature and that of the original artist. He also became a regular on the television chat-show circuit, demonstrating his clever signature-forging skills live on air and becoming, with his bald head, round physique and broad grin, something of a viewers' favourite. When he died in 2000, he left such a famous legacy that his canny great-niece, Petra Kujau, was herself convicted of selling fake versions of his fake paintings.

The years after the Hitler hoax have been less kind to Gerd Heidemann, however. After serving his prison sentence he found himself ostracized by a media unwilling to help him resurrect his career. Now in his mid-seventies, living in a small apartment in Hamburg and crippled with debt, he blames his former brilliance as a journalist for the attitude his old colleagues now take to him: 'I was the big scapegoat for them. They all ganged up on me. There was a lot of envy and schadenfreude involved . . . At last star reporter Heidemann had made a mistake,' he told the newspaper *Bild* in 2008.

In 2003 a twist in the tale was revealed, and old interests in the case were revivified. After Stasi files about him were released it was widely reported that Heidemann had been working as an East German spy from the mid-1950s until the late 1980s. Although the files described him as an agent whose only interest was in earning as much money as possible, they gave ammunition to the conspiracy theorists who claimed the entire hoax was a money-spinning exercise by East German officials. The reasoning behind this theory was that silly little Kujau himself could not have produced all the material so must have been helped by a larger organization. Heidemann has denied these claims, and continues to profess his innocence as a mere pawn in Kujau's grand deception. But there is no denying that the huge scandal of 1983 was caused, at least in part, by his uncontrollable greed: for money, for fame and for professional success. Otherwise he – and his colleagues on the magazine – would surely have looked more closely into the provenance of the manuscripts that seemed too good to be true.

5

AUSTRALIA

WHAT IS IT about Australia? A country whose ratio of literary hoaxes to genuine literary successes is so high must surely be guarding a fascinating cultural secret. Or is the Antipodean profusion of writerly tricks merely the result of a publishing scene desperate for a short-cut to established literary identity? It is telling that every single one of Australia's hoaxes involves race. Nino Culotta's books are about Italian immigrants; Norma Khouri writes about Islamic honour killings; Marlo Morgan and Wanda Koolmatrie both ape Aboriginals (albeit from diametrically opposing viewpoints); the unsavoury Helen Demidenko was inspired by the openly white supremacist context of her upbringing to write a fake memoir in support of Nazi soldiers. And even the most famous of them all, the Ern Malley poems, were created by a pair of young Anglo-Saxon fogies who wanted to poke fun at a trendy Jewish poetaster and his modernist crowd.

ERN MALLEY

SPRING 1943 FOUND James McAuley and Harold Stewart, two rather traditional Australian poets, doing war work in the Victoria Barracks in Melbourne. The kind of verse they created when not on army duty was the romantic, neo-classical lyricism you might associate with the Englishman Rupert Brooke. Across town, however, their nemesis was at work: twenty-four-year-old Max Harris was busying himself being the *enfant terrible* of radical new literature and had just moved from Adelaide (itself the *enfant terrible* of Australia's cultural landscape at the time), having published reams of experimental poetry and an epic prose-poem called *The Vegetative Eye*. He was now fronting an avant-garde poetry and painting movement called the Angry Penguins (a quote from one of his own works) and edited a cutting-edge literary magazine of the same name. He did not yet know McAuley and Stewart, but the three young men were about to come together over a literary sensation that would not only alter their lives for ever, but redefine the course of Australian letters in surprising ways.

McAuley was a formal poet who loathed bohemians, loved jazz, smoked and drank like a machine and was obsessed with the sanctity of Christian marriage. A complex, not very gentle soul. Stewart was a middle-class drop-out with a passion for Buddhism, and himself a composer of old-fashioned, whimsical verse. The two friends were united in their hatred of the long-haired, anarchistic (and, in Harris's case at least, Jewish) young thinkers who were being feted as the next big things in contemporary letters. They agreed that while some early modernist poetry had been quite beautiful – both adored Eliot's 'Prufrock', for example – the current vogue for 'pretentious nonsense' based on the free association of ideas and an unstructured syntax was abominable to anyone with an ounce of real literary sensibility. They felt that the anti-establishment approach to poetry espoused by the likes of Dylan Thomas, William Burroughs and the new Australian experimentalist poet Kenneth Rexroth, who *Angry Penguins* promoted as the future of verse, all represented a pathetic diversion from the real, robust magic that poetry could do. So, with a glint in their eyes but a seriousness of intent at heart, they decided to teach Harris and his 'Angry Pungwungs', as they called them, a lesson.

Holed up in their quarters on the army base, over a number of weeks (probably not, as they initially boasted, in the space of a single afternoon) they composed a string of surrealist, stream-of-consciousness poems by an imaginary car mechanic from the backstreets of Sydney called Ern. They jotted down any funny-sounding nonsense that came into their heads, supplemented by a few words and phrases chosen at random from the dictionary and complete works of Shakespeare they happened to have on the desk in front of them. The only rules, they would later recall, were that no poem should have a single theme; there should be no distinct poetic technique (but rather a deliberate mish-mash of rhythms, rhyme and scansion); and that the general tone of the things ought to reflect the rambling sensuousness of Dylan Thomas – the poet for whom they reserved their deepest disdain.

They called the collection *The Darkling Eliptic* and composed a preface in which the author, Ern Malley, set forth his statement of intent as a writer, which was 'to discover the hidden fealty of certain arrangements of sound in a line and certain concatenations of the analytic emotions' and to produce work 'free of unfulfilled intentions. Every note and revision has been destroyed. There is no biographical data.'

McAuley and Stewart knew that to submit the poems alone might not be enough to prove that Harris and his ilk were undiscerning poetasters. The realized that a concocted back-story for Ern which made him as obscure and raw a figure as possible would give him instant cachet amongst the left-leaning readers and editors of *Angry Penguins*, so set about creating the other character in the Malley hoax, Ern's sister Ethel. Ethel, they decided, had found the poems among her deceased brother's meagre possessions in his bedsit in South Melbourne, where he had moved from his native Sydney to seek work. Not being poetically minded herself, she had decided to send them off to the most talked-about literary magazine of the day for a 'professional' opinion before consigning them to the bin. In her letter to Harris she would outline the short, sad life of her brother, a barely-educated car mechanic who had tried to make a life for himself in Melbourne but had returned to his hometown sick with the thyroid disorder to which he finally succumbed in July 1943, aged just twenty-five. None of the family knew he had been writing poetry, and no one knew much about his doings in Melbourne in the years before he died.

When a sample poem and a covering letter arrived on the desk of Max Harris one morning, he had no reason to think it was anything special. Hurrying to get together the next issue of his magazine, as well as working on his own writing, he probably assumed it was the hopeful submission of yet another fired-up student radical, long on ambition but short on talent. But then he started reading *Dürer: Innsbruck, 1495*, and he could not take his eyes off the page. He reread it. He was transfixed. He felt that he was in the presence of a tremendous and revolutionary talent, and he wanted more. So he wrote immediately to Miss Malley begging for the other fifteen compositions she said she had in her possession, and poem by poem Malley's oeuvre unfurled its strange leaves, revealing to a stunned Harris something he had been looking for his whole life: the true new voice of modern Australia.

The next instalment of poems came accompanied by another letter from Ethel which gave a potted history of her late brother's life that Ernest Lalor Malley was born in England in 1918; emigrated to Australia as a child; was educated at Petersham public school and the Summer Hill Intermediate High, where he failed to achieve academic success; and left school shortly after his mother's death in 1933.

After showing the work and Ethel's letter to his peers, including his co-editor and investor John Reed, it was agreed that a whole issue of *Angry Penguins* should be devoted to this extraordinary discovery, and to mark the occasion a painting for the cover was commissioned from one of the hippest painters of the day, the Melbourne artist Sidney Nolan. In an introductory article, Harris wrote that in Malley he had found 'a poet of tremendous power, working through a disciplined and restrained kind of statement into the deepest wells of human experience. A poet, moreover, with cool, strong, sinuous feeling for language.'

Due to the war, getting anything printed (especially something not exactly crucial to the national effort) took much longer than usual, so it was not until June 1945 that the special Autumn 1944 edition came out. The firebrand young editor would have been taking a risk staking his name on the tiny oeuvre of a dead, unheard-of motor mechanic even if the author had turned out to be a real person. But when, within days of publication, readers, writers and critics began to cast aspersions on the veracity of Malley's work, he must have felt the first stirrings of the humiliation and regret that he would go to great pains to deny for the rest of his life.

Almost immediately, literary Australia smelled a rat. And, desperate for some diverting story to relieve them of the steady diet of depressing war news, the mainstream press picked up the scent of this unfolding literary drama as well. Either, ran the stories in publications from the *New York Times* to the *Spectator*, Australia's greatest poet had indeed been discovered in a mess of papers at a humble house in Sydney or the coolest cat on the literary scene had been royally duped and the whole modernist project looked as if it might fall in shame-faced ruins around him. Either way, it was a great story. In fact, the very first person to tell the press about the hoax was probably a friend of the hoaxers themselves: although they had agreed to keep their prank a secret for the time being, hoping to spectacularly 'slay' (as McAuley put it) Harris by revealing his gullibility themselves, McAuley couldn't help but boast of what they had done to a young woman of his acquaintance, Tess van Sommers. Tess was an aspiring journalist, and had just made contact with the editors of the *Sunday Sun* newspaper in Sydney hoping for work. No doubt she saw the Malley scoop as a way to impress her would-be employers, and she went to them with the story the very week that the autumn *Angry Penguins* came out.

At the same time, a group of academics in Adelaide was beginning to smell a rat as well. Harris had shown the Malley poems to one of his teachers from university, Brian Elliot. Elliot had always been supportive of his highly motivated former student, and thought the poems were indeed impressive. But he confessed that he thought they were the parodic work of Harris himself; there was just something that didn't ring true about them. Panicked by this and the rumblings from the Sydney journalists, Harris went so far as to pay for a private detective to stake out the address in the Sydney district of Croydon from which Ethel Malley's letters had come. The address was in fact Stewart's own, and when the gumshoe knocked on the door he was told, quite truthfully, by the woman who answered it that the only person attached to that household who might know anything about a poet was currently indisposed in hospital. (Harold Stewart was indeed in the infirmary, having minor surgery on an abscess.)

Finally, the two hoaxers were invited to confess in the pages of the national press and they did so in horribly smug terms. They boasted of their creation of 'nonsensical sentences' and 'bad verse . . . utterly devoid of literary merit as poetry' and privately rejoiced even more heartily in getting one over on Harris, who they had long considered to be a figure deserving of public ridicule.

You might think that at this point the story would go away. And perhaps at another moment in history, or in another country, it might have done. But something about Ern Malley caught the imagination of the Australian reading public, and that had a lot to do with the quality of his verse. Too many people agreed it was too good to forget. Reading it now, when we are so much more inured to the vagaries of the late modernist style – when the last few decades have produced so much work like it – it is easier than ever to see why not everyone thought it was laughable. Look at these pieces of poems, imagining, perhaps, that they are by a poet you like:

From 'Sybilline':

> It is necessary to understand
> That a poet may not exist, that his writings
> Are the incomplete circle and straight drop
> Of a question mark

From 'Palinode':

> I snap off your wrist
> Like a stalk that entangles
> And make my adieu.
> Remember, in any event,
> I was a haphazard amorist
> Caught on the unlikely angles
> Of an awkward arrangement. Weren't you?

From 'Petit Testament':

> And having despaired of ever
> Making my obsessions intelligible
> I am content at last to be
> The sole clerk of my metamorphoses . . .
>
> Reserving to myself a man's
> Inalienable right to be sad
> At his own funeral . . .
>
> I have split the infinite. Beyond is anything.

And most famously, from 'Dürer: Innsbruck, 1495':

> I had read in books that art is not easy
> But no one warned that the mind repeats
> In its ignorance the vision of others. I am still
> the black swan of trespass on alien waters.

'The black swan of trespass', the culmination of that first poem seen by Harris, the one about the struggle for true originality, has become one of the most famous lines in the Australian canon. The image of the black swan has long been central to Aboriginal and white cultural histories in the Antipodes and Malley's poignant use of it as an image of creative anxiety struck a deep chord. It became the title of Humphrey McQueen's seminal history of modernism in Australia, as well as the name of the numerous plays and even musical compositions which have sprung up around the Malley story.

Of course, there are many lines in the Malley poems which, whether taken in context or out, are plain ridiculous. Just try pretending your favourite poet wrote these beauties:

From 'Perspective Lovesong':

> Princess, you lived in Princess St.,
> Where the urchins pick their nose in the sun
> With the left hand. You thought
> That paying the price would give you admission
> To the sad autumn of my Valhalla.

From 'Egyptian Register':

> The long-shanked ibises that on the Nile
> Told one hushed peasant of rebirth
> Move in a calm immortal frieze
> On the mausoleum of my incestuous
> And self-fructifying death.

From 'Documentary Film':

> The young men aspire
> Like departing souls from leaking roofs
> And fractured imploring windows to
> (All must be synchronized, the jagged
> Quartz of vision with the asphalt of human speech)
> Java:

Whatever you think of the poems (and they really are worth reading), there is no doubt that the extraordinary afterlife of the Malley hoax has taken on an enigmatic momentum of its own. He is nothing short of one of Australia's favourite cultural figures and, still, one of her most talked-about poets. The highly respected Australian novelist Peter Carey recently produced his novel *My Life as a Fake* out of his fascination with the story and there are endless replayings of the phenomenon on stage, screen and radio.

Equally fascinating is what became of the key players in the saga after the dust had settled. None of the three men was able to resume their life where they left off after the hoax had spiralled so out of control, but for some the shadow of Ern Malley was longer than for others.

McAuley continued to become more and more reactionary, joining his country's sizeable band of committed right-wingers and founding the anti-Communist publication *Quadrant* which is still flourishing today. He continued to bask in the glow of his grand refutation of left-wing silliness and ultimately became a very conservative professor of English at the University of Tasmania. Privately, however, he would confess to feeling guilty for what he had done, because the effect of the hoax on young Max Harris was seriously deleterious. And as it turned out, Harris himself was to retain little of the free-thinking passion that once riled McAuley so much: later in life the two men would meet and drink the night away together, putting at least some of the Malley era ghosts to rest.

Long before that, however, in the immediate aftermath of the debunking, Harris must have hated McAuley with a passion. Especially when the police barged in to the offices of *Angry Penguins* and charged him with printing obscene material – a very serious blot on the copy-book of a publisher at the start of his professional life. Evidently, a few lines of the Malley poems were considered too risqué for public consumption. However, references in the poems 'Young Prince of Tyre' and 'Documentary Film' to 'the woman who scarcely would/Now opens her cunning thighs to reveal the herb/Of content' or indeed 'The blood-dripping hirsute maw of night's other temple' are surely more self-consciously chthonic than deliberately pornographic. The obscenity trial that resulted took place in Adelaide and caused predictable outrage: the defendant was spat at in the street and his name was tarnished forever in the small town. It was, to Harris's mind, just the establishment flexing its muscle again, but mud sticks and he knew it. Soon after, his beloved magazine folded after his investor-cum-business partner John Reed, who was a key member of the bohemian incestuous artistic sect which included the artist Nolan, became incapable of continuing with the venture. And after Harris fathered a child with his childhood sweetheart, Yvonne Hutton, whose family strongly disapproved of this heathen and hairy peddler of left-wing filth, he decided to set up as a bookseller in Adelaide in the hope of garnering enough income and respectability to be considered a worthwhile citizen.

Although his literary ambitions as a poet and editor never survived the Malley debacle, he did succeed in becoming a much-loved figure in his hometown, ending up dealing rare books and cutting a swathe through artistic Adelaide with his trademark hat and cane and endless supply of literary anecdotes. But he would be best known for the ranting opinion pieces he regularly wrote for Rupert Murdoch's newspapers, holding forth on the state of modern society rather than advocating art and free expression as a path to greater understanding as he might have done back in the days of *Angry Penguins*. In fact, by the end of his life in 1995 he had come far closer to the opinions of his former enemy McAuley than anyone who had known the pair in the 1940s could have anticipated.

The oddest coda to the whole affair is what happened to McAuley's sidekick, Harold Stewart. Stewart, a middle-class boy from Sydney who had never been able to stick at anything, had always had two private obsessions: poetry and the culture of the Far East. He briefly held down a job in a Melbourne bookshop but in the mid-1960s decided to flee Australia and make a new life in Japan, where he could teach English and learn the Japanese language. This he did, going on to publish translations of Japanese poetry, write reams of his own, and ultimately live a reclusive life in Kyoto, never again returning to the land of his birth. If any reporter or acquaintance ever asked him about his role in the Malley hoax, he would reply that his days in Australia were as a dream to him now, and he had nothing meaningful to say about them. His real life, he maintained, began when he arrived in Japan.

If McAuley and Harris continued to bask in the publicity brought to them by the Malley affair for the rest of their lives, and Stewart tried his hardest to forget it, that only leaves Ern to wonder about. No doubt he is laughing away on his imaginary cloud at the trouble and fame his lack of existence brought to so many people who never knew him.

NINO CULOTTA

MOST HOAXES HAVE an air of sadness about them. Rejection by parents or publishers and a bitterness that overflows into a lack of self-respect are what characterize their perpetrators. All too often their hoaxees end up equally badly hurt, both emotionally and reputationally, and in the case of Australian literary fraudsters in particular we see an anxiety about race and multi-culturalism that leads to some pretty unpalatable sentiments being expressed. The case of Nino Culotta, however, is different. It is blissfully free of such complications.

Yes, his work is ethno-centric in theme, focusing on a new Italian immigrant to Australia; and yes, a few critics have debated whether the author's attitude is paternalistic if not over-patriotic. But everyone who has read the book agrees that the main feeling you get from reading Nino Culotta's journal (and learning about the O'Gradys' unusual life) is pure, unbridled joy. Put simply, the books, and their real-life author, manage to be brilliantly funny while also enunciating some abiding truths about Australian culture. And best of all, no one got hurt.

Nino, we read, is an educated Italian journalist sent over from his homeland to chronicle the ways of the Australian working man. To this end, he arms himself with a phrasebook and a job as a bricklayer's assistant and sets about immersing himself in the life of a good honest Aussie bloke. The first thing he notices is that the English he has learnt from books in Europe bears little or no resemblance to that spoken in the pubs and building sites in 1960s Sydney. To get along with this 'mob' he is going to have to learn to speak, think and, crucially, drink differently. There'll be none of the working-class wine-quaffing he knew back home in northern Italy, and certainly none of the passionate interpersonal relationships. Nino must become a bloke. And in charting his transformation into this particular species of man he creates one of the funniest and most endearing tributes to a people the English-speaking world has ever known.

They're a Weird Mob opens with Nino addressing the reader thus: 'Who the hell's Nino Culotta? That's what you asked yourself when you first picked up this book, wasn't it? Well I'm Nino Culotta.' Only it turns out that actually he isn't:

> My father had me baptised Giovanni – John – well Giovannino is like Johnny, and Nino is an easier way of saying it. Or a lazier way, if you like. The Culotta family is not famous for doing anything the hard way. It is not famous for doing anything. Because as far as I know it doesn't exist. Not in my family anyway. My family name is something quite different, but I can't use it here.

Was this playing with identity meant as a clue to the fact that the given author of *Weird Mob* was not who he said he was? Certainly, none of the thousands of readers for whom the book became an instant cult hit seemed to suspect anything. But then they barely had time to consider the question before the real author outed himself voluntarily; and nor did they mind particularly when he did, fresh off the plane from Samoa and wearing a grass skirt.

John O'Grady was an eccentric man with an unusual history. Born just before the First World War to Irish immigrant parents, his first few years were spent in the Waverley district of Sydney where his father was the editor of the *New South Wales Agricultural Gazette*. But when an opportunity to run their own farm came up, the O'Gradys moved their household of eight children out to a remote area of Australian New England to bring them up more or less wild. The nearest school was several hours' walk away, so for the next few years young John and his siblings had little formal education. However when drought decimated the area O'Grady Senior, now in his fifties, upped sticks again and moved the family back to the city, where he retrained as a barrister. Out of this upbringing of changing scenes and revolving identities came not one but two published authors: John's younger brother Frank grew up to make his living writing historical novels.

Unlike many literary hoaxers, however, John never dreamed of being an author. Instead, he pursued a career as a pharmacist, dabbling in amateur dramatics on the side but largely remaining committed to working across Australia, New Zealand and the South Pacific to bring better healthcare to remote communities. After enlisting in 1942, he spent nearly a decade with the Army Medical Service.

It was a throwaway remark over the family dinner table that spurred him on to become Nino Culotta. His son (also called John O'Grady) picks up the story in an article in the *Sydney Morning Herald*:

> Every Sunday the family would gather at my grandparents' home at Bronte. One Sunday my Uncle Frank had a new book out and foolishly asked Da what he thought of it. My father used to refer to Frank's books

as 'library novels', because they were researched in the library. Da said: 'Not much, and if I couldn't write a better book than that I'd give up.' So Frank bet him $10 that he couldn't write any sort of book and get it published. He said, 'I'll take the bet.'

It seems he was inspired by his recent experience of life on a building site. He had taken leave from work to help a friend build a house (which was no uncommon thing at that time – Sydney in the 1960s was in the grip of an unprecedented housing boom, as upwardly mobile families created their dream homes on relatively cheap plots of land). John had evidently been fascinated by the fact that he, an Aussie born and bred, couldn't understand a word of what his co-workers on the site were saying; their accents, vocabulary and strange in-jokes all had him stumped. This sparked off in his mind the idea that a genuine new-comer to the country – someone just off the proverbial boat – would have to find novel strategies to fit in with these loud, incomprehensible, beer-swilling but good-natured men or risk total isolation.

Six weeks later, *They're a Weird Mob* was completed. And no sooner was it finished than it was stuffed in a drawer and the author was off on a plane to Samoa, where his professional services were required. It was while he was away on this trip that his son John came across the manuscript and felt sure it was good enough to be published. John Junior knew a thing or two about the market for humour because he worked at a major television company producing light entertainment (and indeed would go on to be head of sit-coms for ABC). He duly sent the manuscript to the publishing house Angus & Robinson who admitted the book was laugh-out-loud funny but didn't see it selling well. John felt sure that they were wrong, and submitted it to the next publisher on his list, Sam Ure Smith. Smith took the bait immediately and accepted the manuscript with relish. Naturally, Smith wanted to meet this comic genius Nino Culotta, but John, acting as agent, played for time by saying that the author was abroad. Which he was – in Samoa working as a pharmacist.

Happily, John Junior decided to come clean rather than get himself – and his father – involved in a pointless and potentially damaging fraud. He admitted to Smith that Culotta was in fact a middle-aged Australian eccentric and Smith cared not a jot. He still loved the book and knew that with the right sales and marketing strategy, readers would too.

So O'Grady's debut was published *in absentia* and much to his surprise began to fly off the shelves. Posters emblazoned with 'weird mob' slogans and phrases were circulated; bookshops were given only a little stock at a time to create the impression of desirability; and through radio and newspaper marketing a combination of reviews and extracts made the whole Culotta phenomenon so popular that by the time John Senior came back to Australia, people were having 'weird mob' parties dressed as builders, and he was nothing short of a celebrity.

Of course many if not most of the 130,000 readers in the book's first year must have believed it was written by a bemused Italian immigrant. (His jacket photograph had him sitting on a kerosene lamp with his back to the camera.) But because the publisher only let people believe that the author was the character Culotta, rather than explicitly telling them he was, nobody felt hard done by. And when newspapers finally made it common knowledge that Culotta was made-up, sales, according to John Junior, 'skyrocketed'. And when John Senior stepped off the plane from Samoa wearing the grass and floral garb of that island and waving happily to the assembled press, his status as a lovable eccentric was confirmed. As his son says, 'He didn't pretend to live that existence. He thought it was a hoot!'

Perhaps it was this good-humoured, honest authorial attitude that ensured *They're a Weird Mob* stayed in print constantly for nearly forty years and enabled its true author to give up being a pharmacist and write more books – some by Nino and some by himself.

However, as far back as 1958 O'Grady expressed a desire to leave Nino behind him, writing to John Junior that he had 'no interest in Culotta any more . . . Mr Culotta has had his day. Let him die.' He even held a mock funeral for him (albeit in a bar) in 1960. But his rejection of his alter ego was always complicated by an interest in where he could take him as a professional writer. In the same breath he would dismiss the idea of writing a magazine column as Nino and yet wonder, in a letter home from another trip to Samoa, whether 'Nino's wanderings in NZ and Samoa, presented in column-narrative form, for collection later into book form, [would] be of any use?'

Was O'Grady hoaxing for money and fame? Emphatically not, at first. But when a whole nation is bursting with love for a writer's work and that love enables the writer to leave his day-job – and when nobody is accusing him of cheating or lying or pretending to be someone he's not – that writer would hardly be human if he refused all of what was on offer. The Nino Culotta hoax, it would seem, is one which genuinely took on a life and momentum of its own, much to the surprise of its light-hearted perpetrator. And due to the affection with which he told his story and the refusal to take himself too seriously, O'Grady will go down in history as the eternal Good Bloke of Australian literary hoaxes.

MARLO MORGAN

*A*NYONE WHO HAS spent any time trawling second-hand bookshops in Britain or America will have come across Marlo Morgan's 1990s bestseller *Mutant Message Down Under*. Its subtitle is 'A Woman's Journey into Dreamtime Australia' and it has caused more offence and upset to the Aboriginal people than any other book before or since. The refusal of the author to admit that she invented the story of her walkabout with a lost tribe of nomads resulted in a delegation of Aborigine Elders seeking permission to fly to America to confront her and stop a blockbusting movie being made of her exploitative work. She did, eventually, apologize, but the million-dollar industry which had sprung up around her books in the States saw to it that her admission of guilt received hardly any publicity.

The story of Marlo Morgan began, like that of so many new-age attention-seekers, in a boring suburb. Born and raised in Idaho in the 1930s, she moved to Kansas, Missouri to become a wife and mother and work in a pharmacy. After twenty-five years of marriage, however, she got divorced and headed off to Australia for a trip of several months. It was there she became interested in the natural remedies and folk culture of the native population, and when she returned to America she gave up pharmacy work to become a peripatetic salesperson for a company specializing in tea-tree oil. After a while of giving potential clients the specified blurb about the products, her sales pitch for the Melaleuca brand of herbal remedies began to include a rather extraordinary story. She told people that when she was in Australia she had been kidnapped by a tribe of native people who had never seen a white person before, and over the course of a four-month trek across the parched country with them they taught her the secrets of health and wellbeing, curing her sore feet with tea-tree oil and coming to respect and even honour her as a member of their group. At some point she started to write this story down and sell it in pamphlet form along with her wares, at which point her company realized she was making unsubstantiated claims for their product (which is a natural antiseptic, not a mystical cure-all), and they – and the Missouri Department for Consumer Affairs – had to reprimand her.

But by this time she knew she was on to a good thing. It was 1990 and self-help books were flying off the shelves as fast as new-age remedies and healing aides, and the industry was no longer limited to the cash-rich, reason-poor burghers of California. She decided to make her tall tale into a full-length book, adding descriptions of the health and lifestyle secrets of her Aboriginal friends (who she called the 'Real People'), and tried to get it published. Initially unsuccessful, she resourcefully went ahead and published her spiritual travelogue herself, enlisting the help of her children to illustrate and publicize the work. That was in 1991 and soon after it seemed her prayers had been answered when the publishing arm of a new-age centre in New Hampshire, the Stillpoint School of Advanced Energy Healing, bought the rights to her book for $2,500. Just days before the presses began to roll, however, Stillpoint decided to heed the warnings of the experts they had asked to look over the book for authenticity, and cancelled the whole project, selling back the rights to the author and reckoning they had escaped an embarrassing reputational crisis.

Across the country in California, however, an agent with her eye on the new-age dollar had heard about the book and, recently disappointed by having missed out on the chance to represent the author of *The Celestine Prophecy*, contacted Morgan with an offer. Now big money was being talked about, and with a bit of editing by one of her associates in the mainstream publishing world, Candice Fuhrman sold the manuscript to HarperCollins for an astonishing $1.7 million. To top it all off, United Artists bought the film rights and began a series of meetings to set up production.

Morgan's cottage industry, based on the fanciful holiday myth of a middle-aged divorcee, was suddenly one of the hottest commodities in American media. And happily, on publication, the book proved to be every bit as successful amongst the snake-oil-hungry reading public as everyone had hoped. Those inspiring pep-talks the author had been giving to her tea-tree customers in Missouri had blossomed into full-blown lectures, where she spoke to hundreds at a time about her experiences as 'walkabout woman' and the marvellous truths she learned in the bush.

But while America was lapping up her spurious literary product, the book – although not published in Australia

– had reached some key Aboriginal commentators in the southern hemisphere. Copies began to be circulated privately amongst writers and readers in indigenous communities and without exception everyone was utterly horrified. What they read in *Mutant Message* was a hotchpotch of offensive, ill-conceived lies – not even half-truths – based, seemingly, on a smattering of knowledge about Native Americans and a thorough grounding in *Crocodile Dundee*. On almost every page there were glaring inaccuracies, cruel misrepresentations and, it was widely claimed, out-and-out racism.

To list every one of the errors in Morgan's account would take up as many pages as are in her book, because almost every claim she makes about Aboriginal culture is unfounded. To name but a few, her 'Real People' are supposed to be nomadic, but they travel with an astonishing amount of paraphernalia such as cooking utensils and musical instruments. They have a designated tool maker and a counsellor called Secret Keeper who helps people with their emotional problems: anathema to a people for whom everyone is a tool maker and there is no therapy culture. They praise Morgan's remarkable talent for self-sufficiency. They use the Native American phrase 'the medicine of music', the European concept of the composer, and eventually put on a Western-style concert for Morgan: none of the ritual 'singing the country' that Aboriginal culture is famous for. They call each other by clumsy made-up names rather than the authentic 'skin' or family names. They approach Morgan unbidden and are not afraid to whisk her off on walkabout with them nor instantly initiate her into their group, whereas in fact even indigenous groups who have known many white people are still slow to integrate with them. Finally, one of the nomads speculates that Morgan must be from 'outer space' – a phrase and a concept that no tribesperson who has never had contact with the white world would be able to enunciate.

Of course, Morgan's get-out clause was her assertion that these people were a hidden, secret tribe who had escaped the attentions of the authorities and never been moved into reservations. So whenever anyone criticized her she merely responded that of course no one could verify her memoir – no one but her had ever known these people. But what about spinifex? Famously, that viciously spiny plant grows all over the dangerous 'red centre' of Australia and anyone claiming to have walked for months across the bush would necessarily know a thing or two about it. They would know, for example, that far from growing in an unbroken 'lawn', cutting your feet to shreds wherever you step, it grows in clumps surrounded by sand which are easy to circumnavigate. And then there is the highly secretive ceremonial artefact of which Morgan claimed first-hand knowledge, the bull-roarer: an instrument it is forbidden for women ever to hear. Apart from in the film *Crocodile Dundee*, that is . . . And how about the phone box that Morgan claims she chanced upon on her way out of the desert? It took a quarter, she said. But every Australian knows that in the 1980s you needed two coins to make a local call (let alone one to America). After making the call, she claims she used a telegraph office to have money wired to her – but there was no such thing in the area.

There was no good reason for her to lie about these elements of mainstream Australian life, so her fate as a fantasist seemed sealed. Just to make sure, however, a group of Noongah Elders organized a survey of all the people on the land she claimed to have travelled through. None of them knew anything of a group of sixty heavily-laden, concert-playing, white-woman-revering Aboriginals having passed by at any time in living memory – and with the deeply ingrained traditional law of always alerting others to your presence when crossing their land, they all agreed that these 'lost people' could not be Aboriginal at all.

Letters and papers were written but to no avail. In America, Morgan answered critics with accusations of racism, claiming that nobody black had ever criticized her worthy work, only bitter white people. Finally, determined to get an apology out of her, a group of Elders sought a grant from their government to make a trip to America to confront this woman who had belittled their precious culture and made them look stupid to millions of foreign readers. Lead by Robert Eggington, the coordinator of the Dumbartung Aboriginal Corporation, seven men arrived in America and arranged a press conference and a meeting with the team at Warner Brothers who were planning the *Mutant Message* film. Stating their case, they managed to get Morgan on a telephone conference call from New York and each man put to her their doubts about elements of her story. Quietly, she assured them that the matter of her official apology would be settled by her lawyers, who would forward them a written confession that the story was made-up. Those who heard the call say she seemed contrite and willing to make up for any hurt she had caused. Doubtless she had also been advised to avoid a PR disaster by placating this pesky delegation from the bush.

But the *Message* machine trundled on: reprints, lecture tours, an appearance on Oprah and new spin-off titles such as the spiral-bound *vade mecum, Making the Message Mine*. In 1997 a lecture tour to Japan was beset by PR problems when another band of visiting Aboriginal critics gained access to a talk in front of a thousand people in Kobe and protested using music and traditional cultural displays. Undeterred, readers still bought more and more copies of the book and a few months later HarperCollins sold its millionth copy.

Morgan never reaffirmed her apology to the race she had disrespected, and continues to be vague about which bits of her book were imagined, which were distorted to protect the identities of the people she went walkabout with and which were true. Her final word on the matter, printed in the *Seattle Times* in September 1994, seems to be this:

> The Australian government says these people don't exist; they couldn't still be there after the last roundup to send Aborigines to the reservation. In the eyes of the government, they would be criminals, walking on government land without a permit, not on any census or tax rolls, not registering births. But the government doesn't pursue fictional people or places . . . I did go on walkabout. Everything that I say happened did happen. Nothing in the book is embellished. It's fiction because of what I left out, not what I put in.

But anthropologists, Aboriginal commentators and historians all agree: if Morgan really did find a lost tribe of nomads in the bush who bear little or no resemblance to any other indigenous

Australian group known to man, her achievement is far greater than even she is giving herself credit for.

HELEN DEMIDENKO

*T*HE STORY OF the Australian hoaxer Helen Darville aka Demidenko has attracted indignant interest from all corners of the globe thanks to the subject-matter of the book that made her famous. *The Hand that Signed the Paper* won the Australian/Vogel literary award in 1993, the Australian Literary Society Gold Medal in 1995 and the prestigious Miles Franklin award in the same year. The book claims to be written by the daughter of a Ukrainian peasant and his brother, now living in Australia, who in the 1940s decided to join the Nazi death squads after being mistreated by Russian Jewish 'commissars' in their homeland. These hated communists, Demidenko wrote, inflicted terrible institutionalized suffering on the native population, causing them to rise up in anti-Semitic hatred and join Hitler in his fatal cause. In the book, Demidenko says that as an Australian-Ukrainian she often found herself having to explain why her forebears acted as they did, and from these discussions grew the idea for a book in which she could retell a particular chapter of twentieth-century history from the less well-known side. The side of the perpetrators. Of course there is nothing wrong with this, as sensitive and gifted German writers like Sebastian Hafner have shown. But coupled with a sideline in anti-Israeli journalism and a prose style that is at best hysterical, at worst sensationalist, Demidenko immediately attracted the attention of Jewish groups in Australia and beyond.

After accusing her of writing a book that hardly sought to disguise its pro-fascist sympathies, commentators from the Jewish and non-Jewish intellectual communities alike began to ask just who this Helen Demidenko was. She replied that she was a young woman in her twenties who had an uncle and other relatives who were keen for her to tell – perhaps to justify – their side of a very dark story. Her family had allegedly been blighted by events in Eastern Europe before fleeing to Australia: events which included witnessing loved ones being killed by Stalin's invading Jews, then being liberated by the Nazis. Ultimately, one member of the Demidenko clan had become a concentration camp guard and another took part in the 1941 massacre of Jews at Babi Yar, a ravine outside Kiev. 'An apology for genocide' is what one highly respected Australian academic called it.

If the testament of the Demidenko uncle had been proven to be true, *The Hand that Signed the Paper* could be relegated to an unpleasant but necessary footnote in the annals of Europe's lowest decade. But the fact that after only a little nudging by resourceful readers and critics Helen Demidenko admitted that she made it all up, casts it in a far stranger and more unsavoury light.

For Helen Demidenko was actually Helen Darville and her Australian family, far from fleeing the horrors of 1940s Ukraine, had come over from Great Britain and lived in the suburbs of Brisbane. They were neither educated nor rich, but Helen was studying English at the University of Queensland when the book was published. In 1993 she was an unworldly twenty-year-old, as evidenced by the fact that she made public appearances wearing Ukrainian folk costumes and regaling fans with tales of her vodka-soaked heritage.

There was no very dramatic debunking of Helen Demidenko, because everyone who knew her at university and at home was well aware that she was 100 per cent English-Australian. As she said herself, in her trademark plain dealing style on Australia's Radio National, she just got tired of putting on the Demidenko act: 'I felt trapped by constantly having to go out and perform it . . . I can pull the wog accent, and sound like Effie and do the Ukrainian-Australian accent really well . . . I grew up around these sorts of people.'

One of the striking things about Helen Darville, as we can now call her, although recently she has been going by the name Helen Dale, is that far from slinking away with her tail between her legs, she has swept off accusations of being a racist fantasist with élan. Some might say that is easier to do in Australia than it might be in the UK, say, because of the comparatively mainstream nature of far-right politics there, but it is also credit to her self-confidence that she has reinvented herself as a right-wing lawyer and commentator for ultra-conservative magazines like *Quadrant* (the right-wing publication founded by the Ern Malley hoaxer) and blogs like Catallaxy. She is now happy to give interviews and write articles in which she discusses her youthful escapades as a literary trickster. And although she never admits to being a hoaxer *per se*, claiming her book was always supposed to be a work of fiction but that she felt a Ukrainian name would give it more credibility, she agrees that she was keen to prick the 'pretentiousness' of the literary scene – just like McAuley, the Jew-baiting *Quadrant* founder did before her

– and decided to start blogging against the left-wing critics in order to 'humiliate a group I considered spineless'.

But deeper clues to the motivation behind her hoax came in a surprisingly revealing interview she gave to the ABC programme *All in the Mind* in April 2006. In it she reveals that far from being the ordinary child of quiet suburbanites, she faced challenges from the outset. Badly dyslexic, she recalled 'not being any good at anything – well certainly not anything academic – when I was young. I can still remember the sensation of being the class idiot.' But a keen intelligence meant she found strategies to overcome her literacy problems, as many clever dyslexics do, and so went 'from the bottom to the top of the class inside six months, and that was very freaky. I've never forgotten that.'

If this sudden success and respect at school was thrilling, there was little such upward mobility at home, where her loving but uneducated mother was battling to keep the family together in the face of that recurring figure in the annals of literary hoaxers – the absent father. And Darville's was absent in a quite spectacular way. Always what she called 'a serial philanderer and petty criminal', her dad, she says, 'wasn't worth too much'. After years of humiliating the family with his infidelities and run-ins with the law, he finally died while *in flagrante delicto* with a prostitute at a local brothel.

What did young Helen have to lose? Merely a past filled with ignominy which was leavened only by her discovery that she was smart enough to outwit the powers that be. And so she did, for a while. But doubtless she considers herself to have got the last laugh, as she is on the way to becoming a high-earning lawyer. Literature, she has said, was never going to earn her a decent crust, and 'If I'm going to cop that much aggro, I want to be paid better for it'. Fair dinkum? You decide.

NORMA KHOURI

*F*ORBIDDEN LOVE IS the story of Dalia, an ambitious, compassionate, beautiful young Jordanian woman who, after falling in love with a Christian man, was murdered by her father in a so-called honour killing. Throughout her short life she had had but one confidante, her best friend Norma – they not only shared their romantic dreams and secrets, but even set up as hairdressers together in a ground-breaking unisex salon in Amman. But when Dalia was stabbed to death with the full knowledge of her family, her friend was determined to tell the world about her unjust end – and to publicize the shameful institutionalized killings that went on behind closed doors in the Middle East. Moreover she wanted to tell the story of her and Dalia's lives in repressive Amman. To do this, however, she would have to get out of the strict, secretive world of 1990s Jordan. It was only with the help of Dalia's boyfriend, Michael, that she was able to be smuggled out of the country, initially to Greece and then to Australia, where she made a new life for herself as an author and campaigner for women's rights.

Writing Dalia's story was, Norma told journalists on the book's publication, a very hard thing to do because it brought back so many painful memories of her dear friend, the beguiling young woman whose affair with the wrong man had, anyway, been totally chaste. But ultimately she found the experience cathartic and was motivated by the desire to tell the world of the injustices perpetrated in the name of Jordanian patriarchy and the chance that by raising awareness – and money, with the proceeds of her book – she might be able to save just one girl's life.

She called her memoir *Forbidden Love* and as soon as it was published in her new homeland in 2003 it became a runaway success. Hundreds of thousands of copies were sold, and Norma Khouri – highly marketable, with her ravishing good looks, sympathetic tone of voice and propensity to public tears of anger over the cause of women's rights – became an overnight star. She trawled bookshops, festivals and rallies speaking about the experiences in her book, and Australia felt blessed that she had chosen that country as a refuge from the irate Jordanians now apparently hell-bent on dispatching her as they had Dalia.

The critical response to the book was muted in terms of its style, but the consensus was that this was one of those books that worked despite, and in a way because of, its unpolished prose. This was the grief-stricken lament of an angry young woman, determined to make her voice heard. And the story it told spoke volumes about the different lives led by women in the modern world. In an online interview with a website for reading groups, amongst which *Forbidden Love* was becoming hugely popular, Khouri was asked how living in a Western country had changed her. She confessed to coming round to the idea that intimacy before marriage might not be the terrible sin she had been brought up to believe it was, although she was of course still a virgin. The same interviewer asked what kinds of responses she had had from readers of Dalia's story, and she replied, 'shock, outrage and disgust'.

These words would taken on a prophetic edge when, only a year after publication, her story would be exposed as a fabrication. Norma Majid Khouri Michael al-Bagain Toliopoulos left her native Jordan before her fourth birthday and, until fleeing to Australia lived the life of a suburban housewife in Chicago, married to a Greek-American with whom she had two young children.

She had never been back to Jordan as an adult, apart from for a brief visit to secure identity papers. She barely spoke Arabic, and her mother and siblings, with whom she had grown up in Chicago, had no idea she was interested in women's rights. In fact her mother, who was tracked down by the Sydney-based journalist Malcolm Knox after he became suspicious of Khouri, said her daughter had suddenly fled America in 2000, leaving her family distraught and missing her. Knox set out his scrupulous debunking in a *Sydney Morning Herald* article that had literary Australia reeling, and asking itself why it should be such a Mecca for audacious literary hoaxers.

But even before Knox's careful investigation, eyebrows were being raised in Jordan even before the book itself had been seen. The leader of a women's rights organization there, Amal al-Sabbagh, had received an anonymous email from someone asking for a bank account in which to deposit a charitable donation to the anti-honour-killing cause. Apparently this person was writing a book on the subject and proposed to give away the royalties. Al-Sabbagh was not in the habit of replying to nameless correspondents asking for bank details, but when, some time later, she saw the book for herself, she knew instantly that its author was not who she said she was. Aside from topographical inconsistencies which cast doubt on Khouri ever having lived in Amman, there were cultural misunderstandings which no Jordanian would make. For one thing, the notion of a unisex hair salon such as she claimed she and Dalia ran together, was absurd – such a venture would have been entirely illegal, and would have been shut down immediately. Besides, none of the hairdressers or barbers in the city had ever heard of these two women. Then came the more serious revelation that if Dalia had indeed been killed in the way Khouri described, al-Sabbagh or one of her colleagues would likely know about it. Amman is a small city of interconnected family and social groups, and scandalous Muslim-Christian relationships resulting in death by stabbing are the sorts of things people talk about. In total, al-Sabbagh found more than seventy inaccuracies in *Forbidden Love*.

Once Knox went public with all this information, it became clear that Khouri had in fact published this story before. In America, the book was called *Honor Lost*. She had sent the manuscript to a New York agent who had secured her a deal, but it hadn't sold particularly well, getting lost in a slew of not-very-well-written misery memoirs and post-9/11 exposés of the 'real' Middle East.

When invited by Knox and others to account for herself, she was living in very nice enclave of Bribie Island off the coast of Queensland, where she, John and the kids had a smart house with a pool. She said she was utterly appalled that anyone would question her authenticity, and flatly denied that she had ever set foot in America until the book tour for *Honor Lost*. She maintained that she had no family in Chicago, no husband and no children and suggested that the enraged Jordanian establishment trying to discredit her.

Her protestations were not enough to prevent her publishers, Random House Australia, from withdrawing the book. However they still hoped to publish the sequel to *Forbidden Love* later that year, a book which, it was suggested, would contain some kind of revelation or confession pertaining to the hoax. The debacle was doubly embarrassing for them because their backing of Khouri had been instrumental in her being awarded an Australian visa on the basis of 'distinguished talent' two years previously. However by the time the Department of Immigration came to investigate her right to remain in the country, she had skipped town again, apparently back to face the music in the US. The book-length confession never came to pass.

A final weird twist to the story comes in the form of *Forbidden Lie$*, the documentary Khouri agreed to take part in to 'clear her name' in 2007. This film, made by the Australian director Anna Broinowsky, followed Khouri back to the streets of Amman where she said the Dalia story took place. It makes for awkward viewing, as an increasingly flustered Khouri fails to find the places she seeks and displays a command of Arabic shockingly meagre for one who claims to have grown up in Jordan. At one point she admits that the person 'Dalia' is based on (by now she was freely admitting that she had changed names and dates to protect the identities of those involved) had in fact been shot, not stabbed, and was accused of pregnancy outside wedlock rather than being in love with a foreigner. At one point she even allows herself to be filmed being reunited with her father, who seems delighted to see her and radiated pride at the big media success his book-writing daughter has become.

At long last, after months of unconvincing protestations, in August 2004 Norma Khouri made something akin to an admission of guilt. She appeared on the television programme *A Current Affair* and said she was moved to 'apologize to all the readers, publishers and agents out there for not telling them my personal, full story'. She had, she now admitted, lived in Chicago (but had lied about it to protect her family there) and was indeed a wife and mother also known as Mrs Toliopoulos. But she maintained she had spent many years in Jordan and did indeed know a girl who was killed by her family.

The proposed sequel to *Forbidden Love* is no longer scheduled for publication and for the time being at least the author has sunk back beneath the radar. The full story of why she perpetrated the first major literary hoax to be unmasked in the twenty-first century may never be known, but from what is known of her fractured immigrant family and, crucially, her inability to get that first, highly personal memoir published, it is easy to see all the hallmarks of the classic hoaxer writ large on Norma Khouri. Perhaps she thought her anger at men (and publishers) would be assuaged if she could prove her worth to them. Perhaps she was just greedy for money. Most likely it was a commixture of all those impulses and more that led her to believe that the best route to professional and personal self-worth was to take on the identity of someone who never existed. After all, she was only trying to do right by her oppressed sisters, right?

WANDA KOOLMATRIE

*I*N INDIGENOUS COMMUNITIES in Australia, storytelling has been the glue that binds generations since time immemorial. But only recently has the written, printed word played a part in the transmission of their culture. For the last twenty years, one of the vanguards of this new writing movement in Western Australia is Magabala Books, who work with local people and the literary establishment to nurture new writers. There are others like them but as ill-luck would have it it was here that the pair of hoaxers calling themselves Wanda Koolmatrie sent their manuscript in 1994.

The book was called *My Own Sweet Time* and announced itself as the memoir of a fifty-year-old Aboriginal woman who had been brought up by white people after being forcibly removed from her Pitjantjara mother as a baby. There is relatively little insider literature of the national scandal that was the 'stolen generation' – those taken from their black parents to be re-educated in white Australian culture in the first half of the twentieth century. So this book was important. Better still, it was funny.

Wanda was a girl who would not give up. She battled on through a life lived on the margins of society – ostracized by both cultures and never able fully to identify with either – but by retaining a strong sense of self and a stiff upper lip, she never succumbed to self-pity. She spoke of the moment she realized she was different from everyone around her in the Caucasian world of suburban Adelaide but resolved not to let it get to her: 'I'd seen my universe twisted, but I made a point of sticking to my habits.'

Her good humour shone through the pages of what reviewers were soon calling one of the funniest books of the year, and she was not only added to a compendium of Australian literature and put on the national curriculum, but shortlisted for a number of prizes. One, the Nita May Dobbie Award, she won, taking the $5,000 prize money bequeathed annually by one of the great feminist figures of Australian literature. The happy story of one woman's rise from criminal cross-racial adoption to mainstream literary success was, it seems, complete.

It was only when the editors at Magabala Books sought a face to face meeting with Wanda to discuss her next book, a follow-up to her acclaimed memoir, that 'she' decided to unmask herself. She was, she jovially admitted, not a she at all. Nor was she Aboriginal, adopted or once married to a man called Frank Koolmatrie. The author of the book that had had literary Australia reaching for the laurels was in fact a disgruntled cab-driver from Adelaide called Leon Carmen.

Why was Carmen disgruntled? Because, of course, he had tried and failed to get his writing published before. And why had he failed in his literary endeavours? To him the answer was obvious: because he was white.

This might seem strange to British readers, even those who use the phrase 'political correctness gone mad' with a straight face. But in Australia, unlike anywhere else in the English-speaking world, there is a popular white ideology which holds that positive discrimination has made life easy for Aboriginals and impossible for whites. And this includes writers. Since it had been decided that Australia's First Nation people had been wronged by years of social and economical abuse, so the rights-for-whites brigade says, the only way to get published as an author is to be black and preferably female and old as well.

When Carmen outed himself in a piece in the *Australian Telegraph* in 1997 and gave this ethnocentric reason for his previous lack of success as a writer, he knew he would have the support of many readers and writers. And indeed letters to the press in the weeks that followed were often along the lines of this one:

> This is yet another case where mainstream Australia is subjected to racial discrimination because privilege, entitlement and opportunity are being restricted on racial grounds . . . Until this racial discrimination against mainstream Australia is abolished, I don't see much chance of reconciliation.

Politicians, too, weighed in with assertions like this one from the reactionary Premier of New South Wales, Bob Carr (whose literary prize had in fact shortlisted Koolmatrie's book two years before):

> This silly chasing after fashionable status in the area of Aborigine studies [sic] is only retarding the cause of better health, better education, better jobs for Aboriginal people . . . By focusing on the damage to the 'fashionable' publishing of indigenous work, the politically correct clique so vociferous in its condemnation of Mr Carmen has succeeded in diverting attention from the real and arguably more important issues.

But Carmen had had support from a much closer quarter from the outset of the project: his friend the writer John Bayley. Bayley had had marginally more success as a playwright than Carmen had had as a novelist, and as a one-time member of the South Australian Writers Centre had more of an idea about how the publishing industry worked. He offered to help Carmen perpetrate his hoax, acting as his agent when sending the book off to publishers, all the time sharing and re-enforcing the view that as white men they were getting a raw deal in society and the arts. Carmen was known to be associated with the publishers of Peace Books, a far-right offshoot of the racist Adelaide Institute, and indeed it was with their help that he went on to release one final gasp of publicity in the form of his tell-all book about the hoax, *Daylight Corroborree*, speaking of his desire to circumvent 'an anti-white male bias in Australian publishing'.

Together, these two unfortunate angry men set about fooling the fashionable world of letters, just as James McAuley and Harold Stewart had done with Ern Malley in 1944. However, Carmen would have us believe that although his aim in publishing pseudonymously had the welcome effect of humiliating a publishing scene quality-blind through colour-sensitivity, there was also a deeper, more personal reason for creating the character he did: 'I needed a charismatic narrator, someone who'd shaken difficult beginnings . . . discouragement, a few bum steers, bewilderment and doubt. Someone who refused to buckle, mope or compromise. In short, Wanda became a symbol of what I might have been myself, had I shown more courage in my youth.'

Carmen's youth, from what little we can know of it, was not a happy one. (He never gave revealing interviews and has now disappeared completely, reportedly having moved to Ireland.) Growing up in the uninspiring suburb of Torrens Park, Adelaide, he lost his father at the young age of fourteen and went on to join a very alternative rock band called Red Angel Panic. After a few years of playing local gigs and festivals the band failed to find success, and Carmen drifted from one low-paid job to another. After decades picking fruit, driving taxis and failing to get his writing recognized, he moved to Sydney and started to formulate the hoax that would afford him both revenge and acceptance:

> The time seemed to be ripe. Authors as personalities were attracting more attention than their books. And the publishing world seemed to be regulated by academics promoting their various hobby horses. As we delved deeper into this kind of chatter, the idea of a hoax gained ground. It seemed the only way to get into print.

Hijacking the voice of an Aboriginal woman may have got Carmen into print, but it also got him painted as a corrupt and insensitive schemer by critics and readers from both sides of the ethnic divide. The indigenous writer Ann Heiss lamented that 'Aboriginality had been appropriated and exploited, yet again, by a white person for the purpose of profit.' Bruce Sims, the director of the publishing co-operative who had published *My Own Sweet Time*, immediately withdrew the book in disgust at what its author had done, and spoke of 'a very elaborate web of deceit involving Carmen's literary agent . . . Now that the facts have surfaced, [Magabala Books] condemns strongly such deception. Trust is an important part of Aboriginal culture. In this respect Magabala Books has been too trusting and fallen perhaps into the same trap as the ancestors of Australia's indigenous peoples.'

In the end, Carmen gave back the $5,000 in prize money he had received and, despite a police investigation into the fraudulent activities of his friend and *ad-hoc* agent Bayley, no criminal convictions were made. Both men have been allowed to crawl back under the rock of ignominy to observe from places of obscurity a publishing scene that will forever be more on guard for phoney Aboriginal authors. If one positive thing came out of the Wanda Koolmatrie hoax, however, it is a consensus amongst Aboriginal writers that the more con-artists try to steal their voices, the harder they will try to nurture the real voices of a new generation of native writers.

6

MEMOIRS

*T*AKE A LOOK at the non-fiction bestseller charts and today, as ten years ago, you will see one trend which (apart from TV tie-ins and recipe books) dominates. The tell-all autobiography. Whether the author is famous already or merely hoping to become so as a result of laying bare their struggle with addiction, abuse, illness or loss, there is a seemingly inexhaustible market for the ever more incredible memoirs of the heirs of Dave Pelzer, the American who blazed the trail with his phenomenally successful *A Child Called 'It'*. Pelzer, like a more recent British exponent of the genre, Constance Briscoe, has had to face accusations from family members that his tale of childhood misery is not authentic. But those allegations pale into insignificance next to the master of the dodgy misery memoir, James Frey: his revolting, brilliantly written *A Million Little Pieces* fooled Oprah Winfrey and millions of others until he was forced to apologize in one of the most unforgiving trials by talk-show host ever broadcast.

His story is instructive and says a lot about the desperation of US publishers to produce the next worst life story. But two generations earlier, amid the heady literary salons of pre-war New York, a plucky young hoaxer with an equally eye-popping tale to tell set about writing a memoir which was only marginally less outrageous than Frey's. She called herself Joan Lowell and, although now largely forgotten, she was the true progenitor of the phoney genre that continues to strike fear into the heart of publishers everywhere.

JOAN LOWELL

IN NEW YORK in the 1920s there was no shortage of glamorous, independent young women who liked nothing more than to prop up bars and be bought lunches while telling outrageous stories to enthusiastic male listeners. This was the age of female pilots, female lion tamers, female sharpshooters and a host of other newly trouser-wearing, cigarette-smoking girls. One such woman was young Joan Lowell who, in 1928, was the talk of the town not only for her impressively robust physique, spirited personality and deep brown eyes, but for the wonderful tales she told about her time at sea. Apparently a very accomplished sailor and swimmer, she would from time to time give lectures about her exploits on her father's trading vessel, the *Minnie A. Caine*, on which she had spent the first seventeen years of her life as the only woman on board.

One day the PR man Edward Bernays, who was a friend of hers and knew she had been thinking of making her memoirs into a book, introduced her to a literary agent called George Bye, who in turn was so impressed by her anecdotes that he set up a meeting with her and the then editor of the *Pictorial Review* with a view to getting her published. That editor, Arthur T. Vane, was so impressed by her tales of seafaring derring-do that he was inclined to publish them without delay; but after every other person in his office implored him not to on the basis that they were too far-fetched to be believable, he held his fire. And how pleased he must have been.

The two publishers Max Schuster and Richard Simon, then just at the beginning of what would become one of the biggest ventures in global publishing, were not so sensible. They had in fact rejected some proposed manuscripts of Miss Lowell's some months before on the basis that the writing was too rough, but now, thanks to George Bye, who introduced them to the appealing authoress at one of his regular literary lunches, they decided to take a punt on her. With a little polishing, they decided, her memoirs could be formed into just the sort of book that their adventure-hungry readers would devour.

So, delighted to have finally scored an inroad into the hottest publishing house in town, Joan Lowell set about completing her manuscript. She called it *Cradle of the Deep* and filled it with breathless accounts of all the extraordinary things which had befallen her as a young girl at sea. She told of how the sailors dressed her in flour-sack dresses as a baby and put her in the care of a kindly old sail-maker called Stitches. By her third year she could swear outrageously, and not long after that she learnt to play poker. Strip poker, if you please. When she was old enough, she was covered in tar and coconut husks in a secret seaman's initiation rite, and then at sixteen she not only watched a man be eaten alive by sharks but performed an amateur amputation on one crewman's gangrenous limb. Although rarely putting in to port, the ship, with its cargo of dried coconut, occasionally alighted on South Sea islands where young Joan witnessed all sorts of unusual scenes, such as the mass-consummation of a group marriage on a windswept beach. She traded trinkets, picked up various local patois and then, when tragedy struck and the boat caught fire and sank off the coast of Australia, she found herself swimming for a mile against a powerful rip-tide to shore, carrying two mewling ship's kittens on her shoulders.

Unbelievable though it sounds in retrospect, the two experts (a pair of aged former sailors) to whom Simon & Schuster sent the text for authentication decided it would pass, and advised publication to go ahead. The buyer of Baker & Taylor, a major book distributor, however, was not so sure. He told the publishers straight that in his opinion *Cradle of the Deep* was 'the biggest hoax of the century'. But he knew that people would want to read it anyway. Perturbed by this, Simon, who had a particularly close relationship with Joan, appealed to Joan to tell them whether parts of the book hadn't been somewhat embellished for effect. He assured her he'd publish it anyway, but needed to know the truth so he could market the book correctly and avoid embarrassment for everyone should things turn out not to be quite as they seem. But Joan swore a seaman's oath that her stories were all true, and the book went to press in March 1929.

As soon as it was published, copies went out to nautical experts on all the major newspapers. The *New York Times* gave it a fairly noncommittal appraisal, but the literary editor of the *Herald Tribune* sent the book to be reviewed by one of the most formidable seamen in America. Lincoln Colcord had himself been born at sea – in a squall off Cape Horn – to a ship's captain father and a tough-as-old-boots mother who had circumnavigated the globe three times prior to her son's birth. He knew the ways of ships and sailors better than anyone, and as soon as he had ploughed his way through Miss Lowell's volume he wrote a review that utterly demolished it, taking its author's credibility down with it. The terms in which he couched his disregard for the book – which, he said, contained scores of basic nautical inconsistencies and made-up terms – were so strong that his editor, Irita van Doren, refused to publish it in case the paper were sued for libel. But she did contact her friends at Simon & Schuster and suggest a meeting between them, their author and her reviewer.

This uncomfortable get-together happened a week later at the publishers' head office. Colcord, a domineering man and a plain speaker, put a series of questions about life at sea to the young author, none of which she was able to answer to his satisfaction. He then listed the fifty or so inaccuracies he had identified in her text and asked her to account for them. Indignant, her dark eyes flashing, Lowell at one point flexed her powerful swimmer's biceps and invited her interlocutor to take off his glasses and prepare for a drubbing, if he were going to continue calling her a liar. But a few minutes later, realizing she was heaping unprofessionalism on unprofessionalism, Joan burst into tears and had to be comforted by Mr Schuster who, like his business partner, still had a considerable soft spot for her.

Joan never actually admitted her deception that day, but her publishers knew they had to limit the damage she had done with her lies, so made sure that the bestseller lists on which *Cradle of the Deep* was already beginning to appear classified it as a fiction title rather than a non-fiction. They also released a statement explaining the developments and saying that the book had been 'published in good faith, not as a literal autobiography but as a teeming yarn, fundamentally a true narrative but inevitably . . . embroidered with some romanticised threads'.

Despite making an offer to refund any customer unhappy with their purchase of the memoir, Simon & Schuster received hardly any requests for money back, and with the book selling so well it was making a tidy sum for all involved. But it was not long before one New York newspaper decided to look more closely in to the real story of Joan Lowell, and what the investigative journalists on the *Evening Post* found would destroy the book's reputation forever.

She was not Joan, daughter of a Montenegrin-Australian father and a mother who was a member of the prestigious Boston Lowell family. She was Helen Joan Wagner, a bit-part actress and performer from California who had hardly spent any time at sea at all. Her father had once worked on a ship called *Minnie A. Caine* for about a year, and at one point she and her mother had made a trip on it with him. But no one from that voyage remembered anything about initiation rites, under-age gambling or a shipwreck: the worst that had befallen the vessel was a small fire while in dock in the Antipodes, but there was no record of Lowell, then thirteen, even being on board when it happened. The ship had never plied tropical waters with a cargo of copra and, far from having sunk in fiery circumstances, it was currently languishing happily in port at San Francisco.

The full extent of their author's bold fabrication had the ambitious young publishers Simon & Schuster well and truly rattled. Rival bookmen – and some in their own house – were openly laughing at their credulity in the face of a pretty, sassy girl with a tall tale to tell. Simon was said to have suffered a minor nervous breakdown over the affair, and an unrepentant Miss Wagner went off travelling and then pursued a new career as a journalist, aided, no doubt, by the $40,000 she had received for the book – a huge sum for an unknown writer in the 1920s. As for Mr Simon and Mr Schuster, they were terrified of making the same mistake twice, and it was probably because of this anxiety that they turned down another fantastical-sounding volume of memoirs that came their way a couple of years later: *Education of a Princess* by the Grand Duchess Marie of Russia, a book which went on to sell 200,000 copies for rival publishers Viking.

The feisty Lowell, for her part, continued to live her life large and undimmed, working for a time as a newspaper reporter in Boston before moving to Brazil to live out her retirement surrounded by wild nature and exotic men, just as she had always wished.

CLEONE KNOX

VERY OCCASIONALLY A literary trickster comes along who is universally forgiven for their deception and whose writing continues to be enjoyed by anyone fortunate enough to find a copy of their out-of-print masterpiece in a second-hand bookshop. The young Anglo-Irish writer Magdalen King-Hall, who *Time* magazine described in 1926 as 'brown and shingled of hair, blue of eye, pert and minxful as her [heroine]', was one such character, and her *Diary of a Young Lady of Fashion* still stands today as an unparalleled meditation on the subject of lusty eighteenth-century aristocrats abroad and the increasingly difficult romantic and sartorial decisions they must make.

Magdalen was the youngest child of Admiral Sir George King-Hall, at whose family seat in Ireland she spent her early years. In 1911, when she was seven, the family followed Sir George to Australia where he had been made a naval commander-in-chief, but two years later they were back in England for good, living in the quiet south coast resort of Hove, near Brighton.

It was here that Magdalen took up writing as an antidote to the decidedly staid and geriatric social scene in her new hometown. Having enjoyed the benefits of extensive foreign travel, and having a mother, Lady Olga, who not only wrote books herself but did so in Italian as easily as in English, it was no surprise if Magdalen felt a little more sophisticated than her peers – and by the dawn of the roaring twenties she had cut her hair short and set her heart on a career as the author of fiction. Medieval history was her passion, and she studied keenly the background to the stories about crusaders and feudal lords that she loved to write and would, eventually, become known for. But her attempts to get published so far had rewarded her only with a stack of rejection letters. She began to wonder if historical fiction was such a good idea after all. Perhaps her talents would be better spent in a different genre? Then, one slow summer's day in 1924, she struck upon an idea. As she said later, 'I got the idea of writing a "diary"'.

Those inverted commas are crucial because it was not her own diary she had decided to write (although that would have been of more interest than the diaries of most girls of her age). What she came up with was the ventriloquized journal of an eighteenth-century 'young lady of fashion', Miss Cleone Knox. Still a teenager when she started researching the book, Magdalen knew that, although her idea for crafting a picaresque romance in the mould of Tobias Smollett (but a whole lot girlier) was a good one, her historical knowledge of the period was sorely lacking: 'I'm afraid I knew very little about the 18th Century when I began. It is really the Middle Ages that thrill me. However, I went to the town library at Brighton and read up several 18th Century books. They were really all I had to go on. I was so surprised when my "diary" was printed . . .'

But printed it was, and with a considerable fanfare. Magdalen had had the nous to know that an American publisher would be the best target for her Englisher-than-English creation, so with an editorial note explaining that the diary had come into her hands as a descendant of Miss Knox, she sent it off to the popular publishing and retail company D. Appleton in New York. As soon as Appleton's readers had a taste of the book's heady mix of almost-titillating romance and rare historical record, they knew that this would be one of the books of the year, if not the decade. In the publicity campaign that followed, potential readers both lay and academic were promised private encounters with figures like Louis XV and Voltaire that young Miss Knox had written about in her intimate, gossipy journal.

The book tells the story of a romance-obsessed young Irish gentlewoman being taken on a tour of Europe by her father, and trying desperately to avoid being married off to a dry but suitable old bachelor instead of the dashing Mr Ancaster, with whom she is secretly, passionately in love. On every page there are minute descriptions of lovely dresses, irascible aunts, splendid country houses and men who look marvellous in riding boots. And no sooner has one of these sights been colourfully evoked than a bitingly bitchy remark about some *beau monde* luminary would be delivered. Cleone Knox was the impossible love-child of P.G. Wodehouse and Jane Austen.

Her impression, for example, of the great Enlightenment writer Voltaire (who, she recalled 'received us in a chintz dressing gown') was that he was 'Peevish. To tell the truth, he reminded me of nothing so much as a chattering old magpie. We listened, silent, with the Respect which is due to Genius, however Wearisome it may be.'

Note her frequent use of capitals, which was one of the short-cuts to authenticity she learned from the old books at Brighton public library. This simple technique, alongside a few examples of strange, old-fashioned spelling, gave the manuscript a veneer of authenticity which ran deep enough to have many critics and reviewers fooled on the book's publication. By the time it appeared in bookshops in January 1926, *The Diary of a Young Lady of Fashion in the Year 1764–65* by Cleone Knox was being compared, earnestly and rapturously, to the diary of Samuel Pepys. The real author must have been astounded. One critic enthused that: 'No modern girl will ever write a diary like this. Cleone Knox breathes the very spirit of the witty, robust, patriotic, wicked, hard-drinking, hard-swearing 18th century.'

Six months after publication, with the book going down a storm on both sides of the Atlantic and already being spoken of as one of the most important – not to mention diverting – literary discoveries of a generation, the essentially fair-playing King-Hall decided she really ought to confess her little 'joke': the stunt she had pulled to spice up a boring summer in Hove was plainly getting out of hand. So she told her publishers the truth, concerned about what their reaction might be. They did not, however, run to the newspapers with the story or send out a heart-felt apology to all the critics and historians who had printed encomia about the book. In fact, as was revealed in a magazine article some weeks later, D. Appleton and Co. did absolutely nothing to alter the sales and advertising blurb for her *Diary*. Once the story had finally leaked out to enough journalists to make further denials futile, however, a representative from the firm assured *Time* magazine reporters that they had been quite convinced the work was genuine when they published it, and were as shocked as anyone to discover it was not.

Unlike the publishers Simon & Schuster, who were also hoaxed by a fake memoir-peddling young woman in the 1920s and, realizing they were dealing with a serious con-artist, made a public vow to reimburse any reader who felt let-down, King-Hall's editors knew they were dealing with a good-hearted girl whose prank had inadvertently taken on a life of its own. It was not even a particularly carefully crafted hoax, and she had certainly engaged in no further deception after her initial submission of the manuscript. Therefore, no dramatic acts of apology were required of anyone involved.

As Magdalen herself said, 'I wrote the book in a few weeks, but, if I had realized so many distinguished people would have taken it seriously, I should have spent much more time and pains upon it.'

The book went out of print in 1984, but, despite going on to develop a prolific career as the author of such rip-roaring historical novels as *Jehan of the Ready Fists, Gay Crusaders* and *Sturdy Rogue*, Magdalen King-Hall has been largely ignored by compilers of literary encyclopaedias and histories. Yet there was a time when her work was considered the best example of its kind. Writing for both children and adults, her passion for history and love for the Irish countryside where she lived most of her life was infectious and anyone with an interest in the castles and manor houses of old Ireland should seek out her many novelized histories of them.

As a hoaxer, she sought neither wealth for herself nor humiliation for others. She was simply a girl with a fun idea who loved writing and whose amused enthusiasm for her chosen subject bursts off every page of her *Diary*. And although no one ever debunked her, leaving her to do the honours herself, like all good literary tricksters, she had left a clue in her text which would have eventually led any sceptical critics to the real truth: the name of the seat of her heroine's family was the Irish version of her own.

BEATRICE SPARKS

I F YOU WERE a young reader in the seventies, eighties or nineties, the chances are that you got your first taste of what class-A drugs might be like by reading the salacious book *Go Ask Alice*. The anonymous 'diary' of an innocent middle-class girl turned drug-fiend, it was published in 1971 and almost immediately became a huge success for its author. But it would be several years before the world found out who that author really was.

The work is most famous for its lurid descriptions of being high, paranoid and hallucinating, but its graphic sexual references were what got it banned or restricted from school libraries. 'Another day, another blowjob' is one memorable quote from the section where the narrator (not, in fact, called Alice – the title refers to a quote from the Jefferson Airplane song 'White Rabbit' but the unnamed protagonist has come to be called Alice for convenience's sake) turns to prostitution to feed her habit. But perhaps the most shocking element of it is in fact the way the diarist gets involved in drugs in the first place.

Unpopular and unhappy, having moved to a new town, Anonymous is concerned at first only with looking nice and meeting boys. Then one day she gets invited to a party where her sensible soft drink is spiked with a large dose of LSD. Tripping wildly, she is of course terrified and goes home to let the strange feelings and visions wear off. But everyone knows one drug leads to another and before the month is out she is injecting speed, smoking dope and embarking on a year of psychotropic experimentation that will land her in hospital. Her poor parents, we are told, 'keep saying that they know I am a good, sweet girl, but I'm beginning to act like a hippie'. Soon she is having sex with dealers, suffering pregnancy scares, running away from home and encountering America's sleaziest low-lifes. Periodically she returns home, seeking familial forgiveness and help, and the book almost ends on a happy note when she seems to have got clean. But a chilling afterword records that she was found dead soon after the last entry.

If the book was meant to warn children off the dangers of drugs and under-age sex, as it turns out it was, the author ought perhaps to have made the narrative a little less extreme and the bizarre symptoms of the drugs a little more believable (no one is going to be put off doing LSD by the fear of feeling a bit itchy). And the fact that drug use and general delinquency has increased amongst teenagers since the book was published in 1971 suggests that Beatrice Sparks, the middle-aged Mormon woman who actually wrote the book, was barking up the wrong tree.

Sparks came forward nearly a decade after the book's publication – when it was being roundly praised by teens, librarians and drug-counsellors alike (albeit for different reasons). She admitted at first that she had 'edited' the diaries of a girl she had counselled who had indeed died after being addicted to drugs. But copyright records have her listed as the sole author of the work and she has never been able to substantiate claims that there was a real diary and real girl on whom Alice was based. She was also unable, in that first confessional interview with Aileen Pace Nilsen of the *School Library Journal* in October 1979, to provide details of the doctorate that allows her to call herself Dr Beatrice Sparks. What did come across plainly was that as a respected member of the Mormon community, she felt it was her duty to warn young people off the dangers of un-Osmonds-like behaviour, and was prepared to sink to any literary depths to do so. Being unable to provide the original documents from which *Go Ask Alice* was produced – she claimed she had thrown the loose sheaves of paper away after transcribing them – immediately sets her alongside the panoply of hoaxers who make up tall tales about manuscripts found in caskets or given to them by anonymous strangers. But what sets her apart from most others is her strong religious conviction and the fact that she was almost certainly not doing this for money: her husband, Lavorn Sparks, was a wealthy property developer who donated millions to charity and moved their large family from California to the well-to-do Mormon enclave of Provo (where the Osmond family live, in fact).

Regardless of Sparks outing herself as the 'editor' and considerable flesher-out of *Go Ask Alice*, the book continues to this day to be read as pure fact. There is everything about the look of it and the words 'diary' and 'Anonymous' on the cover to suggest to a thrill-seeking teenager that it is real, and nothing to suggest it is the weird propaganda of a smart old lady you might think would be more at home doing the church flowers than writing about drug-fuelled sex sessions. It would of course be wrong to suggest that Mrs Sparks got any kind of pleasure from vicariously living the life of a crack-whore, but she did get a taste for something about that kind of writing, because she would go on to write many more such fake teenage diaries on subjects ranging from teenage pregnancy to satanic cults and devil-worship.

It was her inability to know when to stop that would finally discredit her. When should she have stopped? Before devil-worship, as it turned out, because it was her Satanism-themed 'teen diary' that did the most damage of any of her books. *Jay's Journal* describes a downward arc much like that of Anonymous in *Go Ask Alice*: nice, hard-working boy from a God-fearing family who gets sucked into the 'weirdo sick . . . superstitious, stupid, childish . . . kookie, hair-brained thing' that is killing kittens in the name of devil-worship. These words, from the supposed diary of Jay, who ended up committing suicide after fully losing his soul to the forces of darkness, are not, you will notice, the kind of words that teenage boys use. 'Kookie' particularly. Certainly, that was what the parents of the real-life boy behind Jay's diaries thought when they saw what Sparks had done with their son's story. Mr and Mrs Barret of Sparks' adopted Utah had initially approached her with the diaries of their son Alden, a highly intelligent young man who had succumbed to depression and died several years earlier, hoping that she could make something worthwhile out of Alden's writings which would encourage other young people in his position to seek help before it was too late. Absolutely nowhere in any of his diaries was there the merest mention of devil-worship.

Clearly, the tragic demise of an adored son was not juicy enough for Sparks, who knew full well that it was *Alice*'s salacious content that kept it flying off the shelves. To cynically insert a made-up, uncharacteristic and silly element into the story of Alden's life and to let readers believe it was real – just as they believed Alice was real – was an act that incurred the wrath of all those who knew the real-life Jay. The vast majority of journal entries were not Alden's and even if, as may well be the case, the remaining ones (including the Satanism sub-plot) were based on what Sparks knew or thought she knew about other disturbed teens of her acquaintance, that was no comfort to a family and a community who felt their son's memory had been outraged. Such was the anti-Sparks feeling in Utah in the 1990s that a rock-opera based on Alden's life and the *Jay's Journal* outrage was staged in 1997, painting Sparks as a ruthlessly ambitious writer with much less compassion for her subjects than she would have us believe.

The truth about Beatrice Sparks is doubtless somewhere between angel and devil, just like the rest of us (even Mormons). Now in advanced old age, widowed and living out her days in comfortable seclusion in Provo, the creator of *Go Ask Alice* will never have to answer for her actions in this world, but we can assume that a woman of such strong religious conviction believes that what she did, she did to save our souls: to stop us from killing kittens and injecting speed and running away from home and fornicating.

LAUREL ROSE WILLSON

*T*HE CASE OF Laurel Rose Willson is particularly horrifying. Not because, as she testified in her memoir under the pseudonym Lauren Stratford, she was imprisoned by ritual sexual abusers and made to sacrifice three babies to the devil. Nor because, as she later claimed under the alias Laura Grabowski, she was an Auschwitz survivor who had been tortured by Josef Mengele. It is horrifying precisely because all her claims are untrue, and were used by her to elicit attention, fame and money from a number of people who really had been abused by Satanists and Nazis.

Needless to say, Willson was seriously emotionally disturbed and did not make up her stories with the same calculating knowingness that a cold-blooded hoaxer might have done. But neither was she unaware of her lies or the effects they had on others. Sometimes, throughout her lifetime of concocting increasingly far-fetched tales, she would admit to friends that she had made up stories to impress people and get attention; and her habit of changing her name and identity after each hoax was uncovered points to high levels of self-awareness as well. But one of the most surprising things about her story is that she was a committed member of various Christian churches on the west coast of America where she lived, and was intricately bound up in the religious communities she lied to for so long. She was, everyone who knew her agreed, the very picture of a good Christian woman. At least until you saw her close up.

Her real story, as uncovered in a painstaking and sensitive investigation by the Christian magazine *Cornerstone*, bore some structural similarities to the autobiography she detailed in the first of her three books, *Satan's Underground: The Extraordinary Story of One Woman's Escape* (Harvest House Publishing, 1988). Adopted as a baby into a strict Christian household after her unmarried Polish-Catholic mother gave her up, she and her sister Willow were often afraid of their parents' bad moods and marital problems. After some years of domestic discord her father, a doctor, left and moved away from the family home in Tacoma, Washington, and an increasingly unstable Laurel, who had already run away from home once, went to live with him in California while she finished her education. Her teachers reported that she was an excellent student and her greatest talent was music, which she went on to study at university and make the centre of her contribution to the churches with which she became involved. But even as a teenager she showed signs of pathological lying, telling friends she had been sexually abused by a teacher, or driven to a part of town known for kerb-crawlers to be pimped out by her own mother. When staff looked into these stories and questioned her on the details she admitted they were made-up to 'impress' her friends. At one stage she even pretended to have gone blind, until she accidentally pointed out a local monument from a moving car.

A sad history of self-harm and suicide attempts began when her father, Frank, died in 1960 but she stayed on in Southern California where they had lived together, attaching herself to various other families she met through church but always ending up alienating them with her obsessive, attention-seeking behaviour and constant emotional crises.

It was in the early 1980s that her neighbourhood, Bakersfield, was first rocked by stories of a satanic sex cult which had been using young girls as slaves. A popular memoir of one victim was published and Laurel was apparently glued to the book. It was not long before she managed to attach herself to the case by befriending the families of people involved, setting up a support group and ultimately pretending that she too had been a victim of a sex cult.

She began to appear on radio and television and eventually put her bogus memories into a book-length manuscript which, with satanic abuse being such a hot topic at the time, Eileen Mason, the editorial director of Harvest House, jumped at the chance to publish.

Satan's Underground, published under her new, made-up name of Stratford, tells how she was used as the plaything of devil-worshipers, pimps and pornographers for her entire childhood, with the full knowledge of her family. She was repeatedly raped, beaten and forced to witness rituals of human sacrifice. As soon as she was old enough, she was made to produce two babies which were sacrificed in front of her, and another one which she had to give up for adoption. Eventually she graduated to become the personal sex slave of the group's charismatic leader, Victor, who used her to satisfy his many extreme perversions. Only after the death of her father had she been able to break away from the cult and work through her feelings with therapists. She still bore the physical and mental scars of her years in slavery, she said, particularly from cuts to her arms and wrists.

The poor woman's book was a sensation. All America was up in arms about the appalling new scandal of satanic sexual abuse (a phenomenon that was making headlines across Europe as well) and Laurel became a spokesperson for recovering victims. The popular television talk-shows *Geraldo* and *Oprah* had this fluffy-haired, bespectacled, crucifix-wearing woman on to talk about her trauma, and the royalties and accolades came flooding in. But a year after publication, spurred on by other abuse victims who claimed Laurel's story didn't ring true, the magazine *Cornerstone* outed her as a fake after it uncovered her real identity as Laurel Rose Willson. They contacted her publishers, who admitted they had seen no evidence to support her claims, and asked friends and family from her school days whether she had indeed been pregnant three times, drugged and covered in injuries. But the most people recalled of her troubles was her inveterate lying.

The book – as well as her subsequent self-help titles on how she had managed to heal herself – was recalled by the publishers, who realized they were dealing with an unstable fantasist rather than a greedy extortionist, and Laurel was shamed into changing her name and starting a new life away from the Californian evangelical scene.

What did she do next? She reinvented herself as a Jew. And not just any Jew, but an important victim of the infamous Nazi doctor Mengele, whose cruel experiments had rendered her infertile. Her new identity was Laura Grabowski, a Polish-Jewish war orphan who had been sent to an orphanage in Krakow after doing time in Auschwitz and then was adopted by a Christian couple in America in the mid-1950s. Just as she had once pretended to friends that she was blind, she now said her eyes had been irrevocably damaged by having had chemicals injected into them by Mengele. And just as she had pretended that it had taken years for her to confess to her involvement in the satanic cult, she now told people at survivors' groups that she had never told anyone about her time in Auschwitz until now, half a century after the event. Although she stopped short of publishing a book about her supposed Holocaust trauma, she did write and distribute a poem, 'We Are One', in honour of her fellow survivors, and she struck up correspondences – in a spidery, copperplate scrawl such as you might expect from an old Eastern European lady – with elderly Jews who had lived through the Second World War. And most famously, she made contact with Binjamin Wilkomirski, the fellow Polish child of the camps who also turned out to have added a Holocaust element to his own difficult childhood for the media.

Another exposé in *Cornerstone* followed, and by this time Laurel, now becoming frail and losing her grip on reality once and for all, had not the energy to re-invent herself. Some of her friends both from the cult survivors' groups and the Jewish groups stood by her until her death in 2002, but by and large she had alienated everyone who might have helped her find happiness.

There are no winners in the sorry tale of Laurel Rose Willson, but there are many casualties, not least the fragile voices of those genuine witnesses to the abuses she described, who feel diminished every time a hoaxer is found in their midst. No one knows the precise nature of Willson's mental illness, but whatever it was, it reacted spectacularly with a media that was, in the early 1980s, just gearing up for the great era of confessional misery literature which would spawn more hoax memoirists than ever before. She was simply the wrong person in a strange place at the right time.

ANTHONY GODBY JOHNSON

*I*N 1993 A fourteen-year-old boy dying of AIDS in New Jersey wrote a memoir that brought him considerable celebrity and also brought a number of celebrities to him, seeking to help him live out his final days in comfort. His book was *A Rock and a Hard Place*, his name was Anthony 'Tony' Godby Johnson and he was living with his saintly adopted mother, Vicki Johnson, who had rescued him from a life of appalling sexual abuse at the hands of his biological parents. He had been eleven when he discovered he was infected with the virus and by the time his book was published he was seriously ill; but with the support of Johnson, her husband and a coterie of admiring, kindly adults, including an AIDS counsellor from Arkansas called Jack Godby whose name Tony had taken, he was making the most of what time he had left. Vicki had always encouraged him to write his feelings down, and when the Make A Wish Foundation bought him a computer, he was able to complete the manuscript of his memoir, writing against the clock through every numbered day.

The vogue for misery memoirs was in full swing, but his was not so much a grisly account of being locked in a cellar by his father and raped by paedophiles (although that is what he said happened), but a heart-warming redemption story about how wonderful his new mother was, and how his love of literature had helped him through the dark times. One of the writers he particularly admired was Armistead Maupin, whose *Tales of the City* had recently been aired on American radio, and when Vicki encouraged him to make contact with Maupin the pair began a telephone relationship which would bring great comfort and inspiration to them both.

Anyone who has read Maupin's *The Night Listener*, which he based on his experiences with Tony, or seen the film version starring Robin Williams, will know how things turned out. Because although Vicki Johnson (real name Joanne Vicki Fraginals) swears to this day that she did have a poorly, adopted son who wrote a book, every investigator who has looked into the case is certain she made the whole thing up.

Tony would only communicate by letter, fax, email or telephone. And when he called up his 'friends' for one of his long discursive chats, he had a voice that was not only very feminine-sounding, but noticeably similar to Vicki's. Maupin's business partner Terry Anderson was convinced from early on that Vicki and Tony were one and the same, but Maupin, who had spent hours talking to the remarkably wise and witty Tony, was confused: 'My brain was divided down the middle. There were days when I would talk to Tony and think, "this is clearly a boy, why would I ever doubt this?" and other days when I would think, it's her.'

The agent Ron Bernstein, who represented Tony and was in the process of selling the rights to his story to HBO, also happened to be working with Maupin in the mid-1990s, and when the two men got talking about their young associate, alarm bells began to ring for them both. Neither Bernstein nor anyone he knew had ever laid eyes on the child because, Vicki said, he was too sensitive to germs to see visitors or even go outside. But during their cell-phone calls, exterior street noises were clearly audible. Maupin knew that other supporters of Tony, including a rabbi, had flown in to New Jersey to call on the ailing young writer but had been turned away at the door by Vicki, who refused to admit anyone to her apartment – an apartment into which no neighbour had ever seen a child enter, and from which no youthful sounds had ever been heard. Nor had a husband ever been seen or heard of by the many people who lived near her town-centre block or patronized the pharmacy downstairs.

Due to Tony's inability to show his face in public or face a film crew, the HBO production was scrapped and his key role in an Oprah documentary about child abuse had to be played by an actor. As the 1990s wore on Tony, now communicating via a blog, announced a series of increasingly terrible physical ailments that were besetting him: paralysis, a stroke, the amputation of a leg and a testicle and TB were just some of the hardships he suffered; but despite having had full-blown AIDS for nearly a decade, he was still very much alive. Maupin, who had written a blurb for his book, was starting to be seriously doubtful that a boy with no immune system could weather so many new illnesses: 'It did get more and more melodramatic,' he admitted later. 'And as it did, my doubts grew.'

By 2000, with not one of his famous correspondents (he had added Jermaine Jackson and Tom Robbins to the list) ever having seen him or heard Vicki in the background when talking to him on the phone, the ABC news programme *20/20* decided to investigate. At the same time, *New Yorker* journalist Tad Friend was also researching the case of the 'invisible boy', and together they made a very convincing case for Tony being a figment of Vicki's imagination.

Vicki, it transpired, was actually a lonely, overweight former schoolteacher living in a small flat above a shop in Union City, New Jersey. Her former students and colleagues from Sacred Heart Grade School in North Bergen remember her as being extremely involved with every aspect of her charges' education, often volunteering to help with extra-curricular activities, but being somewhat self-pitying when it came to her personal life. There was no sign of a husband until some time after *A Rock and a Hard Place* was published, when she got together with a man called Marc Zackheim, a child psychologist whose work with troubled youngsters nearly came to an abrupt end when he was put on trial for abusing children at a care home in Indiana in 2004. By the time he was acquitted, Tony's website had been long dormant and nobody apart from the Arkansas AIDS counsellor who shared his name seemed to be getting any more phone calls in that strangely lady-like voice.

In 2007, a follow-up investigation by the *20/20* team who first exposed Vicki's double life added a new piece of evidence to their dossier: one of the rare photographs of Tony which she had allowed journalists to see, which shows a cute, dark-haired boy with a cheeky smile and a big red baseball cap, turned out to be an old snapshot taken by Fraginals of one of her former students, Steve Tarabokija. The mother of one of Tarabokija's classmates had seen the image on television and alerted him to the fact and he, now in his mid-twenties and in good health, was astonished to learn that his face was being used to illustrate a story about a young AIDS victim. He appeared on the ABC show to set the record straight and said he hoped for an apology. Another former acquaintance from Sacred Heart went on the show with him and agreed that, although Vicki was a kind woman, she was an inveterate attention-seeker.

Faced by such seemingly incontrovertible evidence, it might be supposed that Vicki would finally admit what she had done and say sorry to the people she deceived; but all the Zackheim household has put out is a legal document containing a sworn statement that Tony did exist. The reason, apparently, for keeping him so secret was not only his ill health but the fact that evil paedophiles were trying to track him down and stop him from identifying them.

To this day, Vicki has never admitted her deception. But looking back over the life of her young alter ego, she must realize that her biggest mistake was not learning enough about HIV/AIDS to know that while you can live for many years with HIV there is no way – least of all back in the early 1990s when drug therapies were so much less sophisticated than they are now – that a boy could have had full-blown AIDS for as long as Tony did. Her next mistake was actually imitating him on the phone: when ABC retained the services of the same voice recognition expert who had identified Osama bin Laden on a scratchy voice recording, he said it was obvious that the two Johnsons were one and the same. But although she might have executed her hoax more carefully had she been less desperate, damaged or deluded, she could not have hoped for a better response – or literary afterlife – than she got from Armistead Maupin, the big-hearted American writer who was happy to help a child in need and never really let go of him even after he realized he didn't exist. As he said after Vicki's hoax was debunked: 'I think maybe Tony was her imaginary friend. He was certainly mine.'

J.T. LEROY

*T*HE NEW YORKER Laura Albert is not the first literary hoaxer to employ a stand-in to appear in public as their fictional author, but she is by far the most talked-about. Few readers of books pages of fashionable magazines around the turn of the millennium can have failed to notice the enigmatic figure of J.T. LeRoy, the cross-dressing teenage prostitute and junkie who had dragged himself out of the trailer park to pen a series of shocking autobiographical writings. He first came to public attention in 1997 when one of his stories, 'Baby Doll' – about a dress-wearing boy locked in competition with his mother's lover – appeared in a collection of new writing. His author profile, which featured hard drugs, cheap sex and gender-bending against a backdrop of truck stops and anonymous American downtowns, made him an instant hit with publishers and editors seeking the latest, hippest thing. Commissions to write journalism and requests for interviews began to flow in, and as soon as his first full-length book, *Sarah*, came out in 1999 LeRoy's trajectory seemed unstoppable.

Sarah told the story of a boy called Jeremiah (the 'J' in LeRoy's name – the 'T' standing, apparently, for Terminator) who lives in a motel at a truck stop with his prostitute mother. Sometimes dressed as a little girl, and known by the nickname Cherry Vanilla, Jeremiah's ambition is to become an even more successful 'lot lizard' than his mother and after a few years as a petty shoplifter he finally graduates to working for a sadistic pimp, who abuses him terribly. The jacket image featured a mussed-up Barbie doll in a silver mini skirt tip-toeing across a dark parking lot towards a Tonka-toy vehicle. The whole package was positively dripping with edgy cool and reviewers marvelled at the young author's lyrical evocation of the lowlife. Soon a number of celebrity fans jumped on the bandwagon as well, kick-started by the pop star Shirley Manson, lead singer of the band Garbage (most famous song: 'Stupid Girl') who wrote on her blog that she was reading and loving the book. She then became one of LeRoy's email buddies, and even wrote a song about him called 'Cherry Lips (Go Baby Go)'.

By the 2001 publication of LeRoy's second book, *The Heart Is Deceitful Above All Things*, all the coolest players in the American film and music scene were queuing up to be friends with the damaged, reclusive young writer: Winona Ryder, Courtney Love, Billy Corgan of the Smashing Pumpkins (who it is widely believed was in on the deception from quite early on) and even Madonna were all said to have pledged support and friendship to the ailing youngster. And ailing he was – he let it be known that not only was he pathologically shy, but he was HIV positive. This was also of great concern to the group of well-known contemporary American writers like Sharon Olds and Mary Gaitskill whose personal attention and professional advice he had been seeking (again, never in person but by fax or telephone) since the mid-nineties.

It was the crippling shyness that was blamed for him not appearing in public but rather conducting his interviews and business meetings over the telephone or by email. But in 2001, this suddenly changed. J.T. began to turn up to photo-shoots and public readings of his work. As everyone who saw him agreed, the figure who appeared at these events was clearly a bundle of nerves: a whispering, twitching, ungainly gamine who was always protected from the world by sunglasses and a hat (both of the coolest possible varieties of course) and a close-knit group of friends. His long, straw-like hair looked like it could be a wig, but he was such an extraordinary character all round – hiding under tables while others read out extracts from his books at signings; bouncing up and down with a fairy wand in his hand – that a wig seemed like the least weird thing about him.

While the cult of personality could have sustained him for a while, the fact that he spent the entire first half of the 1990s consistently visible above the cultural radar was due, undeniably, to the quality of his writing. His journalism as much as his stories displayed a witty, unusual, intimate prose style that readers simply wanted more of. He was commissioned to profile other celebrities, to write tongue-in-cheek travel pieces and even to create a screenplay for the 2003 film *Elephant* by cult director Gus Van Sant. And a production company called Antidote Films was collaborating with him on a film version of *Sarah*.

In short, Jeremiah Terminator LeRoy's zeitgeisty star was very much in the ascendant. That is until 2005 when, after years of personal appearances in which his undeniably feminine appearance was put down to his being in the process of gender realignment (another of his outlandish claims), a number of American journalists decided to go public with their misgivings about him. The unmasking of LeRoy, and the revelation that his creator was a struggling musician in her forties called Laura Albert, was more akin to the slow exposure of a Polaroid than the sudden swishing back of the Wizard of Oz's curtain, and it began with a piece in *New York Magazine* in October 2005 by the writer Stephen Beachy. The article, headed 'Who Is J.T. LeRoy? A Search for the True Identity of a Great Literary Hustler', was a masterpiece of investigative journalism. Beachy, who had been following LeRoy's career with interest since its outset, managed to identify and analyse almost every named person with whom the young author had been publicly associated, and one by one to weed them out of his long-list of potential targets. The only people he was left with after questioning the various editors, publishers, directors and writers who had known J.T. as a correspondent but never spent any length of time with him (and if they had, they seemed convinced that the figure in sunglasses and a hat was not the same intelligent, lucid figure with whom they had been corresponding), were the two people with whom he lived.

These were his adopted family, Speedie and her partner Geoffrey, sometimes known as Astor. Speedie had been appearing alongside J.T. for years at his public events, helping him cope with the crowds and often speaking and reading for him. Sometimes, when Speedie was not there, a woman who looked uncannily like her, calling herself Emily and speaking in a British accent, would be there instead: she said she was the outreach worker who had rescued J.T. from the streets. Now, not only was J.T. living with Speedie and Geoff and claiming to be helping them raise their young child, but he said he was in a band, Thistle, with them. And this is where Beachy struck gold: Speedie had been a singer in bands before, on the San Francisco gigging circuit, including one called Thistle. Astor had been her guitarist. And one very telling track from the pair's incarnation as a group called Daddy Don't Go features Speedie enacting a sexually explicit conversation with her partner which could have come straight from the pages of *Sarah*: in twisted, mother/lover tones, she upbraids a young boy who might be a girl, saying he/she is nothing more than a tease and deserves to be pimped out to paying customers. This – along with reader reviews on the website amazon.com in which someone with the same name as Albert praised *Sarah* as 'the most extraordinary and lucid book I've read in a long time' – was evidence enough to suggest that J.T. and Laura Albert were in fact one and the same. Who it was behind the sunglasses and wig was not yet known. Nevertheless, this opened the floodgates for all the people who had secretly suspected J.T. of not being who he said he was, and three months later another article, this time in the *New York Times*, saw the journalist Warren St John revealing photographic evidence that the person playing the part of J.T. in public was in fact Savannah Knoop, the half-sister of Laura's partner Geoff.

Only Geoff was an ex-partner now, and a few weeks later, although he never sought to humiliate the mother of his child, he felt more free to speak candidly about her writing life. On 7 February 2006, St John wrote a follow-up article containing an interview with Geoff in which he told Laura Albert's secret to the world. He admitted that Laura had written all the books and articles by LeRoy, who she had invented as an alternative literary persona, but said 'It's not a hoax. It's a part of her,' calling the reasons for her act 'very personal'.

In the face of this, and with the newspaper and magazine editors J.T. had written for hurriedly reassessing their relationships with him, there was no way Albert could go on with the deception. She confessed, agreeing to only one interview (with the *Paris Review*, which famously allows its subjects copy approval before going to press) but pleaded for understanding on the basis that she herself had suffered an abusive childhood just like J.T. and the only way she could deal with it was by taking on another personality to write through the trauma. When, some time later, she agreed to a recorded conversation with James Stafford, a friend who was also a journalist for the *Independent*, she tried to explain further (22 July, 2007):

I don't go to sleep and another personality takes over. I'm aware, I'm conscious, but it's like I've moved to the back of the bike and they're driving. . . J.T. was the more dominant twin. I was just an appendage. But I loved him . . . I was never laughing at people thinking 'Ha Ha, I'm fooling them.'

And of the patriarchy that led her to take on a male persona:

'I grew up believing that a boy's pain was always more valid. An abused girl must have been flirtatious, somehow deserved it. An abused boy was more transgressive.'

Albert's troubles did not, however, end with professional ignominy: in 2007 she found herself defending her project to a courtroom full of jurors in New York, after being sued for fraud by the film company which had paid thousands for the right to develop *Sarah* into a movie. Ordered to pay $60,000 in damages, she was faced with the miserable prospect of being in debt for the rest of her life. However, certain pressure groups have since lent their support to her suggestion that the court's guilty verdict was a 'first-amendment issue'. In August 2008, for example, the Author's Guild released a statement which spoke of the 'repercussions extending into the future for many authors' of Albert's conviction. It said that 'the right to free speech, and the right to speak and write anonymously are rights protected by our Constitution, and the district court's decision which holds that Laura Albert's use of pseudonym breached the Option and Purchase Agreement, is one that will have a chilling effect upon authors wishing to exercise their right to write anonymously.'

None of which has stopped Laura writing as J.T. LeRoy. In 2005 a new book was published, along the same lines as the others but with a slightly cuter twist: *Harold's End* is beautifully illustrated by the Australian artist Cherry Hood, bound extravagantly and decorated with a plush satin ribbon, and tells a tale not only of under-age rent-boys and heroin addicts on the streets of San Francisco, but of the animals the young boys take as pets. A delightful snail is one of the protagonists. *Labour*, a sequel, also in collaboration with Hood, is in the pipeline, and fans of LeRoy's output will no doubt keep buying copies – and there are still many, including Dave Eggers, whose praise of J.T.'s 'perfect and bizarre eloquence' adorns Albert's lovingly maintained website jtleroy.com. Maybe even enough for Albert to make a dent in her legal costs.

It is now more than a decade since the teenage rent-boy, who claimed an intellectual patron at the truck-stop had got him into literature, slunk on to the literary scene. And still, we are no close to working out what exactly this complex chimerical figure really represents. Is his success a function of our desire to turn suffering into art into money, or simply of his creator's personal problems? Was it, as the *San Francisco Chronicle* said, 'the greatest literary hoax in a generation', or should Albert be believed when she promises J.T. was never a hoax, merely a veil? Ultimately, the strange case of the cross-dressing rent-boy who never was raises more questions than it answers. Only one thing is for certain: for those few years that he was real, he was the coolest guy on earth.

TOM CAREW

*H*EREFORDSHIRE IN WESTERN England is where the formidable Special Air Service is based, and in certain parts of the county you can't move for burly, steel-eyed men with half-moon moustaches and checked shirts looking strangely out of place but utterly unarguable with. In the 1970s and eighties, one of these men was Philip Sessarego. To an outsider's view, he looked just like one of the club. But in fact – as his wife Diane and children Claire and Paul well knew – he was a pretender. Having failed the SAS's punishing entry tests due to an injury, he was never allowed officially to join the group he had idolized all his life. Having done a few years in the regular army, he had a taste for military hardware and fatigues, and even managed to get a job as an assistant to an SAS leader. But although he drank in the same pubs, wore the same clothes and talked the same talk as the big boys, he always felt a failure.

But in the late 1970s there was a growing sector in the UK which gave mercenary and intelligence roles to tough ex-soldiers, ex-policeman and general hard-nuts. What is now a multi-million dollar global private security industry was just emerging as a legitimate (albeit informal) profession, and as luck would have it Sessarego was invited to join a number of foreign missions as a paid gunslinger.

First there was a trip to Sri Lanka to help train their army in new techniques, then a role in the attempted coup on the Maldives. Neither of these postings gave Sessarego the real battle experience he craved, but before long, in the early 1980s, the call came to go out to Afghanistan to assist the Mujahidin in their fight against Soviet forces.

Finally, he had got what he wanted: to run around in hostile environments with a big gun in his hand.

During this tour he proved himself to be a brave and competent soldier, and after his return soon won contracts in Africa, South America and the Balkans. Now divorced from his wife and estranged from his children, in 1991 he committed his first act of extreme dishonesty: he faked his own death, putting it about that he had been blown up in an explosion in Croatia. He re-invented himself under a new name – Philip Stevenson – and told army friends that he had been forced to do this for mysterious international security reasons. Many suspected that the real reason, however, was to escape alimony payments to his wife.

It was while living as Philip Stevenson that he – like the rest of the English-speaking world – learnt of Andy McNab, the *Bravo Two Zero* author who was making a killing out of his books about killing for the SAS. In search of a new project, new money and, no doubt, a new way to assert to himself and others that his experiences in the field were every bit as valid as those of an official SAS man, he put pen to paper and started to write about his experiences in Afghanistan:

The butt of my deadly Kalashnikov pressed into my shoulder as I let go a long, vicious burst of fire. A Russian special forces soldier and two Afghan regular troops clambering over the wall only noticed me as they were poised in mid-air. By then it was too late. My weapon bucked and climbed as it spewed out bullets. They had no chance . . .

This was the *Boy's Own* tone of his book, which was to be called *Jihad!* and published under the pseudonym (for security reasons, he claimed) of Tom Carew. Not long after it was submitted to the literary agent Andrew Lownie, Mainstream Publishing in Edinburgh paid a six-figure sum for the book. The fact that a small independent Scottish publisher was willing to stake so much on an unknown first-time writer was testament to the huge market in real-life war diaries, and that market did not disappoint: sales were good enough to warrant translations into several foreign languages, a high-profile extract in the *Sunday Times* and a fair amount of press coverage for the big blond author.

A year later, the paperback edition came out. Most publishers cannot hope for even more coverage of a paperback release than an original hardback, but it just so happened that it hit the shelves (and newspaper editors' desks) on a rather pregnant day: 10 September 2001.

No 9/11 conspiracy theorist has yet been mad enough to link Sessarego directly to the timing of the attacks on America, but certainly, within twenty-four hours, he was one of the most sought-after media commentators in Britain. With a book title like *Jihad!* and a blurb that touted him as the first British soldier to go out and train side by side with the Mujahidin, his twenty years of experience with extremists made him the natural choice for editors seeking an expert view. He wrote articles for national newspapers and appeared on the BBC and CNN looking and sounding for all the world like a genuine SAS fighter. And, as even his detractors in the army community will admit, apart from the fact that he was not a member of the SAS, much of what he said was probably true. But masquerading as something you're not is, in the eyes of the very close-knit Special Air Service, a very serious breach of etiquette. And as so many people in Hereford and abroad knew of his true identity, it was not long before television news reporters were tipped off and a very public unmasking was orchestrated.

Asked to come to the BBC2 studios to be interviewed by *Newsnight's* George Aykyn, the unsuspecting author arrived thinking he would be talking about Afghanistan but was alarmed to find himself being questioned about his own shifty identity instead. Asked directly whether he was not Philip Sessarego, he denied it emphatically, took a swing at a cameraman and hot footed it out of the studio. Ignominy ensued for his publisher, agent and all the editors who had employed him to write pieces and appear on news programmes. In one fell swoop, his career as a phoney SAS memoirist was over.

The following decade brought less and less good news for Sessarego: he had burnt so many bridges with the military, media and publishing worlds that he fell into the refuge of the brawny unemployed: security work. He ended up in Belgium, reputedly working for criminal gangs involved in extorting protection money from nightclub owners and pimps. Cut off from friends and family in northern England and reduced to living in an Antwerp garage lock-up with only a camping gas stove and a camp-bed, it was several months before his badly decomposed body was found. He had died – for real this time – as a result of accidental carbon monoxide poisoning from his gas burner. Those who knew him in his final years reported that he always kept himself fit and ready for action, waiting for the call that never came. But although the end of his life was tragically pathetic, little love was lost between him and his firstborn, Claire, who told the *Mirror*: 'He never served in the SAS. He's just a fantasist who's trying to make money on the back of other people's reputations . . . Basically, if I'm going to be blunt about it, I think he is a twat.'

A tough epitaph for a tough but not quite tough enough guy.

MICHAEL GAMBINO

*A*T THE TURN of the twenty-first century there was nothing so marketable in the American media as mobsters. Except, perhaps, for misery memoirs. And the book that was about to leave Simon & Schuster with egg on its face was a too-good-to-be-true amalgamation of both of those things.

In 1999 Mario Puzo had died, leaving a gap in the market for inside accounts of Mafia life. *The Sopranos* had just debuted on HBO and it could be argued that America was keen to look back to a more traditional kind of violence than crack-heads with guns or foreigners with bombs. So when the bosses at the American publishing giant who had first been hoaxed by Helen Joan Wagner in the 1920s were contacted by the grandson of the infamous crime boss Carlo Gambino and offered a fictionalized account of the inner workings of one of the country's biggest crime families, they quite understandably jumped at the chance. The call came via an agent at the now disbanded Artist's Management Group who had in turn heard about the book from an associate who had met the author, Michael Gambino, in LA a few years previously. The agent said that

Gambino, just out of jail after serving more than a decade for various organized crime activities, was ready to 'cleanse his soul' with some cathartic writing which would also, as it happened, give the reading public exactly what it wanted in terms of authentic mob drama. Simon & Schuster reckoned about half a million dollars would be appropriate for a book with this much potential, and were hoping that a whole series of books like Puzo's could be spun out of this man's bloody life story.

Michael Gambino had started writing his book while still in prison. Although not blessed with much in the way of natural literary talent, he had enough raw material to ensure that his proposal would strike editors as something that, with the help of a ghost-writer, could be turned into gold. And so it was, albeit fool's gold. Gambino was paid his handsome advance, and even after paying his agent's fees he had enough to start living considerably better than he had before he went to prison. Even before the book was finished, Simon & Schuster began the publicity campaign to end all publicity campaigns. They touted *The Honoured Society* (fans of the Sicily-loving English novelist Norman Lewis will recognize the title) as the work of 'the highest-ranking mob member' ever to describe the 'innermost workings' of the Mafia. And as soon as the book was published, Gambino was sent to appear on television and radio and booked in for signings and personal appearances. 'In these days of fake television gangsters and wannabe gangsters, Gambino is the real thing,' trumpeted the *Daily Telegraph*.

He certainly looked the part, with his stocky figure, greased-back hair and flashy clothes lending him more than a passing resemblance to a character from *The Sopranos*. What's more, he talked the talk. In a thick New York accent, he would dodge detailed questions about the criminals he had consorted with, just like any former don keen not to name names would do. He spoke of the need to 'cleanse' himself after all the years of ill behaviour on the mean streets of gangland America. He presented himself as the immigrant son of a son of Carlo Gambino called Vito, born in Sicily but brought to America as a boy to be with his family. And as he chugged coffees in diners while being interviewed by journalists, he always had his eye on the door.

What he did not mention in these interviews was that his real name is not Michael Gambino. Nor, it transpires, is it Michael Pellegrino, the name he went by before he wrote *The Honoured Society*, and which he still uses now. It was Michael Budaj, the same name as his German immigrant father, who is a factory worker in Chicago and nothing whatsoever to do with the Mafia. This detail was uncovered, long after Gambino's unmasking, by the investigative journalist Kevin Gray. But before that, only months after publication, much more serious questions were being asked about Gambino than the name under which he chose to write.

It was in mid-December that the real Gambino family's lawyer, Mike Rosen, contacted the offices of Simon & Schuster to tell them that no one had heard of a man called Michael. He recalled telling their lawyer 'You've been had!' and pointing out that the only Michael Gambino who has any connection to the family was a teenager at school in upstate New York – a Gambino grandson, yes, but one far too young and guileless to be able to write a book like *The Honoured Society*.

Other Mafia experts began to weigh in with their opinions of the book as well, and they all supported Rosen's contention that the author was not who he said he was. Evidently, the movie-style executions and wisecracking did not ring true with people like Larry Panaro, a commentator with genuine Mafia connections, who told the journalist Kevin Gray: 'It took me fifteen pages to know he was a phony. There was no way he could have done all this shit and still be walking around.' Gerry Capeci, who has published many books on the Mafia, said he 'suspected its authenticity from day one'.

If Simon & Schuster did not react immediately – which they did not – it was perhaps because they knew full well that Michael Gambino was not their author's real name: the contract for *The Honoured Society* is made out to Michael Pellegrino. Of course, it had been in the interests of everyone hoping to make money out of the book to go along with Pellegrino's chosen surname, but there is some argument about just how much the editors and publicists knew about Pellegrino's true identity. He says they knew full well that his claim to be Carlo Gambino's grandson was based only on 'family legend'. They disagree.

Eventually, more and more facts came to light which proved once and for all that not only was Gambino not a Gambino, he was not a mobster either. He claimed he had spent twelve years in prison for serious crimes. The truth was rather more pathetic.

Michael John Budaj was a small-time crook from Chicago who had spent his adult life in and out of trouble with the police for a string of minor offences and scams. Records show a familiar career trajectory, up to and not including the point where he sold a book for half a million dollars. He did indeed spend a few months here and there in prison, but not twelve years, and not for anything like the bribery, murder, money-laundering and pimping he described in his book.

Being the archetypal unreliable narrator, it is best not to go solely on what Pellegrino says about the affair. But he does point out that the book deal he signed was for a work of fiction, and fiction is what he produced. He claims he spent all the money on lawyers. Friends say he got his teeth fixed and bought a share in a piano bar, and both these things have been easily proven to be true.

His publishers, however, were furious. Yes, it was a novel they had paid him for, not a memoir, but the value of that work was predicated almost entirely on the author having had inside experience of the world he described. Hence the ghost-writer and the florid PR campaign. Before 2001 was out, they began to prepare a case against him and in August 2002 sued his agency for misrepresenting their client. Client and agency were both indignant that the last of the advance ought to be paid and Pellegrino did indeed believe he was the illegitimate grandson of the infamous Carlo. But the more character witnesses came out of the woodwork, the more Pellegrino began to seem like no more than a deluded con-artist on the make. The woman he married – a stripper working at the club where he worked as a doorman – spoke of him knowing all the words to the *Godfather* films and swaggering around like a gangster in his everyday (decidedly un-mobster-like) life.

He claimed to have met famous mobsters in prison, but in fact had never been near the high-security wing in which the Mafia dons were held.

In the end, however, the case against him was unsuccessful and Simon & Schuster settled, awarding him an undisclosed amount which must have convinced him he was having the last laugh. He subsequently retained the services of a PR advisor and was last heard of planning the next two instalments in *The Honoured Society* trilogy, clearly hoping that the notion of 'Michael Gambino' as the creator of a *Godfather*-like serial brand is more than just a dream.

Simon & Schuster, who, as part of the giant global Viacom brand has a seriously big name to protect, will doubtless do its best not to fall victim to a hoaxer like Pellegrino so easily again. But it will take years of careful vetting of potential memoirists to erase the embarrassment caused by the kid from Chicago who convinced everyone – perhaps including himself – that he was a hotshot. Interviewed at the time of his book's publication on *Good Morning America*, Pellegrino recalled his tough years on the wrong side of the law and solemnly opined that those whom you trust the most are 'usually the people that betray you'. Sadly for his trusting readers, it took one to know one.

JAMES FREY

*I*N THE TWENTY-FIRST century, the name most synonymous with the literary hoax is James Frey. Such has been the media frenzy surrounding his unmasking as a very unreliable memoirist indeed that even people who have no interest in books seem to have heard of him. It was Oprah Winfrey who brought his crimes against autobiography to such a wide audience, after she was duped into not only making his *A Million Little Pieces* the book of the month on her highly influential book club, but openly weeping at the honesty with which this marvellous young writer laid bare his experiences with drug and alcohol addiction. And it was Oprah who plotted a devastating trial by television to give him – and his editor Nan Talese – a truly public flogging.

The fuss began when Frey, a thirty-something screen writer and recovering addict, decided to write a book about his adventures in rehab. The resulting work, published by Random House America in 2003, is one of the most harrowing, disgusting and sad memoirs to have hit the bookshops in a long time. Since Dave Pelzer's now-disputed memoir *A Child Called 'It'*, in fact. *A Million Little Pieces* charts the journey of a blood- and sick-bespattered Frey from his arrival in a treatment centre to his ultimate triumph over his demons (which was achieved with willpower alone rather than AA, which he hates). On the way, he recalls such terrifying instances as his involvement in a fatal smash between a car and a train; being in prison for several months; having root canal surgery with no anaesthetic; and repeatedly throwing up on himself in increasingly foul ways. Naturally, it was an instant success. Sales figures were more than healthy even before Oprah discovered it and made it the subject of her monthly book club, but after her programme entitled 'The Man who Kept Oprah Awake at Night', aired in October 2005, Frey started to shift serious copies. Sales figures rose well above one million in one year, and in 2005 his book sold more than any other apart from the new *Harry Potter*. His triumph over desperate obscurity was, it seemed, complete.

Oprah tearfully recommended his memoir to all her viewers, especially those with a friend or family battling substance abuse. (Frey had been into everything, from wine to crack.) She told how the entire staff of her production company, Harpo, was glued to the book, calling it 'like nothing you've ever read before. Everybody at Harpo is reading it. When we were staying up late at night reading it, we'd come in the next morning saying, "What page are you on?"'

However, three months later, on 8 January 2006, the legal news website *The Smoking Gun* revealed that police records from the time of Frey's self-confessed crimes and incarceration did not corroborate what was written in the book. The car-train crash in which two young women died had been in the news at the time, but there was nothing showing Frey's involvement. One of the deceased girls' parents even came forward to say she would have known if Frey had been involved and he emphatically had not. It also seemed that rather than having been in jail for more than eighty days, as he claimed, he had only been held in custody for a few hours. And another of Frey's criminal boasts, that he had been intimidated by FBI investigators over a high-level drugs ring, was, in reality, a not very exciting student pot-selling misdemeanour he had been questioned about while at university.

The editors of *The Smoking Gun* approached Frey with their findings via an off-the-record email, which Frey then reproduced, calling it the latest attempt to discredit him: 'Let the haters hate,' he wrote, 'let the doubters doubt,

I stand by my book, and my life, and I won't dignify this bullshit with any sort of further response.'

When the website finally published their article 'A Million Little Lies: Exploring James Frey's Fiction Addiction', however, the mud they flung at the discredited author proved harder to wash off. Suddenly, the news, television and online media which had once been so impressed by the bestselling memoirist's work all cottoned on to the fact that they may have been taken in and began demanding answers. Especially as Frey's follow-up to that first volume of memoir, *My Friend Leonard*, had recently been published.

Frey decided to go on the popular CNN talk show *Larry King Live* and, sitting next to his mother whom he had brought to the studio with him, attempt some damage limitation. This took the form of denying most of the accusations against him and claiming that the main point of the book – his struggle with addiction – was all true, and he had only changed certain minor details to protect the identities of those involved. Towards the end of filming, King took a phone-call from Oprah Winfrey, who defended her beloved Frey, maintaining that his book could be a valuable resource for anyone coping with alcoholism. Later, Oprah would admit: 'I regret that phone call. I left the impression that the truth does not matter. To everyone who has challenged me about this book – you are absolutely right.'

While, in the days that followed the Larry King interview, Oprah had cause to regret ever endorsing *A Million Little Pieces*, his publishers and agents were getting seriously worried too. Although his editor Nan Talese seemed to be standing by him, Random House's lawyers were realizing that to avoid accusations of consumer abuse they would have to either insert retractions into each new edition of the book, or set aside a fund of money to pay off litigious book-buyers who had been conned into buying something which was wrongly described as non-fiction. In fact, they ended up doing both.

In the Frey household, however, things were going from bad to worse. Kassie Evershevski, who had been James' agent for nearly five years, parted company with the author over 'matters of trust', but conceded in an interview with *Publishers Weekly* that she still considered him 'a very talented writer'. The fatal blow was to come on 26 January 2006 when Oprah invited both Frey and Nan Talese to come and sit on her sofa to discuss the general subject of truth and authorship in literature. What she actually had in mind was a grand public drubbing for the writer who had made her look stupid in front of millions of viewers. During an interview that is most uncomfortable to witness but impossible to look away from (not unlike Frey's book), Oprah – power-dressed and coiffed spectacularly sleekly for the interrogation – repeatedly attacks him over the specifics of his mis-truths. She forces him to admit that he lied about his criminal activities, and to see how much he has embarrassed her. Then she brings in his publisher and compels her to admit that she did nothing to check the facts of Frey's memoir, even though elements of them – the pain-relief-free dental surgery, for example – seem nothing if not far-fetched. Various other commentators such as Maureen Dowd and the *New York Times*' Frank Rich are brought on to add their indignant two penn'orth, and by the end of the show the Frey debacle has been extrapolated to exemplify, along with the war in Iraq and the rise of reality TV, a nation almost dangerously reliant on lies and misinformation. The following days' news reports gleefully echoed Larry King's comment that 'Oprah annihilates James Frey'.

Even though Oprah herself rang to check on her victim a few days later, and make sure he understood that she did what she did because she was so 'disappointed' in him, and Frey himself says he does not blame her for what she did, it seemed like he would never recover, professionally at least, from such a shaming. But the media is forgetful and can be surprisingly forgiving. Amidst rumours of a fall-out between Frey and Talese over Frey's reported claims that his editor pushed him to change his book from fiction to non-fiction because misery memoirs were so much more marketable than novels, Frey quietly got on with doing what he had always wanted to do: writing fiction.

His first official novel came out in May 2008. *Bright Shiny Morning* is set in Los Angeles (where he and his wife and daughter live when they are not in their very swish New York loft apartment), and revolves around a cast of a hundred, offering snap-shots of their very different lives. The opening page of the book says simply: 'Nothing in this book should be considered accurate or reliable', a disclaimer which he told one journalist 'was sort of an acknowledgement of the past, and it was also a way to be really clear – this is fiction. Don't take anything in it literally or too seriously.' As he acknowledged in the same interview, he 'made some big mistakes with my first two books, and I've tried to learn from them and move on'.

In interviews to promote his most recent book he seems, in the words of *The Times'* interviewer Alan Franks, 'beyond unrepentant'. Frey told Franks, in what is probably the closest he has ever come to really explaining himself:

> 'I've been in conflict with everything for my whole life . . . I'm in conflict with what writing is, in conflict with what literature is, in conflict with what people's acceptable standards are. In conflict with the idea of what fiction and non-fiction is, or are . . . I'm not done with twisting the lines of fact or fiction . . . There isn't a great deal of difference between fact and fiction, it's just how you choose to tell a story.'

And for his next trick? No less than a retelling of the final book of the Bible, in which Jesus comes to New York to walk amongst crack-addicts, thieves and prostitutes. It will be interesting to see whether conservative America gets more or less ruffled by his fictional appropriation of Jesus than they did about his deceiving Oprah. It could be a close run thing.

MARGARET B. JONES

I F THE LA gang memoir *Love and Consequences* had been for real, it would have been a very significant book indeed. For the first time, a mainstream publisher would be enabling a female gun-runner and drug dealer for the notorious Bloods to tell her story. At times, Margaret B. Jones' memoir of growing up a hustler was almost too painful to read: it told of how she, a half Native-American, half-white child from a very poor family had been removed from her parents as a five-year-old when she had turned up to school bleeding from sexual wounds. Then, under the auspices of her overworked foster mother 'Big Mom' in South Central LA, she had fallen into the gang culture, seeing it as a way to gain money and respect in a fractured and abusive community. In interviews prior to the release of her book, Jones told – in an African-American lilt, and peppering her speech with words like 'homies' – that 'the first thing I did when I started making drug money was buy myself a burial plot'. She also spoke movingly of her foster-brothers Terrell and Taye who had also fallen in to the thug life.

As soon as review copies were distributed, America's literary press began heaping praise on the brave young writer who was risking serious retributions by exposing the intricacies of gang life. The Oprah Winfrey machine got behind the book too, praising it in *O Magazine* as 'a startlingly tender memoir'; the *New York Times* called it 'humane and deeply affecting' and *Entertainment Weekly* recommended it as a 'powerful story of resilience'. This was exactly the response the book's publishers, Riverhead, an imprint of Penguin, had anticipated, and it seemed that the first print run of 19,000 copies had not been so ambitious after all.

Jones' editor, Sarah McGrath, had been working on the manuscript with its damaged young author for three years before its eventual publication in February 2008, initially having been approached by the agent Faye Bender while she was working at Simon & Schuster. McGrath was so enamoured of the plucky young Margaret that when she moved to Penguin she arranged for Jones' contract to be transferred with her, so the two women could continue working together. Throughout this period, Jones consistently impressed her editor with her desire to get her story out at all costs, and to communicate not only the pain and danger but the unbreakable bonds forged in the crucible of gang warfare. 'She would talk about how she didn't have any money or heat,' recalled McGrath, who, along with her colleagues at the publishing house 'felt such sympathy for her'. Their sympathy was augmented by the fact that Jones was a single mother, striving to make a better life for her young daughter than that which she had endured. And when the time came to crank up the publicity machine in the months leading up to *Love and Consequences*' release date, affecting photographs of the pretty, brunette author were distributed to journalists. Other pictures were made available to the press too, such as the one of Jones with straightened hair, hoop earrings and tight white t-shirt, sitting on a wall in a rough area, every bit the care-worn homegirl; and of her holding up a bandana in the blood-red hues of the gang with which she was affiliated.

But it was an image of her posing with her young daughter, eight-year-old Rya, which would bring about her abrupt fall from grace. When the picture was published in the *New York Times* it was immediately spotted by a woman called Cyndi Hoffman, who recognized the faces in the picture. She recognized them because they belonged to her sister and niece. And far from being a juvenile gangbanger from the streets of South Central, her sister was the privileged daughter of wealthy, loving, white parents who had raised her in a smart district of the San Fernando Valley. She was not called Margaret B. Jones, but Margaret 'Peggy' Seltzer. And instead of having learnt about the world in crack-houses and stolen cars, she had been educated at the exclusive Campbell Hall, an Episcopalian private school in North Hollywood. Hoffman told all this to McGrath at Riverhead Books in a phone-call she felt duty bound to make as soon as she realized what he sister was doing. McGrath was astounded.

Having been outed by her own flesh and blood, there was nothing much Seltzer, now living in Oregon, could do. The media were chasing her for a statement, but initially had to make do with some words from her mother, whose defence of her apparently well-meaning daughter turned on her having been caught up in the drama of other people's lives.

Eventually, a tearful and apologetic Seltzer herself agreed to talk to the press in a telephone interview in which she explained that during her years working in the voluntary sector to help combat the evils of gang violence, she had collected and in some way assimilated the experiences of her friends on the street.

Seltzer's unmasking came just days before she was due to embark on a publicity tour to promote *Love and Consequences* to readers all over America. The tour was hastily cancelled, the 19,000 copies of the book were recalled, and Penguin's imprint Riverhead was left not only with egg on its face but with a genuinely hurt editor. There was no way a book so explicitly autobiographical could be quietly re-issued as fiction, and there is no way certain members of the African American community will ever forgive this poor little rich girl for aping their language, lives and stories and very nearly getting away with it. However good her intentions might have been.

7

POST-MODERN VENTRILOQUISTS

FERN GRAVEL

IN 1940, A new American poet burst on to the scene who was quite unlike any other. For one thing, she was not strictly new: her writing career had begun at the turn of the century when she was only nine years old only to burn out two years later when she took early retirement at the age of eleven. For another, her scope was parochial to say the least: all her poems were about the daily life of the small Iowa town where she lived. And almost without exception the poems are terribly bad. Yes, she charmingly evoked the nostalgia of a forgotten America, but she was certainly no infant prodigy, as is plain from one of her more accomplished works, 'Winter Music':

> Oh, it is wonderful in Millersville
> On many a winter night,
> When the ground is covered with snow
> And the moon is shining so bright.
> You can hear the sleigh-bells jingling

Everywhere around.
I don't think there could be
A more beautiful sound.

Her one and only collection was called *Oh, Millersville!*,
after her hometown, and having been handed to an older
relative for safe keeping soon after the author's retirement,
it finally saw the light of day in 1940 when it turned up in the
postbag of an up-and-coming Iowa publisher called Carroll
Coleman. Coleman was an interesting character himself:
obsessed with the beauty of traditional typographics and
often choosing to use old-fashioned manual printing
presses, he had recently set up Prairie Press, one of the few
independent publishing houses in the country devoted to
bringing out original work instead of trusty old classics. He
was madly in love with his home state, finding it every bit
as charming and beautiful as Fern had a generation earlier,
and was determined to help protect it from the onslaught
of industrialization. Although starting up a publishing
company during the Depression years brought him much
financial uncertainty, he was completely committed to his
regionalist agenda and launched the company in the mid-
1930s with the following rabble-rousing statement:

Here on the rolling prairies, on the hills along the rivers,
in the endless fields of corn that bend before the summer
wind in green waves, in the soft little cities hardening
under the growth of industrialism, these writers, artists
and printers might record and preserve, for all to see, the
form and direction of life here in the Middlewest.

Just five years later the poems of Miss Fern Gravel came his way. As soon as he read 'Iowa', the opening poem in the manuscript, he knew this was a girl who would appeal to the ladies in book groups as much as to the thoughtful country folk and academics who bought his prettily designed volumes:

> I am writing another kind of poetry,
> And some of my poems are beautiful to me.
> I hope, someday, people will travel
> To see the home of the poetess, Fern Gravel,
> Like they go to Longfellow's home, and Whittier's,
> And then I'll remember the day I wrote this verse.

Fern would never attain anything like the status of Longfellow, but she did, for a while, get an astonishingly good reception in the press. Responding not only to her youth and optimism but her delight in the simpler, quieter side of America (at a time when the rest of the country was obsessed with war and cars and money), critics decided she was destined for 'immortality'. The *New York Times* jokingly called her 'the Sappho of Iowa', *Time Magazine* spoke of this 'precocity in pigtails' and the reviewer for Iowa's *Des Moines Register* spoke of her work's 'warm feeling of validity'.

But validity, at least in the conventional sense, was the last thing *Oh, Millersville!*'s readers were getting. For after six years of excellent sales for Prairie Press, the true author of the poems decided the time had come to reveal himself. As it turned out, he was indeed a proud native of the Tall Corn State, but not only was he not a girl called Fern, he was a rather successful writer of adventure stories and First World War memoirs. In fact, he was none other than James Norman Hall, the well-known author of the *Mutiny on the Bounty* trilogy, *Falcons of France* and regular contributor to the *Atlantic Monthly*, in whose pages he eventually made his confession.

He began with the customary self-flagellation of the guilty hoaxer, saying he was 'shame-faced' at having misled people for so long. But he went on to account for himself in most unexpected terms. He had been motivated not, he said, by a love of mischief or a bet with a fellow writer or any of the other usual reasons an author might perpetrate a deception. Instead, little Fern had come to him 'in a dream' and started dictating her poems to him. Now, Hall was not, as far as anyone knew, at all mad. But he was a prolific and sensitive writer who had perhaps become trapped in a *Boy's Own* genre not entirely of his choosing. He was also someone who cared so deeply about the changes overtaking his beloved Iowa and other rural places like it that he could not bear to live in America any longer and was relocating to Tahiti, where the pace of life was slower and more natural. It seems, then, that Fern was in a way quite real to this clever and highly creative man, albeit as a semi-mystical facet of his subconscious.

Just like Carroll Coleman, Hall longed so much to make people see the evils of industrialization that he believed in ends justifying means. He explained how he had been musing on his idyllic childhood days back in Colfax ('All my roots are still in the prairie country of the Middle West') when this little, very local girl started to invade his thoughts, not only when he was asleep but when he was at his desk, too: 'She dictated so fast that I got writer's cramp . . . She told me things about people in our hometown that I had completely forgotten, or thought I had.'

Clearly, Hall's imaginary dictator is intricately bound up with his literary identity and methods, and although it seems strange for a writer who is not a raging post-modernist to play with ideas of real and unreal in this way, his entire life story betrays a talent for using imaginary sources to create good works.

In the 1910s, Hall was studying for a master's degree at Harvard while working as a social worker in some of Boston's more impoverished communities. Each experience fed into the other, and he seemed well on the way to getting his first stories published when, in 1914, the First World War broke out. It just so happened that Hall was on holiday in England in July that year and, seizing the opportunity for adventure, he pretended he was a Canadian and signed up with the Royal Fusiliers. He fought bravely at the Battle of Loos but when his true nationality was discovered he was sent back home to America, where he found he had more than enough to put into his first published book, the gripping war memoir *Kitchener's Mob* (1916). As soon as he could, he joined the US Army and when they entered the theatre of war he returned to France, achieving the rank of Air Captain and being awarded a Croix de Guerre for his good work. Towards the end of the war he was captured by the Germans and incarcerated, during which time he bonded with another American writer-pilot, Charles Nordhoff. The two men kept their spirits up by planning the books they might write together, and after their release in 1919 they launched a collaborative career that would make them both, for a while, household names. Their three books

Mutiny on the Bounty, Men At Sea and *Pitcairn's Island* are still enthusiastically read by fans of adventure fiction today.

Hall would go on to write a dozen more books on his own, many of them inspired by his life in the South Seas, where he settled in a humble wooden house with his half-Polynesian wife Lala and became increasingly preoccupied with the lost innocence of pre-war America. It was into this middle-aged homesickness for a world that no longer existed that Fern Gravel appeared. She had the power to take him right to the heart of the kind of simple family home he had loved and felt safe in while at the same documenting the irrevocable social changes affecting Midwestern society in the new century. In these terms, a poem like 'Visiting Cards' starts to seem less like doggerel and more like a cunning and very modern piece of artistry:

> My mother has had some calling-cards printed.
> The reason is Mrs Smouse.
> She thinks she ought to leave one
> When she goes to their house.
> Mrs Smouse was the only one
> Who had calling cards before;
> But now that my mother has them
> I expect there'll be more.
> My mother has put a little table
> In our vestibule.
> You leave your card there, in a cut-glass dish;
> That is the rule.

Will Hall/Gravel one day be lauded as a radical, ventriloquistic sage of his times? A strange hybrid of

Garrison Keillor and Daisy Ashford with a message for the America of tomorrow? If so, critics and literary historians will have to work hard to pluck him out of the near total obscurity into which he has sunk. But you never know, perhaps in a hundred years' time the tattered manuscript of *Oh, Millersville!* will turn up on the desk of some unsuspecting young publisher and Fern Gravel will live again.

ARAKI YASUSADA

IN THE EARLY 1990s, the work of a unique poet began to appear in American literary magazines. He was Araki Yasusada and, although he had died in 1972, his son had found his notebooks in 1991 and had them translated into English. The central theme of his work, and the cataclysmic centre of his tragic life, was the bombing of his hometown, Hiroshima, on 6 August 1945. Although his son was out of town that day, Yasusada had watched his beloved wife and youngest daughter die horrific deaths, only to lose his older girl to radiation poisoning a few years later. He himself fought a long battle with the carcinogenic effects of the bomb until his death in the 1970s.

His writings – called, collectively, *Doubled Flowering* – replayed the world-changing events of that day again and again, reframing the experience with a variety of seemingly typical Japanese images, such as flowers, lakes and clouds, and in styles like the haiku which immediately speak – to Western readers – of all things Eastern. But Yasusada's imagination and intellectual life were far from parochial – trilingual in English and French, he had studied Western literature at Hiroshima University and developed an interest in the works of Roland Barthes and the developing avant-garde poetry movement. Traces of these influences can be seen in works like 'Dream and Charcoal', which opens with that typical cipher of poetic modernism, the word 'And':

And then she said: I have gone toward the light and
    become beautiful.
And then she said: I have taken a couple of wings and
    attached them to the various backparts of my body.
And then she said: all the guests are coming back to
    where they were and then talking.
To which she said: without the grasp-handle, how would
    you recognise my nakedness?
To which she replied: without nothing is when all things
    die.

It was to respected modernist journals like *Conjunctions*, arts magazines like *Grand Street* and even the Japanese quarterly *Abiko* that the poems were initially sent, appearing on the editors' desks in packages postmarked London, Tokyo, Chicago or California. Covering letters said that several translators had worked on bringing Yasusada's oeuvre to English readers, and the editor of *American Poetry Review* even got a portrait of the author with which to illustrate his work.

Over the next few years, Yasusada began to be seen as the only true poetic voice to have survived the devastation of Hiroshima. This was 'witness poetry' at its most raw and personal, and thanks to the biographical details with which his anonymous editors had seen fit to annotate his poems, lines like 'You are a little girl with blistered face, pumping your legs at a great speed beside the burning form of your Mother' from 'Suitor Renga' took on a horrible poignancy. Critics the world over praised these remarkable evocations of the horrors of war, and as more of his notebooks began to leak out of Japan, everything from his thoughts about Zen Buddhism and rough drafts of letters were pored over by an increasingly devoted band of readers.

It became obvious that there was enough interest and more than enough material to justify a book-length edition of Yasusada's work, and Suzanna Tamminen, the poetry editor of Wesleyan Press, the Connecticut University's famously *au courant* publishing arm, put herself forward for the job. She set about collecting all the known poems and notebooks, which would amount to more than a hundred pages, and also sought more information about the author himself. But the book would never come to light, and Tamminen would speak of 'a personal feeling of being humiliated'; because long before the presses started rolling, rumours about the Yasusada poems' true authorship became too loud to ignore.

Key figures in the avant-garde poetry world had been hearing stories for some time about the real origins of the work, and the finger of suspicion pointed most directly at a language teacher at a very minor university in Illinois who had written very knowledgably about Yasusada and even composed some similar poems himself. An article in the *Boston Review* by the respected critic Marjorie Perlof made the accusation directly. This man was Kent Johnson and, despite officially being a Spanish teacher, he was known to have a strong interest in oriental literature, to be a keen contributor to debates on subjects like witness poetry, to be something of a joker and in fact to have told various poetry editors that he knew who the real Yasusada was.

Johnson initially responded to the claims that he was the real Yasusada by asking, wide-eyed, how on earth 'a community college Spanish teacher with little poetic talent could have produced work that caused fairly unbridled admiration amongst such a range of well-placed arbiters in the world of poetry'. Pressed further, he claimed that the real poet was in fact his old flat-mate Tosa Motokiyu, a secretive poetic genius (also pseudonymous and also now dead) who wished, for complex creative reasons, to be known only as the work's translator and not its author, and for Johnson to help deliver it to the world. Pressed even further, and shown the startling similarities between the Yasusada poems and his own 'From the Daybook of Oshimora Okiyaki' – a series of verses written many years before in the voice of a Hiroshima survivor – he was forced into an even tighter corner. The reason he gave this time was that Motokiyu had been so impressed with Johnson's Hiroshima poems that he had asked permission to include them in his 'hyper-authored' Yasusada collection. At this point, a resounding 'Hmm' could be heard emanating from editorial offices and lecture theatres across the American poetry scene.

Yet still, Johnson would not admit the hoax was all his own doing, and does not to this day. And in the years since *Doubled Flowering* was revealed as a hoax, the evidence has mounted up spectacularly. Firstly, there are a number of basic historical errors in Yasusada's notebooks, such as the fact that he claimed to have attended Hiroshima University twenty-four years before it existed, and read Roland Barthes' *The Empire of Signs* before it ever came out. Then there was the poetry itself: critics argue that it misunderstands basic elements of Japanese style and culture as only a foreigner could, for example figuring the act of bowing as humiliating rather than merely polite. Were these textbook errors planted deliberately to test editors and readers? Or were they genuine mistakes which must have left the American author of the poems kicking himself in annoyance? Until Johnson reveals the extent of his involvement in the project, we shall never know. And it seems unlikely that he ever will now, partly because the moment for a dramatic revelation has passed as interest in the work has dissipated, and also because he is so busy writing long, strange, obscene, gossipy poems as part of the new post-avant-garde poetry movement. And therein lies the final piece of evidence that suggests he wrote Yasusada's work: his current output, published by online post-avant-garde journals and the experimental publishing house Skanky Possum (yes, really), seems more Yasusada-like than ever. Take his recent *Miseries of Poetry: Traductions from the Greek*. These are loose translations of sexually and scatologically explicit works unearthed in an archaeological dig in Egypt and translated by Johnson and a mysterious woman who was then, allegedly, murdered. Or his new poems on the theme of war and torture in Iraq, which revisit a distinctly Yasusada-like propensity for detailing America's appalling degradations of the human body under foreign suns.

Today, as in the early 1990s, the idea of a privileged Western orientalist hijacking the experiences of real historical sufferers is not popular with many, if not most, people who encounter fake witness poetry like Yasusada's. The motivations behind the hoax may indeed have been intellectual rather than financial or playful, but, unlike the fake oeuvre of Fern Gravel, the ten-year-old bard of Iowa who wrote mostly about dear little sunbeams, these works force us to confront some difficult questions about our roles as readers and observers of history: how does suffering improve art? Is it ever OK to lie about being tortured? And, most importantly, has the idea of 'the death of the author' stolen literature's conscience?

ANDREAS KARAVIS

'I remember the wine was
sweet
and the bread always fresh.
We conversed in Lyric, rich
and passionate,
and the young girls, intact
for marriage,
blessed their men in every
dialect.
In the village
curling like a sprig of
jasmine by the sea
it was almost impossible
to imagine betrayal: sour
wine, stale bread,
bad verse, unfaithful wives.

*T*HIS IS THE work of the Greek fisherman-poet Andreas Karavis who was, for a brief period at the turn of the twenty-first century, hailed as the modern Homer and a strong contender for the next Nobel Prize. His poems had been translated and presented to the Canadian literary journal *Books in Canada* by the poet and critic David Solway, who also wrote a companion piece outlining Karavis' autobiography. He was, Solway wrote, a sixty-year-old native of Chania in Crete who had spent his life sailing between islands selling poems along with the fish he brought into port each morning. After years of peripatetic writing and fishing, he landed upon the island of Lipsi in the Dodecanese and settled into the life of a well-regarded, if reclusive, national bard (his verses were apparently much anthologized by Greek poetry presses and a regular feature on the national curriculum). It was to Lipsi that his fan and future translator Solway travelled to track Karavis down, offering to translate his work into English and bring it to the wider international audience it deserved. Although the sea-worn poet shied away from the limelight himself, he was, apparently, happy to have this adoring Canadian represent his work abroad and even gave a rare interview and supplied a photographic portrait to the editors of *Books in Canada*.

When the journal appeared, in October 1999, it advertised Karavis' evocations of island life as the output of 'Greece's modern Homer' and not only were critics and readers bowled over by his timeless romantic lyrics but academics began to speak of organizing Karavis conferences and inviting papers on this mighty, newly discovered talent. Soon after that first outing of Karavis' oeuvre, Solway, who had only admitted privately to a few close confidantes that Karavis' life and work was a complete figment of his imagination, published *An Andreas Karavis Companion* which contained quotes from critics, further examples of his writing and anecdotes such as the rather cheeky one about the time when he showed the grizzled old Greek a photograph of Andrea Dworkin, by way of explaining something of the North American critical landscape, and Karavis nearly died laughing. Solway was no doubt emboldened to carry on his hoax this far by the earnest pledges of Karavis-philia he kept hearing from fellow poets: at least one correspondent said he had loved the man's work for years and expressed heartfelt thanks that someone had finally brought him to wider notice. But a letter to *Books in Canada* from one Fred Reed which controversially suggested that Karavis had in fact plagiarized his work from the Canadian poet David Solway, was by an amused co-conspirator.

As the months went on, Solway took more and more people into his confidence, one of whom was the press officer to the Greek cultural attaché in Canada, Giorgos Chouliaris. Chouliaris thought Solway's hoax was not only thoroughly amusing but a rather admirable – if elaborate – way of celebrating Greek literary culture. Part of Chouliaris' job was to stage events to promote Greek culture in Canada, so it was easy for him to collaborate with Solway on the event that took his hoax to the next level: a celebration of Karavis' work that would feature a live appearance from the poet himself. The party was also to be the official launch of *Saracen Island*, the book-length translation of Karavis' work which Solway had been working on.

On the night of the party at the Hellenic embassy in Montreal, journalists and critics waited with bated breath to find out whether the elusive scribe would indeed appear. After several hours of quaffing and gossiping, a swarthy old man appeared in the midst of this gathering of well-turned-out Ottawans. He wore a fisherman's cap and muttered enigmatically in Greek. Even before he introduced himself as Andreas Karavis, there was no doubt about who he was. He seemed somewhat bemused by the attentions of his glittering new fan-base, but accepted drinks and praise for the duration of the evening.

But the following day, a columnist called Matthew Hays from the newspaper the *Globe and Mail* looked back on the party with perplexity. Something was not quite right. And of course it only took a modicum of journalistic poking around to unearth a distinct lack of information about this so-called Bard of the Cyclades from his native Greece. Far from being the toast of syllabus-writers and anthologists across the Hellenic world, Karavis' reputation was notable only by its absence. The resulting article, which ran with the headline 'Karavis: Greek god of poetry or literary hoax?' marked the final undoing of Karavis as a supposedly real man of letters.

Solway admitted, not ungleefully, that he had fooled the editor of *Books in Canada*. And he conceded that many other readers had been hoodwinked too. But, he said, he had not done it to make people look stupid, but rather for a combination of two very pressing intellectual reasons: that he felt 'exhausted and in need of replacement'; and that, much as he loved living and working in Canada, he had come to the conclusion that 'Canadians are not a very exciting people . . . they need to be poked'.

Whether playfulness or the desire for a new poetic voice was the main motivation behind the Karavis hoax will only ever really be known to Solway himself. But considering the energy he devoted to creating eighty pages of poetry and thousands of words of commentary, it is safe to assume that the latter reason was the most pressing. For a poet in his sixties to have found a second wind by, as he says, 'creating a style' rather than 'perpetuating a deception' is actually rather heartening. And as with many hoaxes, most of those who were wounded by it were the ones who were pompous enough to have pretended to have known about the poet for years. And the character who turned up at the book launch? That was none other than Solway's dentist in a funny hat.

8

HOLOCAUST MEMOIRS

*T*HE DISCOMFORT INSPIRED by the Yasusada poet's use of Hiroshima in his hoax is as nothing compared to the fury invoked by literary hoaxers who pretend to have suffered in the Holocaust. It is hard to believe that anyone would want to spend their time making up stories about Nazi horrors, but to go out into the world pretending they happened to you – to point at the scar on your arm and whisper 'Mengele's child', as Misha Levy Defonseca apparently did – is surely the work of a damaged mind. Certainly, the writers in his category have all had some traumatic childhood experiences which merged with their interest in the events of the Second World War and resulted in them feeling entitled to use the Holocaust as a cipher for their personal pain. This was what Binjamin Wilkomirski, the most famous of them all, explicitly said, and what the others have implied. Facts were not checked and vulnerable people – not least the genuine victims of the horrors these phoney memoirists describe – were undermined.

BINJAMIN WILKOMIRSKI

IN 1994, A Zurich literary agent, Eva Koralnik, received in the post a manuscript from an unknown writer called Binjamin Wilkomirski. What she read had her captivated from the first page. It was the heart-rending memoir of a boy, too young to understand what was happening to him, being taken from his Latvian home by Nazi soldiers and moved through a series of concentration camps where he was experimented on, beaten and abused, and where he watched his mother die. The simple, crystalline prose and the author's perceptive afterword about how children, back then, were not supposed to have a voice, much less speak of the horrors of the Holocaust after the war ended.

Wilkomirski, now in his sixties, had worked as a professional clarinet player and musical instrument maker in Switzerland all his adult life but had only now, after years of analysis, been able to articulate what happened to him during those dark years. Only now, he said, could he divest himself of the memories so painfully written down in his book, which he called *Bruchstücke. Aus einer Kindheit 1939–1948 (Fragments: Memories of a Wartime Childhood 1939–1948)*. There were memories of seeing a man who may have been his father crushed to death against a brick wall by a mob of German soldiers; of glimpsing his dying mother for one last time in a concentration camp; of rats feasting on corpses; and then, after liberation, of experiencing the loneliness of being an unwanted orphan as he was passed around foster homes in Switzerland. Throughout, there is an overwhelming feeling of young Binjamin's powerlessness at the hands of the adult forces – both evil and good – who have total control over his fate.

Piecing together these fragments may have taken him a whole lifetime, but it was the work of moments for Eva Koralnik to see that this was a book that had to be published. In no time at all, she had secured him a publishing deal with the very highly respected Jüdischer Verlag. *Fragments* appeared in German in 1995 and Carol Janeway's English translation was released soon after by the Jewish publishing house Schoken Books.

Fragments was, as Koralnik had predicted, an overnight success. Laudatory reviews compared Wilkomirski's slim but weighty 155-page volume to the works of Primo Levi and Elie Wiesel, the two acknowledged stars of Holocaust memoir, and sales figures across Europe and the English-speaking world were impressive. It won the prestigious Prix Memoire de la Shoah in France, the *Jewish Quarterly*'s prize in London and also its American equivalent, the National Jewish Book Award. Feted by critics, historians and book-buyers alike, Wilkomirski found himself fending off interview requests from television, newspaper and magazine editors, and for the next three years rose to become one of the most sought-after and well-loved survivors of Hitler's atrocities. He was even sent on a lecture tour of America by the United States Holocaust Memorial Museum.

It was not until 1998 that a Swiss journalist called Daniel Ganzfried – himself the child of a survivor – began to go public with his suspicions about Wilkomirski. Writing for the news magazine *Weltwoche*, he presented his dossier of research into the man he had been secretly studying for over a year: a close reading of *Fragments*, he argued, showed that the author had not actually been in the camps at all – his accounts of the workings, layouts and customs of those places simply did not chime with the testimonies of those whose presence in them could easily be verified (which Wilkomirski's could not). He also put it to his readers that if indeed Wilkomirski was born in 1939, he would have been far too young to process or even correctly identify the horrific sights he claimed to have seen in camps such as Auschwitz. Furthermore, he wrote, after a thorough investigation into the clarinettist-turned-memoirist's background, the man's true identity seemed to be Bruno Grosjean, not Binjamin Wilkomirski. And Bruno Grosjean was not a Jew. He was not even born in Riga, as the book claimed. Rather, he was a Swiss-born child of Christian parents who had abandoned him to an orphanage as a baby. An uncle, Max Grosjean, had been found who hinted at Binjamin/Bruno's involvement with the unsavoury Swiss post-war practice of putting orphans to work (*'verdingkinder'*) as indentured domestic servants, and suggested that this might be what damaged the young boy and left him feeling abused.

Although Ganzfried's research seemed scrupulous, so many people had already pledged their love and support to poor old Wilkomirski that the journalist found himself shouted down by a number of irate critics, and Binjamin did the round of television studios again to protest his innocence. By 1999, however, Koralnik herself was starting to doubt her client's testimony, so she retained the services of the historian Stefan Machler to try to separate fact from fiction. Until then, it was only Wilkomirski's work against Ganzfried's. Six months later, in 1999, Machler's report was complete. Regrettably for everyone involved, it upheld every single one of the doubts expressed in the articles in *Weltwoche*.

It found that Wilkomirski was born in the Swiss town of Biel in 1941 to a poor young woman called Yvonne Grosjean who had indeed given him up for adoption. The child's father had contributed to his foster-care expenses until he was adopted by a wealthy Swiss couple, Mr and Mrs Doesseker, in 1957, from which point he had lived the life his friends and colleagues knew about – that of a talented musician living comfortably in German-speaking Switzerland, where he resides to this day. Machler also discovered that as a young man, Binjamin/Bruno had developed a consuming interest in the history of the Second World War and simultaneously an obsession with discovering more about his true biological identity. Clearly an emotionally fragile man, it was beginning to become clear how he might have conflated these two fixations in a work of autobiographical fiction that he may well believe, in some sense, to be true. Further weight was given to this argument when it was discovered that the pattern of events in his book mirrors almost exactly the circumstances of his unstable 'real' boyhood being shunted around institutions in Switzerland.

It was now clear to his publishers and literary agency that there was something very complex going on in their damaged author's mind. This was not a straightforward instance of hoaxing for political, financial or professional gain, and Wilkomirski genuinely seemed to stand by his explicitly blurred and imagistic story as a fair approximation of what his early boyhood had been like.

Nevertheless, as professionals in an industry fraught with recent examples of memoir-writers who turned out not to be quite what they seemed when selling their manuscripts, it was essential that Jüdischer Verlag took a stand for authorial integrity. People had a right to know what was real and what was not. So, at the Frankfurt book fair in 1999, a spokesperson for Wilkomirski's publishers announced 'with regret' that they had decided to withdraw all copies of *Fragments* from sale. Heide Grasnick, one of his editors, told journalists: 'I feel pity for him because I know him personally. He's not a happy person.'

And his is not a happy story. Academics, critics and psychologists continue to debate the workings of Binjamin/Bruno's mind, but if there is anything approaching a consensus about the man and his deceptions it is that he should not be condemned along with other fake Holocaust memoirists like Misha Defonseca or Helen Demidenko, but rather forgiven, if at all possible, for using the real horrors of other people to illustrate the real pain of his own memories. The fall-out from his debunking heaped yet more humiliation for the lonely Swiss orphan, and the fact that he was not taken to court to account for himself shows a rare corporate compassion.

One of the saddest and strangest postscripts to this sorry tale is that one of the names which crops up in *Fragments* is Laura Grabowski – a fellow survivor who also went on to speak publicly about her experiences in Auschwitz – whom Wilkomirski affectionately mentions having known in the camps. Only Laura Grabowski wasn't real either: that was the pseudonym of the detested serial literary hoaxer Laurel Rose Willson. Seemingly, Grosjean did not subscribe to the magazine *Cornerstone*, in which she had been sensationally outed as a ruthless liar several years earlier.

MISHA LEVY DEFONSECA

*T*HE SAME WEEK that Margaret B. Jones' fake gangland memoir *Love and Consequences* was outed as a hoax, and its author revealed as about as far from a mixed-race gun-runner as she could be, another book, also by an American woman of questionable racial origins, was also debunked. But that other book, and the twisted saga behind its publication, had been turning heads in Europe and America for ten years by the time it was revealed as untrue. And bizarrely, it was the book's own publisher who caused its author to be outed as a fantasist, finally, in March 2008.

The book was *Misha: A Memoire of the Holocaust Years* and its author, Misha Levy Defonseca, claimed to be a Belgian-Jewish immigrant to Massachusetts who had settled near Boston with her husband in the late 1980s. At some point over the next few years this attractive, dog-obsessed woman in her sixties began to tell friends and neighbours the story of how, as a child, she had done a most extraordinary thing: she had trekked nearly 2,000 miles across Europe in the middle of winter to search for her parents, and on this journey had been saved from death by a pack of wolves who had taken her in and raised her as their cub. She recalled how, while she subsisted on a diet of wild meat and scavenged scraps, she sometimes heard terrible sounds coming from deportation trains and once had to kill a German soldier with her bare hands when her life was in danger. She also spoke of darting in and out of the heavily barricaded Warsaw ghetto in search of food, friends and family. Finally, after an odyssey which would have demanded unbelievable stamina and good luck, the seven-year-old Misha finally found her way home. But, tragically, her mother and father had been killed by Hitler's soldiers.

This incredible tale gathered momentum and was fleshed out with new details on every telling. Before long, Defonseca was being invited to speak at synagogues and Jewish groups across New England, to share her story with other survivors and their families. Everybody who heard this charming, voluble, animal-loving woman speak was beguiled by her, and one of her new fans informed the local writer and publisher Jane Daniel that here was a tale which really ought to be put into print. Daniel ran a small, one-woman publishing company called Mount Ivy Press from her home overlooking Gloucester Harbor in Massachusetts, and immediately knew the potential value of a life story like the one she was hearing about. She arranged to meet Defonseca at a nearby restaurant to discuss the possibility of a book, and as soon as she heard her relate her tale in person she decided to go ahead with the project.

She says now that her first reaction was 'I thought it was far-fetched, but who knows?' But her concerns weren't enough, at that stage, to stop her retaining the services of another local woman to help with the project. To craft French-speaking Defonseca's imperfect English into read-able prose, she invited her friend and neighbour Vera Lee, a former professor of French, to collaborate. Daniel too would lend her stylistic hand to the manuscript, and between the three of them it was not long before the book that would go on to be more famous and expensive than any of them could have imagined, took shape.

In 1997 Mount Ivy published the first run of *Misha*, alerting journalists and film companies to the arrival of an extraordinary new voice on the Holocaust memoir scene. Gold-dust was sprinkled on to the book in the form of a flattering quote from Elie Wiesel; Oprah Winfrey's camera crew filmed Defonseca at a local wolf sanctuary in Ipswich, Massachusetts, and Disney came forward to enquire about buying the rights. Eighteen different foreign-language editions were produced across the world and in France the film-maker Vera Belmont was keen to work the book up into a feature film. An extensive book tour was undertaken by the author and for a while, at least, the three women who had made the phenomenon possible could congratulate themselves on a job well done.

But then the questions started, and the cracks began to show. Certain historians of the Holocaust and of Eastern Europe in general began to query aspects of the text. Such obvious errors as the year in which Belgian Jews were taken to camps were highlighted, not to mention the fact that wolves were highly uncommon in the areas mentioned by Defonseca. What's more, experts in lupine-human interaction called the idea of a pack like the one she describes taking in a small child and treating it like a puppy 'absurd'. Ever the professional, Jane Daniel sought the advice of a couple of experts in the field, the historians Deborah Dwork and Lawrence Langer. They immediately found a host of geographical and chronological inconsistencies, but, according to Dwork: 'She kept finding ways to get around my objections. She said, "Of course, she was a young girl at the time. You are a historian. This is a memoir – people make mistakes on details and dates all the time." '

Nothing was done about these doubts however, and as the sales figures continued to climb, Defonseca – and by extension Daniel and her small company – began to make serious money. And this, perhaps unsurprisingly, is where things came unstuck.

Seeing how well the book was doing, Vera Lee became annoyed that she was not being credited with enough authorial input and fell out with her former neighbour. In 1998, she formally sued Daniel for not citing her as a co-author on the book's jacket or publicity material, despite the fact that it was she who had put into words the often incoherent recollections of the book's named author. At the same time, a far more serious case was brought against the publisher by Defonseca herself: an accusation that Daniel had siphoned off millions of dollars of royalties and hidden them in an off-shore account in Turks and Caicos to prevent Defonseca gaining access to them. Unfortunately, this turned out not to be the paranoid babble of a war-damaged woman but a hard fact: Daniel had indeed failed to declare or share large sums of money arising from sales of the books, and had presumably considered Defonseca incapable of catching her out. A long legal investigation swung into action and by 2005 the judge was ready to deliver her decision: Daniel must repay $33 million to Defonseca and Lee, with two-thirds of that amount going to Defonseca who was still, of course, at that point, considered to be a heroic survivor of Nazism. The following year, with the money apparently still not forthcoming, Lee's lawyer brought Daniel back to court to demand that she pay $2,000 a month to his client. Daniel's vociferous protest to the judge resulted in her being held in contempt of court and spending a night in the cells. Finally, she agreed to put her house up for sale as a way to pay back some of the money she had illegitimately taken.

So enraged was Daniel about all this, she decided to get her revenge on her author by returning to the two historians, Dwork and Langer, who had suggested the story was a fake several years earlier. She resurrected their claims and put them up on a website, asking for any expert or genealogist who might be able to help expose Defonseca to come forward. And before long, one did. The findings of forensic genealogist Sharon Sergeant would blow Misha's claims out of the water and, for a while at least, swing the balance of opinion back towards the benighted publisher. Sergeant found out that rather than being called Defonseca, the woman who told stories about wolves was Monique de Wael, a Brussels-born Catholic who had lived through the entire war in perfect safety with her grandparents. She had spent the early 1940s enrolled in a Belgian primary school rather than traversing Europe as she had claimed, and the only echoes of truth in her made-up story came from the fact that her parents, who had been Resistance fighters, died mysteriously in Germany towards the end of the war.

Monique de Wael could not deny any of this, especially when presented with documentary evidence of her true biography. In an emotional statement said:

Yes, my name is Monique De Wael, but I have wanted to forget it since I was four years old. My parents were arrested and I was taken in by my grandfather, Ernest De Wael, and my uncle, Maurice De Wael. I was called 'daughter of a traitor' because my father was suspected of having talked under torture in the prison of Saint-Gilles.

She apologized unreservedly to the readers who had bought her book in good faith, and in the now familiar terms of a hoaxer pleading an alternative truth as a reason for their deception, went on to say: 'There are times when I find it difficult to differentiate between reality and my inner world. The story in the book is mine. It is not the actual reality – it was my reality, my way of surviving.'

Daniel herself has tried to use the revelations of her author's deception as grounds to appeal the multi-million dollar judgement against her, but as her appeal was lodged more than a year after her initial conviction, the statute of limitations had timed out so she has no legal right to do so. Even if she had, the court would most likely hold that the misappropriation of millions of dollars has little to do with the deluded or duplicitous state of mind of her former author. Now, in a final attempt to rescue her reputation, Daniel has written and published her own account of the saga which she refers to as a decades-long con perpetrated against her. Somehow, it seems unlikely that *Bestseller! The $33 Million Verdict. The 20-year Hoax. The Truth Behind the Headlines* could generate anything like the amount of interest *Misha* did, even if Daniel herself turns out to have been raised by wolves. But in a case as bizarre and seemingly never-ending as this one, you never know.

HERMAN ROSENBLAT

O UT OF THE grim darkness of the Holocaust there very occasionally comes a story with an ending so lovely that it offers a real message of hope to the world. Herman Rosenblat's romantic autobiography, which did not come to light until 2008, was one such tale. As he sat on Oprah Winfrey's sofa with Roma, his loving wife of fifty years by his side, he beamed as theirs was called 'the greatest love story ever told'. As Herman told it, he had been taken from Piotrokow in Poland along with twenty-one young boys as part of a larger group of Jews rounded up for transportation to a camp. They ended up in Schlieben, a sub-camp of Buchenwald, where the conditions were as dire and brutal as can be imagined. But one day, when out strolling near the perimeter fence, young Herman spotted something remarkable on the other side: a flash of colour. A red jumper over a blue skirt. This was unusual enough in his world of grey mud, dirty rags and sickly faces. But to find it was attached to a lovely young girl with a kind, healthy face was something like a miracle:

> 'Do you have any bread?' I asked the little girl.
> She shook her head. No bread.
> Then she reached in to the pocket of her sweater, pulled out an apple and threw it over the fence. I grabbed the apple and instinctively started to run away.
> 'See you tomorrow,' I heard her call to my back.

And so began a daily meeting between the two young people. Herman did not know at first that she, too, was a Jew but that she and her family were hiding out in the farm next door to the camp pretending to be Christians. He knew only that she offered him a fix of hope, friendship and, crucially, food. When the day came for Herman to be moved on to another camp, he bade his little friend a sad farewell and they accepted the fact that they would never meet again.

The war ended with young Herman's life intact and he was released in May 1945 from Theresienstadt, the last major camp to be liberated by the Allies. He made his way to England where he lived for four years in London while he trained to be an electrician and then in 1950 he left for the bright new world of post-war America, hoping to fulfil his dreams of success and escape the ghosts of Europe. He ended up in Coney Island, New York, and it was here that he got talking to a pretty, Polish-Jewish woman called Roma Radzicki. Inevitably, they soon began swapping stories about their experiences at the hands of the Nazis and as Roma told him how, back in the early 1940s, she used to venture out of the farm where she was hiding and toss fruit to a boy in a camp, Herman could not believe what he was hearing. He asked her what the boy looked like ('skinny', she said); he asked whether one day the boy had bid her farewell and told her not to come back to the fence again. He had, she said. In a moment of almost unimaginable emotional intensity, the two realized they had been reunited at last. He proposed to her there and then and she accepted.

And that was when their real life began. Madly in love and determined to make amends, as best they could, for the horrible childhoods the war had inflicted on them, they ended up in Miami, Florida where Herman worked as a TV repair technician and Roma took any job she could find that would allow her to make ends meet while raising their longed-for son, Ken.

Some time after 2001, Herman, now retired, decided the time had come to make their story into a book, an inspirational love story that might be just what a shaken

America needed in the light of recent events. In the unpublished manuscript, which was leaked to American journalists in December 2008 just prior to its intended publication, he describes his overriding thought at the time of his reunion with the apple girl: 'Impossible!'

Indeed it was.

The book was about to be published by Berkley Books, an imprint of Penguin USA, when Kenneth Waltzer, a professor of Jewish Studies at Michigan State University, realized that the story which Rosenblat had been putting about via Oprah Winfrey and the Jewish community in Florida, simply could not be true. He had been conducting a study of youth and childhood in concentration camps and, as luck would have it, was looking closely at the stories of the very group of boys taken from Piotrokow to Schlieben that included Rosenblat. Waltzer had been conducting interviews with many of the survivors, so as well as being fully conversant with the physical layout of the camp, he knew something of the relationships between its former inmates. Apparently there had been talk for years about Herman having made up a tall tale about how he met his wife, and neither his two older brothers, with whom he was incarcerated (and who had pledged at the beginning of the war never to leave him) nor his fellow prisoners, were too happy about it. In fact 'ashamed' was the word Waltzer used to describe their attitude to this most imaginative member of the group. There were also stories of ructions within and between the wider Rosenblat clan and Roma's family, and even the couple themselves were reputed to be locked in a dispute about Herman's claims. No one knew for sure whether Roma had been tricked too or was in cahoots with him, but there was no doubt that Rosenblat was known by those closest to him as an unrepentant fantasist.

Waltzer, as conscious as any Jew or historian of the damage done to real war stories by fake ones, approached Rosenblat's agent, Andrea Hurst, with what he knew. He was able not only to quote a very reliable witness, Ben Helfgott, the leader of the Schlieben survivors who had journeyed with Rosenblat to England after the war (and had himself gone on to find fame as an Olympic athlete), but to show maps of the camp's layout which proved that the apple-tossing story could not possibly be true; because aside from the fact that wandering alone along the perimeter of the camps grounds was an infraction punishable by instant death, the only place in Schlieben where anyone outside the compound could possibly approach the fence was in the spot right next to where the SS guards had their look-out point.

At first, according to Waltzer, neither agent nor publisher was interested in his claims. The promise of recouping millions from what was now planned to be a memoir, a children's version called *Angel Girl* and a film too was hard to let go. And besides, Rosenblat was a sweet and kindly old man, clearly in love with his wife of half a century and determined to spread a little happiness in the world before his time was up. But by 28 December 2008, Berkley Books had announced that they were pulling the plug on the whole project. There would be no books and if the film company who had bought the rights to the story still thought they could get investment after the greatest love-story ever told turned out to be a fabrication, well, good luck to them.

Penguin was embarrassed. Oprah Winfrey – hot on the heels of the James Frey debacle – was incensed. And

Rosenblat's son Ken, who had known about the deception for years, was keen to distance himself entirely from the affair, telling the magazine the *New Republic*: 'My father is a man who I don't know. I can't understand it. It's not my way of thinking . . . I didn't agree with it. I didn't want anything to do with it. I tried to just stay away from it. It was always hurtful. I just never dealt with it.'

All that remained was for Rosenblat to account for himself, and, choosing his words carefully to avoid any accusations of greed, he used the *New York Times* to address the dozens of publishers and millions of *Oprah* viewers he had duped:

> To all who supported and believed in me and this story. I am sorry for all I have caused to you and every one else in the world. Why did I do that and write the story with the girl and the apple, because I wanted to bring happiness to people, to remind them not to hate, but to love and tolerate all people. I brought good feelings to a lot of people and I brought hope to many. My motivation was to make good in this world.

No one is suggesting that Rosenblat's motivation was to do evil, but the prospect of a retirement supported by the astronomical fee a good popular memoir can net its author in the twenty-first century would seem delightful to any ageing couple, let alone one who has lived through the horror of the Holocaust and then pulled themselves up by their bootstraps to join America's middle class. And indeed, despite the debunking of his hoax, he might still make some money out of the story, because as of January 2009 his book is slated for release by the New York publishing firm York House Press. They will, of course, be branding the book fiction and releasing it under the new name of *The Apple*, and its new selling point is that it is 'one of the most controversial love stories of all time'. Their website confirms that a film version is indeed still in production and also carries an essay encouraging readers to think about the complex nature of authenticity and authorship in autobiographical writing and to ask themselves whether Rosenblat – a damaged war survivor – wasn't just working through his trauma by writing the book.

All of which is indeed worth thinking about. But the real tragedy of the *Apple* debacle is that a far more moving story – the true story – may never be told. That is the story of the two older brothers who took a solemn vow never to abandon their little sibling, never to let him starve, and to lie about his age to save him from punishment even as they were risking their lives daily to do it. And of the woman – Roma's mother – who in deciding to disguise her children as Polish Catholics and live openly under the gaze of the Nazi occupiers (near Breslau, not Schlieben) had to take the appalling decision to leave her one very dark-complexioned child, who would never be able to pass as an ethnic Pole, behind to die. It is no wonder that the families of Mr and Mrs Rosenblat find it hard to forgive the man who wasted his voice on fantasy when the reality spoke so much more poignantly of the power of love.

9

RELIGION

*H*OAXES INSPIRED BY theological debates might, to an atheist, sound slightly boring. But from the reclusive German priest who wrote the dark, reality-fairy tale *The Amber Witch* to the academic genius who could not rein in his love of practical jokes when he found himself alone in a monastic library in Morocco, these are some of the boldest and best pranks in literature. Not to mention the most influential in terms of the books people believe in now. For without the crazy schemes of a provincial Frenchman in the 1950s there would be no one who believes you can find the secret of Jesus' bloodline in the Louvre. And without the violent acts of a disenfranchised Mormon in the 1980s, one of America's most influential church groups would be resting far more comfortably on its Utah laurels than it is today.

JOHANNES WILHELM MEINHOLD

*T*HE EARLY LIFE of Johannes Wilhelm Meinhold was one not even the most fanciful of German romantic novelists could have made up. Born on the lonely Baltic island of Usedom to an impecunious Lutheran pastor and his wife, his formative years were spent in the company of books, pious adults and nature – he never even saw another child of his age until he left the island to continue his education at the University of Greifswald in 1813. It was always assumed that Johannes would follow his father into the clergy, and indeed that was what the young man seemed to want for himself, but not before spreading his wings for a while in his provincial college town, where he made a name for himself as one of his year's most enthusiastic drinkers. He also began to write poetry, and when a volume of his work was given a small print run it was, to his delight, well reviewed by Goethe himself.

However, Meinhold was an inherently religious young man and after he had got his rebellion out of the way he continued with his theological education, taking his doctorate at the age of twenty and then being posted to a series of dull institutions to further his professional practice. His first job, in 1821, was as rector of the school of Usedom, and soon after he was promoted to the role of pastor at Koserow church on the same island. He moved around the district working at different churches, but it was with Koserow that he would come to be infamously associated in years to come, because it was there that he set his most famous literary creation. In fact, he stayed there little more than a year, moving on to the isolated diocese of Krummin, where he would spend the next sixteen years performing the unchanging cycle of duties of the country pastor.

It was during this quiet time that his literary career began to preoccupy him more and more. As well as poems, he now turned his hand to prose, hoping, no doubt, that his mature talents would be recognized, as his youthful poetry had been. These were the years that the new German Romantics – Hegel, Schlegel and Heinrich Heine – were taking over from classical writers like Goethe and Schiller, and Germany was by far the most happening place on the European literary scene. It was also the time of the Napoleonic wars and most of Europe was in the grip of a revolutionary fever which resulted not only in the creation of fine poetry, prose and music but of philosophical and theological developments which were, to a conservative like Meinhold, utterly shocking.

One of the most famous revolutionary religious thinkers of the day was David Strauss and it was for him and his followers that Meinhold reserved his strongest disdain. Strauss believed that Jesus ought to be seen as a historical figure, not a divine one, and set about deconstructing the Bible to support his thesis, which he published under the title *Leben Jesu* (*Life of Jesus*). In this unprecedented book he rereads Jesus' miracles in strictly mythical terms, ignoring both the rational explanations and the divine ones that had split Enlightenment thinkers into two groups. Strauss was a genuinely radical thinker and by the time Mary Ann Evans (aka George Eliot) translated his work into English in 1846, he was officially the leading subversive writer on Christianity in Europe and had a wide following. He was also very young (twenty-seven when he published the *Leben*) and fiendishly handsome, which may well have inflamed Meinhold's ire even more.

To a man like Meinhold, saying that the virgin birth was merely a silly story invented to please Messiah-hungry Jews in the aftermath of Jesus' death (one of Strauss' most famous theories) was the worst kind of sacrilege. He felt that people who believed this sort of thing would believe anything and were incapable of discerning what was a real historical document and what was not. And in 1839 he began to focus all his literary skills and ideological indignation on proving that this was the case.

One of the most popular subjects in Germany at that time was the supernatural, and literature across Europe was in thrall to the vogue for gothic fiction. Meinhold decided that a 'discovered' book about a medieval witch trial which would also give him the opportunity to pontificate on the history of the Thirty Years' War and the behaviour of the Catholic church in relation to magic and paganism, was just the thing. So the story of *The Amber Witch* was born. The given author was to be Reverend Abraham Schweidler, a pastor at the church of Koserow in the seventeenth century who had nearly lost his only child, Mary, to a witch trial; and in the preface, the 'editor', Wilhelm Meinhold, would describe how the manuscript had come into his possession:

At Koserow, in the Island of Usedom, my former cure, the same which was held by our worthy author some two hundred years ago, there existed under a seat in the choir of the church a sort of niche, nearly on a level with the floor. I had, indeed, often seen a heap of various writings in this recess; but owing to my short sight, and the darkness of the place, I had taken them for antiquated hymn-books, which were lying about in great numbers. But one day, while I was teaching in the church, I looked for a paper mark in the Catechism of one of the boys, which I could not immediately find; and my old sexton, who was past eighty . . . stooped down to the said niche, and took from it a folio volume which I had never before observed, out of which he, without the slightest hesitation, tore a strip of paper suited to my purpose, and reached it to me. I immediately seized upon the book, and, after a few minutes' perusal, I know not which was greater, my astonishment or my vexation at this costly prize. The manuscript, which was bound in vellum, was not only defective both at the beginning and at the end, but several leaves had even been torn out here and there in the middle. I scolded the old man as I had never done during the whole course of my life; but he excused himself, saying that one of my predecessors had given him the manuscript for waste paper, as it had lain about there ever since the memory of man, and he had often been in want of paper to twist round the altar candles, etc. The aged and half-blind pastor had mistaken the folio for old parochial accounts which could be of no more use to any one.

No sooner had I reached home than I fell to work upon my new acquisition, and after reading a bit here and there with considerable trouble, my interest was powerfully excited by the contents . . .

This story is so similar to others of the found object school of literary hoaxing that it is hard not to echo the Shakespeare scholar Malone's response to the William Henry Ireland affair in saying that 'after the demolition of the chest with six keys [Chatterton's], I did not expect to have heard again, for some time at least, of such a repository for ancient manuscripts'.

Meinhold, however, goes on in his preface to play a far more complex game with his learned readers than the boys Chatterton and Ireland, admitting that he has filled in a few of the missing pages in the text himself in a manner he hopes is consistent with the tone and content of the 'original' author's work:

> This I have done with much trouble, and after many ineffectual attempts; but I refrain from pointing out the particular passages which I have supplied, so as not to disturb the historical interest of the greater part of my readers. For modern criticism, which has now attained to a degree of acuteness never before equalled, such a confession would be entirely superfluous, as critics will easily distinguish the passages where Pastor Schweidler speaks from those written by Pastor Meinhold.

The story that follows is an account of Mary Schweidler's wrongful arrest and trial after a spurned suitor decided to get revenge on her by accusing her of magic acts. Unfortunately for Mary and her God-fearing father, the suitor is the local sheriff and he brings all his corrupt power to bear on those trying her for the crimes her father knows she did not commit. Ultimately, the girl confesses that she is indeed a witch in an attempt to avoid the terrible tortures she is being threatened with, and is sent to the scaffold to die. At the eleventh hour, however, she is saved by a valiant man of noble birth who is able to reveal the sheriff's true motivation, prove that she was lying about the witchcraft, and see that justice is done.

The fairy-story structure and convincing eighteenth-century orthography (Meinhold was nothing if not a thorough scholar) captivated audiences immediately, and the text, originally published within a historical journal due to its relevance to the period of the Thirty Years' War, became an instant hit among the German-speakers of Europe. Some libraries even classified it as a historical legal record. Certain experts, however, began to question just how much of it was the work of the 'editor' and how much was Schweidler's, but it was not until one very important reader approached Meinhold for more information that the author was forced to confess.

Friedrich Wilhelm IV, King of Prussia, was an enthusiastic Romantic with a particular passion for all things medieval. He was also a committed Lutheran. As soon as he saw that a learned pastor had produced a historical study of a German girl caught up in a witch trial and saved by chivalric love, he knew he must read it. And no sooner had he read it than he sent to Meinhold praising his marvellous discovery and sensitive editing, and asking whether he wouldn't like it to be published (lavishly, no doubt) as a stand-alone book with the king's help. Appalled that his hoax had gone so far, Meinhold confessed to the king what he had, up until then, denied to everyone else: that the entire thing had been a fabrication designed to show up the poor literary critical skills of his theological bête noir. But the story was so well told that the king cared not one bit and insisted that the work should be published regardless, which it was, under the title *Die Bernsteinhexe* (*The Amber Witch*).

The king was not alone in disregarding Meinhold's confession as a minor detail. Indeed, as happens so often with particularly well-crafted hoaxes, many of the book's fans refused to believe it was the work of a quiet little pastor from Usedom. Meinhold was reduced to showing these determined fans his preparatory notes and rough drafts to prove what they did not want to believe was true.

Eventually, when the book's true authorship was proved beyond doubt, the academic and publishing worlds, humiliated by Meinhold's trickery, repaid him the only way they knew how: by ignoring him for the rest of his life. His literary output (which included another witch novel, about a girl called Sidonia von Bork) was never to receive the attention from German critics that others in Europe felt it deserved.

There is an amusing postscript to this story. In 1861 the eccentric Victorian translator and socialite Lucie Duff Gordon came across the book and knew that the horror-loving readers of her milieu would react enthusiastically to it. An accomplished writer in French and German as well as English, she prepared an excellent translation of *The Amber Witch* and published it in London. But nowhere did it say that the original author was Johannes Meinhold; she blithely passed it off as her own work, making her edition the first example of a literary hoax within a literary hoax. And Meinhold's British afterlife did not end there: his book *Sidonia* was also taken up by an English-speaking lady novelist and translated for her countrymen. Indeed, *Sidonia the Sorceress* went on to be by far the best selling of the thirteen books published by the woman who wrote under the name Speranza. That woman was Lady Jane Francesca Elgee aka Lady Wilde, aka the mother of that real-life victim of a wrongful witch-hunt, Oscar Wilde.

ROBERT COLEMAN-NORTON

S UBSCRIBERS TO THE *Catholic Biblical Quarterly* in 1950 must have raised a quizzical eyebrow when they saw in the contents page that the respected Princeton historian Paul Robert Coleman-Norton had submitted an article called 'An Amusing Agraphon'.

Agraphon is the Greek for 'unwritten' but to theologians it refers to teachings and sayings of Jesus which, although taken to be true, are not written down in the canonical Gospels. There are many examples, but few if any of them could be described as amusing. Coleman-Norton's article began on page 439 of the esteemed journal and over the following ten pages told an extraordinary story. He was a teacher at Princeton when war broke out, and his intelligence work in Europe had, he wrote, taken him to Morocco. It was 1943 and his platoon found themselves in the French-controlled town of Fedhala, where there was a fine old mosque. Knowing his interest in matters of ancient history and literature, his colleagues were not surprised when he ventured inside to look around. He, however, got the surprise of his life when the kindly keeper of the place offered to show him some of the rare books and parchments that were held there, and proceeded to open up a book which contained, in amongst the usual Arab texts, a most unusual piece of Greek. It was one page only and had seemingly been slipped inside this other book at random. It was a Greek translation of a set of Latin homilies on the book of Matthew, concerning chapters 1–13 and 19–25. And there was something there that was entirely unfamiliar to him. It would of course have been a terrible *faux pas* to remove the scrap of paper for further study, and due to the circumstances of war there was no time to go back to his base and fetch a camera. Instead, Coleman-Norton sat down and made a hasty but perfectly accurate copy of the text and slipped it into his pocket to peruse at his leisure.

When he did so, his suspicions were proved correct: he was in the presence of a never-before-seen report of something completely new that Jesus had said. And it seemed to fit exactly in to the known Gospel of St Matthew. Matthew 13:42 finds Jesus delivering a vivid warning to his disciples about all the people and things on earth which offend God and 'do iniquity'. They will, he warns, find themselves thrown by angels 'into a furnace of fire' on judgement day, where 'there shall be wailing and gnashing of teeth'. The image of the gnashing of teeth has become famous thanks to its unusual evocation of the misery of hell as an emotional state as well as a physical one. In the canonical Gospel, that is the end of that. But in the agraphon discovered by Coleman-Norton, there is more . . .

But Rabbi, said one of his disciples, with a look of concern, 'how can this happen for those people who have no teeth?' (It is safe to assume there were a quite a lot of toothless people in biblical times, so this would not necessarily have been as facetious a question as it sounds.) 'Ah, ye of little faith,' replied the Messiah, 'do not be troubled. If some have no teeth, then teeth will be provided!'

Jesus Christ promising false teeth to all on judgement day. Quite a coup. But as soon as it was published, those readers who knew the author smelled a rat. One such reader was the great Bible scholar Bruce Metzger, who had been a pupil of Coleman-Norton's before the war. He recalled his old teacher telling a joke along exactly those lines to his theology students, and lent his voice to the chorus of academics who knew Coleman-Norton who all said that this was exactly the sort of prank the old fellow loved to play. Nobody much minded, of course (least of all the editors of the *Harvard Theological Review*, who had previously rejected the very article that the *Catholic Biblical Quarterly* published), because the author was, by all accounts, a harmless, eccentric professor of the old school. At Princeton he would often take seminars dressed in a dressing gown or cape and smoking a pipe. One old student of his even recalls a song sung by junior members of his faculty that went:

> Here's to Norton PRC
> Of Oxford University
> With cape and cane and pipe and Sapphics
> And Greek and Latin pornographics.

This reference to classical pornographics is testament to Coleman-Norton's considerable powers of composition in the ancient languages he had mastered so well. Whenever the university needed something formal written in Latin it fell to him to do it, but in his spare time – much to the amusements of students and colleagues – he would relish translating and inventing less salubrious texts. Knowing this about him, it is clear not only that he had the ability to compose, in Greek, a convincing fragment of an imagined Latin text, but that the sensitive readers of the *Catholic Biblical Quarterly* were lucky to have been spared exposure to the grinding of something far less polite than teeth.

MORTON SMITH

O NE OF AMERICA'S most fascinating and gifted students of religion was the twentieth-century theologian Morton Smith. His lifelong absorption with the mystical early history of the Christian church began when, as a committed Christian and scholar, he moved to Israel to study Talmudic literature in 1940, becoming fluent in Hebrew, Latin and Greek, and became the first non-Jew to be awarded a doctorate by the Hebrew University. The war trapped him there and he lived for four years in Jerusalem, studying under the great Jewish scholar Gershon Scholem and conducting research on early rabbinical parallels to the Gospels. On moving back to America at the end of the war he briefly became an episcopalian minister but decided that that life was not for him – possibly because he was gay, probably because his intensely questing mind was more suited to academia – and returned to the classroom to become professor of ancient history at Columbia.

It was in 1973 that he published two books that rocked the Christian and theological communities across the world. One was for scholars, published by Harvard University Press and called *Clement of Alexandria and a Secret Gospel of Mark* and the other was a layman's companion to the research in that book, *The Secret Gospel* (Harper & Row).

The books explained that he had been going through the library of the Orthodox monastery of Mar Saba in Israel back in the 1950s when he chanced upon a seventeenth-century edition of the works of Ignatius of Antioch which contained a transcription on the back fly-leaf of a letter from Clement of Alexandria. The contents of that letter were astounding. It described a secret set of magical rites which Jesus had passed on to a few enlightened followers, and linked this to the Carpocratians, a cult of early Gnostics who believed in the contrary-sounding ethic of redemption through sinning. Carnal sinning particularly.

And herein lay the detail that rubbed Christian commentators up the wrong way. Clement's letter spoke of a secret Gospel of St Mark which ought only be seen by those sophisticated enough to receive its unusual news. Here, according to that letter, is what it said on the subject of Jesus and boys:

And they come into Bethany. And a certain woman whose brother had died was there. And, coming, she prostrated herself before Jesus and says to him, 'son of David, have mercy on me.' But the disciples rebuked her. And Jesus, being angered, went off with her into the garden where the tomb was, and straightway, going in where the youth was, he stretched forth his hand and raised him, seizing his hand. But the youth, looking upon him, loved him and began to beseech him that he might be with him. And going out of the tomb they came into the house of the youth, for he was rich. And after six days Jesus told him what to do and in the evening the youth comes to him, wearing a linen cloth over his naked body. And he remained with him that night, for Jesus taught him the mystery of the Kingdom of God. And thence, arising, he returned to the other side of the Jordan.

The homosexual subtext might not be immediately obvious to all readers, but to scholars familiar with the secret initiation rites of the Carpocratians and the fact that in the standard Gospel of Mark there is a strange nonsequitur about a young man present at the time of Jesus' arrest in a flimsy covering of a linen cloth which is torn off him, leaving him to run off naked. Speculation as to who this figure is and what he was doing, half-naked but for his scrap of linen, with Jesus in the garden of Gethsemane, has divided scholars for years.

Now, it would seem, there was a whole aspect of the last days of Jesus' life that had never been revealed and which spoke of him not only as a practitioner of pagan rites but one of a decidedly pederastic bent. Authenticity is lent to this claim when Clement, after revealing the story of the young man, assures the reader that although his is definitely true, the rumours of a further line in the secret text mentioning 'naked man with naked man' was a vicious lie put about by those naughty Carpocratians, who were trying to hijack the story of Jesus' gentle love of men for their own extreme ends.

On discovering this incendiary material, Morton Smith did not rush out into the scholastic community and tell everyone about it. He merely photographed and catalogued the book in which he found the transcript and quietly returned to America to sit on his discovery for several years, musing on it and discussing it only with his closest academic colleagues. But he knew that when he did finally release it, it would cause a major stir. After all, here were new details from Jesus' life story, suggestion of a new, Lazarus-like miracle, and confirmation that Mark had indeed written a second, secret version of his Gospel.

At a conference of the Society for Biblical Literature in 1960 he made mention of it, but it was not until his two books were published, giving the full story, that the theological world at large started to weigh in on the debate. Some critics flatly refused to believe that the Clementine letter ever existed. Many more felt that someone – either themselves or Smith himself – had been hoaxed. Both sides had convincing arguments: although Morton Smith was a highly respected scholar, who had corresponded with his close friend and teacher, Scholem, about the Clementine text (and surely he would have no reason to trick him, of all people?), there seemed to be clues – some deliberately planted by Smith, some accidentally left by him – that he had faked the letter all along.

The evidence for the secret Mark being a hoax is compelling, and was collected as recently as 2005 with the highly detailed (and readable) *Gospel Hoax: Morton Smith's Invention of Secret Mark* by the lawyer Stephen Carlson (Baylor University Press). First of all, there is the absence of the letter itself. It was photographed twice, once by Smith in 1958 and once by a librarian in the 1970s; but the fragment itself, which was removed to the Orthodox Patriarchate in Jerusalem after Smith's 'discovery' was subsequently lost when the librarians decided to cut it out of the seventeenth-century book in which it had been found and file it away separately.

However, even from the extant photographs the hand-writing of the transcript can be seen well, and specialist analysts have shown that it bears all the hallmarks of the hesitant calligrapher forging someone else's hand: the archaic letters are constructed not of naturally flowing lines but broken up ones, studded with concentrations of ink where the scribe has stopped mid-letter and started again.

Then there is the fact that just before the 'discovery' of the secret Gospel, Smith had published a paper on the exact subject which it claims to expose – the relationship between the 'mystery of the kingdom of God' mentioned in Mark 4 with sexuality. And another publication seems pertinent too: the novel published shortly before Smith went to Israel by James Hunter called *The Mystery of Mar Saba* which is about the scandal of a forged document in the very library in which Smith claimed to have found his Clementine letter. Coincidence? Perhaps. But there are several more concrete clues within the text that have left many critics convinced that there could have been no author other than Smith involved in its creation. One of the most compelling arguments is that the style of Clement's supposed letter is utterly, perfectly Clementine. No words or phrases exist there that do not exist elsewhere in his known oeuvre. It is as if someone had an index of all the words he ever used (and such an index would have been readily available to Smith had he needed one) and was careful not to stray one bit from that lexicon. Surely the real Clement would have varied slightly when writing his letter and used a few novel constructions? That would be only human, after all.

And now things get funny. In his books, Smith refers to another important textual fragment he 'found' and photographed while working in the library of Mar Saba. Like the secret Mark, it was written in a distinctive Greek hand and was signed by a scribe calling himself M. Madiotes. This is not a common Greek name at all. Rather, it is a noun made from the verb *madao* whose meaning is, literally, 'to go bald' (which the distinctive-looking Smith was) but which colloquially means 'to swindle'. Could this be the signature-cypher of Smith himself?

Then there is the matter of salt. Alongside the secret Mark passage in Clement's letter was a reference to Jesus teaching his subjects a lesson about purity versus pollution and using, to illustrate this, the image of free-flowing salt being mixed with another substance and so altering the flavour of the salt. Homophobic critics of the main body of Clement's letter passed over this at first, but then the ever-scrupulous Stephen Carlson pointed out that this is an image that a pre-twentieth-century mind could never had thought of. Because until very recently salt came in lumps or cakes, and was never seen in the pourable powdered form we know today. Indeed, the patented process of de-caking salt for the table was invented by a salt company only in 1910. And guess what the name of that company was? Morton.

So convinced – or so keen to convince themselves – are disbelievers in the Clementine letter's authenticity that they have placed Smith's prank firmly in the context of mid-twentieth-century homosexual culture and classified it as, in the words of one critic, 'a nice ironic gay joke . . . [an] amusing bit of post-modern scholarly theatre'. In this reading, Jesus in the garden with the nameless, naked young man is a reference to the infamous 'cottaging' scene of America at the time of Smith's 1958 discovery.

If all this is true, it might seem like Smith was an angry, bitter person, determined to humiliate churchmen and academics alike. But those who knew this clever, complex man suggest that this was not the case. Certainly, at the time of his 'discovery' he had recently been passed over for tenure at Harvard, and he had of course rejected the clergy as a tenable profession for himself. But his close ties with the theological community in Israel and America and his very high standing in both suggest a different answer. One thing that everyone agrees on is that Morton Smith was a funny guy. A laugher, a giggler, a wit, a storyteller and, most probably, a prankster. But because he was so clever – probably cleverer than everyone else he knew – he would never have been satisfied with a minor, throw-away hoax on his fellow academics. If a man of his intellectual stature was going to pull the wool over his fellows' eyes he would do it with massive attention to detail and timing. Moreover, he would be quite happy to play the long game, watching his tall tale spin out over the decades and cause commentators to tie themselves in ever more Gordian knots. Did he hope to reveal the hoax before his sudden death from heart failure in 1991? Or did he always mean to take the secrets of the alternative Gospel according to St Mark to his grave? Or had he indeed found what he believed to be a genuine, inflammatory, Bible-changing piece of writing from Clement of Antioch? Either way, he must have had a stupendously big smile on his face that day in the library of Mar Saba.

PIERRE PLANTARD

*I*N PARIS IN 1920, in the humble household of a butler and a cook, a little boy was born who would go on to commit France's greatest twentieth-century literary hoax. A little boy without whom the most obsessed-over novel of the twenty-first century would not have been *The Da Vinci Code*. The boy was Pierre Plantard and he was born at a time when his country was undergoing a period of great upheaval. Religious and political ideologies were fracturing in the tumult that so many European lands were experiencing in the immediate aftermath of the First World War, and by the time Plantard was twenty he had firmly allied himself with the Catholic right, which stood in violent opposition to the forces seen as dragging France to the dogs: Freemasons, Jews, socialists and Protestants.

Anti-Masonic sentiments on the French right, fomented by an unease at the number of Masons in politics (and conflated with anti-Semitism, thanks in part to *The Protocols of the Elders of Zion*) had reached fever pitch by the time Plantard wrote to Marshal Pétain pledging his support to the collaborationist government and asking what he might do to help. That was in 1940 but for several years previously this apparently devout young Catholic had been taking an interest in another questionable school of thought that was sweeping Europe at the time, that of esoteric religious mysticism.

There was no shortage of senior Catholics willing to engage in arcane practices and explore imaginative avenues of belief in the inter-war period, and Plantard was not the first to see political mileage in combining this passion for pseudo-medieval Christianity with a nationalist agenda. He formed pseudo-political groups called things like French National Renewal and the French Union, which failed to garner much interest, but he was already working with Catholic youth groups and lecturing them on the importance of creating a pure France when, in 1939, he had the idea of forming the Alpha Galates sect.

Alpha Galates, with its far-right publication *Vaincre* (*Conquer*) came at the right time to attract a number of members anxious about goings-on in Europe, and although it would not last long, and never did much apart from publish inflammatory articles and rub Masons up the wrong way, it did result in a well-publicized four-month prison sentence for a delighted, martyred Plantard when the German authorities refused permission for it to be registered as an official group but it carried on publishing his magazine regardless. It also gave Plantard the support and confidence to establish the Priory of Sion a few years later, capitalizing on the support of his vulnerable war-damaged followers to concoct a pack of lies so audacious as to result in his eventual arrest.

The Priory of Sion came about when Plantard, now married to a woman called Anne Hisler, moved his operation to a town near the Swiss border called Annemasse. The war had ended six years previously, but the right-wing movement in post-Vichy France continued undimmed, allowing Plantard to make quick alliances with other Catholics of his persuasion in his new area. His first project was to ally himself with a local church and to start campaigning for low-cost housing for French nationals, but his interest in mysticism was growing too. He began to talk to his cohorts about the medieval origins of Catholic France, pointing out that the nearby hill known as Mount Sion would be a perfect place for a religious retreat, sharing as it did a name with the famous Priory of Zion – a crusader-era order picked up by the Jesuits in the seventeenth century.

By 1956 his supporters were numerous enough to officially register themselves (as all French social or religious organizations had to do) at the local town hall under the name of the Priory of Sion. The founders all gave themselves antiquarian-sounding pseudonyms, Plantard's being Chyren and his friend André Bonhomme's being Bellos. The subtitle of the sect was registered as the Knighthood of Catholic Rule and Institution of Independent Traditionalist Union whose acronym in French was 'Circuit' – the name they gave to their *Vaincre*-like magazine.

The Priory of Sion might have remained just another small-time, eccentric alternative to Freemasonry were it not for the fact that the media at that time was awash with stories of rediscovered ancient texts and pedigrees. The Dead Sea Scrolls had recently been unearthed and, much closer to home, the French hotelier Noël Corbu was claiming that some mysterious ancient parchments had been found by a priest called Saunière bricked up in a pillar on his property in Rennes. Public interest in the prophecies of Nostradamus was at an all-time high and it was no coincidence that the name Chyren was taken from the anagrammatic 'Chyren Selin' with which Nostradamus referred to the great king who would inherit the earth.

It was now, in the late 1950s, that Plantard decided to step up his game and make it known that not only did he hate Jews and Masons and want a Catholic French France, but he was in fact the last true heir to the throne of France: a direct descendant of one of the assassinated Merovingian kings, Dagobert II.

The Merovingians were the Frankish dynasty who ruled what is now called France for several hundred years until Pepin the Short deposed their leader and instituted the Carolingian dynasty. The Merovingians were a highly religious people, obsessed with miracles and saints and enthusiastic founders of grand monasteries. They did not however believe that they were descended from Jesus, although this is the popular myth that has grown up, partly thanks to Plantard, in the last fifty years. Another proponent of the theory of the Merovingian's special bloodline was the Italian esoteric writer Julius Evola whose charismatic public appearances had been much admired by high-ranking members of the Nazi party and whose ideas about pure Christian blood had no doubt influenced Plantard considerably.

So Plantard decided to insert himself into the story of the 'lost' Frankish King Dagobert, and (inspired by Nostradamus) put it about that it had been secretly prophesied that Dagobert's successor would show up one day to claim the throne after a period of terrible turbulence. There was no stopping him. Starting in the mid-1960s, he physically inserted pages of parchment into books in the Bibliothèque National de France in Paris, aided by his friend and accomplice Philippe de Chérisey. They signed the papers Philippe Toscan du Plantier and attempted to authenticate their provenance by calling them the Secret Files of Henri Lobineau. He also resurrected the story of Corbu's parchments, publicizing the fact that details of Plantard's false pedigree were recorded in them. But his *coup de grâce* was persuading the author (and, rather appropriately, surrealist) Gérard de Sède to write a book about the Corbu discoveries in which he would lay out the full story of the Priory of Sion and its leader's links to France's royal lineage. This book, *L'or de Rennes, ou La vie insolite de Bérenger Saunière, curé de Rennes-le-Château* ('The Gold of Rennes, or The Strange Life of Bérenger Saunière, Priest of Rennes-le-Château'), turned out to be a popular hit, even more so when it was released in paperback under the more snappy title of *The Accursed Treasure of Rennes-le-Château.*

With many people now believing that Plantard was more than merely a reactionary butler's son from Paris, his dreams of commanding a grand religious cult with political aims (he had not forgotten his desire to re-create twentieth-century France for the Catholic French) looked within his grasp. And when Henry Lincoln, a British actor, sci-fi enthusiast and producer became interested in his case, it seemed that his story would finally reach beyond France. Lincoln was fascinated and convinced by Plantard's claims, and made a series of documentaries for BBC2 on the subject. Following on the success of these programmes, which attracted hundreds of letters from intrigued viewers, he decided to team up with two other researchers, one French, and prepare a book on the subject. When they came upon the planted pedigrees in the National Library in Paris, they were convinced they had all the evidence they needed to publish the full story of Plantard's claim to the throne, and in 1982 their book *The Holy Blood and The Holy Grail* was published by Jonathan Cape in London.

Now, finally, Plantard's most florid fantasies were portrayed as fact. Lincoln wrote that there was a secret society called the Priory of Sion who had had many illustrious leaders, including Leonardo da Vinci, and that they may well be related to Jesus through his relationship with Mary Magdalene. If this sounds familiar, that is because it was on this hoax-based book that the American novelist Dan Brown based his bestselling *The Da Vinci Code*.

The idea of the Priory of Sion having a string of illustrious leaders like Leonardo was not made-up by Lincoln – it was a mainstay of Plantard's hoax. He had carefully delineated a history of Grand Masters which stretched back hundreds of years. And when he came to the twentieth century and was faced with the challenge of bringing his pedigree up to the present day, he was careful to choose people who – while sufficiently illustrious to merit a place at the head of his fine secret society – had recently died so could not argue with him, such as the cultural icon Jean Cocteau. He was less careful about some of his other dates, claiming that certain of the Priory's Masters had been active when in fact they too had already died.

Ultimately, after decades of successful hoaxing, it was this list that would be Plantard's undoing. One of the names on it – the most recent Grand Master, in fact – was a recently deceased businessman called Roger-Patrice Pelat. Pelat had died of a heart attack in 1989 in the middle of his being tried by the French courts for insider dealing. He was a close friend of President Mitterrand and an associate of many other important political and commercial figures in Paris. The judge presiding over the case was careful to explore every possible avenue relating to Pelat's doings in order to avoid being accused of white-washing a high-profile case, and when he learned that Pelat was named as a member of a secret society, he ordered the headquarters of the Priory of Sion to be searched. The headquarters were Plantard's home. On entering his living quarters investigators found a profusion of faked documents and inflammatory material claiming that this seventy-four-year-old man was the true king of France. Pelat's family knew their relative would have had nothing to do with such a fantasist, and were keen to have him brought before the court.

Under oath, he admitted he had fabricated all the evidence that pointed to his impressive bloodline, and indeed that the entire history of the Priory of Sion had been founded on make-believe. Letters between him and his associates, dating back many years, proved that his aims were to take power and money for himself rather than the good of the country he loved. In these letters he had also discussed various plans of action should anyone become suspicious of his claims. There is some evidence to suggest that even before the Pelat case in 1993 Plantard had tried to distance himself from the information about the Merovingian bloodline presented as fact in Lincoln's book. But after being forced to out himself as a hoaxer before a court of law, he removed himself altogether from society and retired to the South of France. He returned to Paris to die in February 2000 and apparently spent his last days attended by his few remaining followers.

Plantard's legacy lives on, however, and not only in the form of the many treats we can imagine Dan Brown bought himself with the money from *The Da Vinci Code*.

In France, people claiming to be members of the Priory of Sion periodically approach journalists and academics to put forward their versions of French history and their opinions about contemporary culture and in 2002 a man called Gino Sandri announced the official rebirth of Plantard's cult.

And the spin-off conspiracy theories continue apace. 2006's *The Sion Revelation: The Truth About the Guardians of Christ's Sacred Bloodline* by Lynn Picknett and Clive Prince posits that Plantard's hoax was designed to distract attention from the real truth: that Plantard was himself being controlled by an all-powerful, secret group of politicians who are trying to control the fate of Europe and make it into one super-state ruled according to their religious wills.

Echoes of *The Protocols of the Elders of Zion* are impossible to ignore at many levels throughout the strange history and afterlife of Pierre Plantard, and if there is one lesson to be learned from this peculiar affair it is surely that where politics, religion and literature collide, readers should have their hoax-detectors very finely tuned indeed.

MARK HOFMANN

*T*HE HISTORY OF the Church of Latter Day Saints is inextricably entwined with stories of literary hoaxing. The entire movement is predicated on the alleged discovery by Joseph Smith in the 1820s of a series of 'golden plates' bound together with wire and inscribed with a mysterious Egyptian-style script telling of the pre-Jesus doings of God's people in America. Smith claimed to have been led to the plates, which were buried in the ground near his home in

New York, by an angel called Moroni, and to have been given, by divine gift, the ability to translate them. He was helped in the transcribing and publishing by his friend and neighbour Martin Harris, and in 1830 published the first edition of the Book of Mormon, which would become the central text for the millions of followers the group would go on to attract.

Unsurprisingly, given the unusual and private nature of Smith's discovery (and the fact that he claimed to have lost the golden plates soon after unearthing them), many people at the time and since have concluded that the whole thing was a hoax. Tensions between these nay-sayers and the powerful and numerous modern-day Mormons who believe Smith's transcription is indeed a literal record have increased over the years and been fuelled especially by former Mormons who have left the Church of the Latter Day Saints (known as the LDS) and attempted publicly to discredit them.

In the 1980s the anger and greed of one disgruntled apostate, Mark Hofmann, was to lead not only to one of the most damaging literary hoaxes of the twentieth century, but also to the violent deaths of two innocent people. Hofmann was a sixth-generation Mormon, born in Utah to devout parents. Although he never excelled academically, he was known to be good with his hands and to have a natural flair for engineering – as well as manufacturing a metal detector, childhood friends recall him making fire-bombs. His other passion was coin collecting, and he is said to have forged a mark on an old coin which fooled expert collectors when he was still a boy. As is customary in the LDS church, Hofmann was sent abroad to do missionary work when he left school and he ended up in the English city of Bristol. People who knew him at that time say he had already lost his faith, and was devouring Mormon-sceptic literature even as he was officially baptizing new converts into the religion. By the time he went home to Utah, although he enrolled in university to read sciences, he had another plan up his sleeve. Using his engineering and handicraft talents, and motivated apparently by the realization that the masters of his family's religion were gulls, Hofmann set about planning the first of the many hoax materials he would unleash on his community throughout the next decade.

In 1980, Hofmann, still a student, announced that he had found a seventeenth-century Bible which contained a mysterious folded script stuck to one of its pages. This text, it seemed, was none other than one of Martin Harris's original transcriptions of the *Book of Mormon* – the very one he was on record as having given to the Columbia University classics professor Charles Anthon in 1828. Hofmann presented his discovery to the church in Utah, which immediately got its foremost Smith scholar and handwriting expert, Dean Jessee, on the case. Jessee deemed the manuscript genuine and the LDS church gave the hoaxer $20,000 for it.

Emboldened by this early success, Hofmann gave up his place at university and decided to devote himself full-time to playing the church for all it was worth. To account for the sudden influx of old Mormon documents which he was about to unleash on his community, he let it be known that he had developed a network of contacts within the families of early Mormons and also sought out collectors of old letters whose interest was not in Mormonism but in antiquarian stamps and post-marks, so would be willing to part with their collections if the money was right.

Among the many texts Hofmann manufactured in his basement studio were a much-talked-about but never before seen document claiming that Joseph Smith had intended the leadership of the sect to be passed down to his son, not to his acolyte Brigham Young; letters from Smith's mother and three men he claimed had witnessed his work on the golden plates; a printing contract between Martin Harris and a man called Grandin concerning the production of the first edition of the Book of Mormon; and in 1983 a letter supposedly from Smith which confirmed the view, unpopular in the eyes of the church and its leader Gordon B. Hinckley, that Smith was involved in magic and mysticism at the time he claimed to have discovered the plates. This last text, dated 1825 and written, again, in what seemed to be Smith's hand, would be extremely inflammatory if it got out, so Hinckley paid $15,000 for it and resolved to keep its existence secret. But Hofmann tipped off the media and academic community that the letter was in the church's possession, forcing them to admit to its existence.

This particular hoax is telling on two counts. Firstly, it proves that Hofmann's aim was not only to earn himself a good living, but to humiliate the institution he felt had been lying to its followers – and itself – for so long. It also taps into the greatest insecurity – the ideological Achilles' heel – of LDS churchmen: that their esteemed founder was a dabbler in heathen magic rather than a vessel for the word of God. It was the fear that this might one day be proven to be true that ensured the leaders of the church would pay up and shut up whenever Hofmann presented them with a new piece of anti-Smith 'history', and which led to the hoax that would make his name infamous far beyond Utah.

The Salamander Letter must have been written by Hofmann sometime in late 1983 because in the first week of 1984 it was offered for sale to the LDS Church Historical Department. Don Schmidt was the man first approached about buying the letter and when he read it, he must have known there was trouble of one kind or another ahead. It was a missive supposedly written by the scribe Martin Harris to a new convert called William Wines Phelps, and it described the true story of Smith's discovery of the golden plates in terms dramatically opposed to those put about by the church establishment. It painted Smith not as one led by a divine angel to the site of the plates, but as a common treasure-digger on the make. Worse still, it claimed that far from being visited by an angel at the site of the buried texts, Smith had encountered a 'white salamander' which rose up out of the ground in the manner of a daemonic spirit. This salamander then transformed itself into a spirit of questionable affiliation and began to bargain with Smith, denying him ownership of the plates unless he produced his dead brother, Alvin, as an accomplice. This element chimed dangerously with one of the most keenly suppressed rumours put about by Smith's dissenters: that he had been involved in a thoroughly unchristian exhumation of his brother for use in a magical ceremony.

Schmidt, the LDS historian, was being asked for a piece of Mormon gold in return for the letter, but after consulting with Hinckley, made a lesser offer, which Hofmann, acting through an intermediary, Lyn Jacobs, turned down. He then offered it for sale to two prominent critics of the church, thinking they would jump at the chance to have 'proof' that Smith was not as saintly as people said. These two potential buyers, however, immediately suspected it was a fake. Finally, an agreement was reached in January 1984 with a Utah collector called Steven Christensen who bought the letter for $40,000. Christensen's aim was to have the document authenticated then sell it back to the church at a profit, but a year later he was still unable to have its provenance verified. Only a few months later, Christensen would be dead.

What turned Hofmann from an angry hoaxer into a murderer is not clear, but his childhood passion for making incendiary devices, coupled with his increasing feeling of isolation, raises the question of psychopathic tendencies. Certainly, by the time he resorted to manufacturing a series of bombs in his basement studio, he was a man at the end of his tether: after failing to sell the Salamander Letter to his first choices of buyers, questions about the provenance of his discoveries were beginning to be asked publicly and it must have seemed to him that it was only a matter of time before he was unmasked. And like other hoaxers before him, he had promised his demanding clients marvellous new items for sale (such as the famous McLellin collection of papers, pertaining to one of the church's earliest apostles) which he did not have the time or ability to produce. Added to this, the hefty income he was making from the forged texts was not enough to finance his increasingly lavish lifestyle and his passion for collecting rare and antiquarian books. Debt collectors were closing in and in order to divert attention from himself and his crimes, on 15 October, 1985, he took the drastic step of sending the letter-bomb that would kill Christensen. Later that day, he sent another which took the life of Christensen's associate's wife, Kathleen Sheets.

Christensen and Sheets were involved in an investment project together which had gone badly wrong, and

Hofmann apparently hoped to make the attacks look like they were related to that. But when a third bomb exploded accidentally in Hofmann's own car, it was not long before police raided his home workshop which contained not only bomb-making equipment but the tools with which he had created his many forged items. Aided by the FBI's new forensic analysis techniques, the police were able to prove that the inflammatory documents Hofmann had sold to members of the LDS church were hoaxes. Seemingly unrepentant for the crimes he committed, it was decided in court that life should mean life for this particular hoaxer, and he languishes to this day in a Utah state penitentiary. Gordon B. Hinckley, the church leader who believed in Hofmann's literary discoveries, said afterwards:

> I accepted him to come into my office on a basis of trust . . . I frankly admit that Hofmann tricked us. He also tricked experts from New York to Utah, however . . . I am not ashamed to admit that we were victimized. It is not the first time the Church has found itself in such a position. Joseph Smith was victimized again and again. The Savior was victimized. I am sorry to say that sometimes it happens.

He would admit to no sense of satisfaction – or even divine retribution – when it was revealed that Hofmann had lost the use of his forging hand in an accident shortly after his arrest; but no doubt other humiliated bibliophiles of the American Church of the Latter Day Saints were more forthcoming on the subject.

10

Entrapment Hoaxes

*E*NTRAPMENT HOAXES ARE the easiest to enjoy. Not only because within us all there is a naughty school-kid sitting at the back of the class asking the teacher how to say 'tail' in Latin, but because when highly intelligent people turn their talents to mischief-making, the results can be pretty spectacular. In some cases, like that of the Spectrist school of avant-garde poetry in Australia and Romain Gary's Prix Goncourt-winning novel, the hoax text can actually have considerable literary merit in its own right. In others, like the extraordinary case of *I, Libertine* – the book that never was but which had all of New York raving about the made-up Englishman who wrote it – important hypocrisies in the way literary fashions are created are exposed for the first time. Another good thing about hoaxes like these, which are designed specifically to be debunked, is that the perpetrator is usually willing and able to write about what they did and why, giving a valuable insight into the effects hoaxing can have on a writer. But as H.L. Mencken (phoney historian of the American bathtub) and William Boyd (biographer of a non-existent artist) both make plain in their eloquent explanations of the hoaxer's craft, practising to deceive can sometimes be more trouble than it's worth . . .

HAROLD WITTER BYNNER AND
ARTHUR DAVISON FICKE

*T*HE GREAT SPECTRIST poet Emmanuel Morgan, along with the flame-haired Hungarian beauty Anne Knish, exploded on to the American modernist scene in 1916 with a collection of work – and a manifesto – inspired by imagism, futurism and, well, -isms generally. Spectrism was a hoax from the Ern Malley school of intellectual-baiting, and although it has never enjoyed the popular afterlife that the Australian poetry-hoaxers did, it was, while it lasted, a jolly good laugh for all involved, and had unexpected consequences for the two poets who came up with it.

The perpetrators were Witter Bynner and Arthur Ficke, two poets in their thirties who had been best friends since meeting at Harvard in 1900. As typical frat boys they had always been keen on pranks, but when they both became poets after graduating and found that their traditional tastes in verse were at odds with the prevailing modernism of the day, they saw that the time was right for their grandest trick yet.

Bynner had had a job at *McClure* magazine but given it up to write poetry full-time in 1908, and that same year Ficke made the decision to practise law full-time and make writing his second career. But both were deeply committed to and involved in the literary scene. So when Bynner had the idea for the Spectra hoax in 1916 it was only natural that he would call on his friend to collaborate. They had worked together before on more serious joint literary ventures and, lubricated by whisky and laughter, they holed up in Ficke's house in Davenport, Iowa, making occasional forays into Chicago to socialize with the poets and novelists who congregated there. In little over a week their work was complete, after which time Ficke's wife became sick of them prancing around her home talking in Spectrist-speak and advised them to move into a hotel if they had any more to do.

The slim book they came up with was authored by Morgan and Knish and opened with the Spectrist Manifesto. This statement of poetic intent was a pastiche of the various new schools of poetic thought that were emerging, seemingly by the day, all over the English-speaking world. This new 'ism', Knish wrote in her introduction, had a complex tripartite definition: to 'speak to the mind of that process of diffraction by which are disarticulated the several colored and other rays of which light is composed', to illustrate 'reflex vibrations of physical sight . . . and, by analogy, the after-colors of the poet's initial vision' and to connote 'the overtones, adumbrations, or spectres which for the poet haunt all objects of both the seen and the unseen world'.

The poems, which were given opus numbers rather than titles (and what could be more pretentious than that?) were all redolent with the imagists' shifting visions of the natural world, and Knish's, in particular, were possessed of an edgily female sensibility. While Morgan's free-spirited romances spoke of things like 'the liquor of your laughter/ And the lacquer of your limbs' (Opus 6), Knish inhabited a darker domestic world, as evidenced by her Opus 118:

If bathing were a virtue, not a lust
I would be dirtiest.
To some, housecleaning is a holy rite.
For myself, houses would be empty
But for the golden motes dancing in sunbeams.
Tax-assessors frequently overlook valuables.
Today they noted my jade.
But my memory of you escaped them.

The pair of hoaxers had no trouble getting their work into print, and as soon as it was in the public domain it began to attract attention – as would any new poetic movement in those fecund days. Publication was supported by a number of poems being submitted to fashionable literary magazines such as *Others,* the *Little Review* and the highly-respected *Poetry*. To the authors' delight, the big-name poets and critics weighed in with their responses, and they were largely positive. William Carlos Williams admired their work 'sincerely', the Pulitzer-winning poet Edgar Lee Masters wrote to Morgan praising his work highly but admitting he felt Knish's output was rather bogged down in theory; Amy Lowell and the famous editor Harriet Monroe were both beguiled.

Out in Wisconsin, the *Literary Magazine* even published a spoof of the Spectrists, with a manifesto written by 'Manuel Organ' and 'Nanne Pish' who solemnly delineated the artistic aims of 'the Ultra Violet School of Poetry'. Fan letters poured in to the borrowed address in Pittsburgh that the Spectrists gave as their HQ – a town sufficiently obscure to make them seem as marginal as possible – and as the imagined back-story of Knish's tempestuous love-life and flame-headed beauty became well known, it was not uncommon to find a young poet or critic who claimed to have met her and revelled in her gorgeousness. And though her made-up name, Knish, would be instantly recognizable to a New Yorker today as a popular Jewish snack-food, it raised no doubts amongst the less worldly readers of 1916 who were all hungry for exoticism of any sort.

Keen to have a real live woman in the movement and aware that the success of Spectrism might justify enlarging their school, the two men approached another poet of their acquaintance, Marjorie Allen Seiffert. She was a writer of independent means with the time and naughtiness of spirit and disregard for trendy poetic 'isms' to devote herself wholeheartedly to the project. Indeed she had already submitted some hoax poems to a literary journal in the past under the made-up name Angela Cypher. She was an enthusiastic co-conspirator, using her considerable talent as a literary mimic to produce work under the name of Elijah Hay which was as well received as Morgan and Knish's had been.

In 1918, while Spectrism was still being talked about in reverent tones throughout literary America, Ficke was called to France to serve in the First World War. Although he would return intact shortly afterwards, the hoax would not. At one point the subject of modern poetry came up in conversation with an army brigadier and he was directly asked what he thought of the Spectrist poet Anne Knish. He could not contain his amused pride at this question and revealed himself to his astonished inquisitor there and then. Bynner was no more capable of keeping it a secret that he felt he had come up with the hoax to end all hoaxes, and by the time *Dial* magazine ran a story revealing that 'the interruption of the war . . . gave "Miss Knish" a commission as Captain Arthur Davison Ficke' the true nature of the Spectrists was already an open secret.

The literary luminaries who had been fooled had to admit they had been had, but most echoed Carlos Williams when he said; 'I was completely taken in by the hoax, and while not subscribing in every case to the excellence of the poems admired them as a whole quite sincerely.'

But the life of the hoax was not extinguished by its debunking. Although the Spectrists' poems were never themselves to enter the canon in any meaningful way, as literary sensibilities developed in America, the work eventually came to be considered by Bynner, Ficke and their critics to be some of the best work they had ever made. Although they had been joking when they wrote it, they later came to see that in amongst the dross there had been lines and expressions that were far purer and more elegant than anything they had written in their immature incarnations as formalists. And although Ficke was to die too young in 1945 after a protracted illness, Bynner went on to travel the world writing about the things he saw and felt, and ultimately settle in Santa Fe and write poetry – modernist, imagist, not at all un-Spectrist-like poetry, until his death in 1968.

H.L. MENCKEN

THE WINTER OF 1917 was not a happy one in America or Europe. Casualties in the field in France and Belgium were stupenduously high after the battles at Ypres, and in Halifax, Nova Scotia, the biggest man-made explosion ever (until Hiroshima) had just killed thousands when two tankers collided in the harbour. Journalists struggled to find any good news with which to lighten the hearts of their readers, so some took a page out of Mark Twain's book and made it up.

H.L. Mencken was one such writer, and the fake news story he published in the *New York Evening Mail* on 28 December would continue to haunt him for the rest of his life. Known as the Sage of Baltimore, Mencken was at this point halfway through a life which would see him crowned as America's best loved critic, editor and social commentator. He lived almost all his life in the same house in Union Square, and wrote every week for the *Baltimore Sun* for nearly fifty years, covering a range of local and international issues in his famous opinion-editorial pieces, and attracting as much controversy for his political views as he did praise for his witty prose style.

America, he decided, needed cheering up. So he put pen to paper and began to write an article under the heading 'A Neglected Anniversary':

> On December 20 there flitted past us, absolutely without public notice, one of the most important profane anniversaries in American history, to wit, the seventy-fifth anniversary of the introduction of the bathtub into These States. Not a plumber fired a salute or hung out a flag. Not a governor proclaimed a day of prayer. Not a newspaper called attention to the day.

He went on to describe, in a piece of 1,780 entirely mendacious words, how the great American bath had been created by a Cincinnati cotton dealer called Adam Thompson who, on a business trip to England in the 1830s, had picked up the habit of taking a regular bath for the good of his health and wellbeing. Thompson had a sideline in inventing useful things (it was he who pioneered the cotton bags in which legs of ham and bacon are hung to this day). When he decided to bring this invention back home, he commissioned the grandfather of all modern baths – a huge vessel made of Nicaraguan mahogany – and had it installed in his home. Dignitaries from far and wide came to marvel at the invention, and before long the idea caught on, spawning imitators all over the land. But some states began to raise heavy taxes on bathtub owners ($30 a year in Virginia!) and health officials, concerned that plunging one's whole body into warm water every day would bring about a generation plagued by respiratory disease, tried to have bathing stopped by law. But America was by this time in love with bathing, and tubs private and public proliferated, ensuring that the bid to have them outlawed failed. The fame of this newfangled domestic contraption was sealed, Mencken told his readers, when, in 1850, President Millard Fillmore himself visited the original Thompson bath on a tour of Cincinnati and resolved to have one brought into the First Family's official home. Accordingly, he instructed his secretary of war, General Charles Conrad, to put the job out for tender and a year later the Philadelphia engineering firm Harper & Gillespie had won the contract and installed a fine cast-iron bath in the White House. There it remained until the Cleveland administration, when it was upgraded to an enamel one. Finally, after years of dispute, the country was in agreement that having a bath was a good thing, and in 1862 the army even made bathing compulsory among soldiers.

How diverting all this must have seemed to the good people of New York and the other towns to which Mencken's article was syndicated. After all, most people had never stopped to think about the history of this ordinary household object – and why should they? It is, after all, not a very important subject; which is exactly why Mencken had such fun with it. Every detail of his history was fabricated, from the ham-holding sack supposedly invented by the American bathtub's progenitor to the attempted bill to outlaw them heard before Congress. He was, he would protest, just having a bit of fun.

However what happened next he could not have foreseen. The whole story was taken as gospel truth by everyone who read it, and facts from it began appearing whenever the subject of the history of sanitation arose in an article, paper or book. After a few such citations of the Thompson bath, or Fillmore's role in popularizing it, Mencken thought he had better make it clear that he had invented the story to bring a bit of much needed silliness and Christmas cheer into people's lives. So he wrote a confessional article in the *Chicago Tribune* on 23 May 1926 under the headline 'Melancholy Reflections', lamenting the fact that he had deceived so many of his readers but also pointing out that the American public were a gullible lot who would swallow whatever was fed to them. He was particularly annoyed, he wrote, that among the many people who had used his hoax article for their own ends were quack medicine sellers and chiropractors, who used it as an example of 'the stupidity of medical men' and indeed medical men themselves, who used its statistics about the number of private baths in use in 1917 as evidence of a mighty improvement in public sanitation that had not in fact taken place.

Unfortunately, this article was largely ignored. Not only did the public continue to talk about baths as being from Cincinnati, but the junior writers in the very newspaper his confession appeared in continued to quote spurious facts from the original piece whenever a news story about plumbing or engineering or the White House called for fleshing out with historical data. This drove Mencken mad. There was nothing he could do, it seemed, to put the genie of misinformation back in the bottle, and the fact that it was not about anything of great consequence was neither here nor there: it brought it home to him just how gullible not only readers but editors, publishers and writers are too.

Not long before his death in 1956 H.L. Mencken tried one last time to put his hoax to rest. In his book *A Mencken Chresthomacy*, he observed sadly that:

> The success of this idle hoax, done in time of war, when more serious writing was impossible, vastly astonished me. It was taken gravely by a great many other newspapers, and presently made its way into medical literature and into standard reference books. It had, of course, no truth in it whatsoever, and I more than once confessed publicly that it was only a jocosity . . . Scarcely a month goes by that I do not find the substance of it reprinted, not as foolishness but as fact, and not only in newspapers but in official documents and other works of the highest pretensions.

To this day, examples persist of 'A Forgotten Anniversary' being taken seriously, not least by compilers of information about Millard Fillmore, whose famously lacklustre presidency was so devoid of interest that the possibility of him being associated with something so exciting as a cast-iron bathtub is an on-going gift to quiz masters and trivia buffs the world over. And in 1998, the car-maker Kia launched a marketing campaign based on the idea of 'Unheard-of Presidents': they gave away bath-soaps shaped like busts of Fillmore to publicize the fact that that particular unheard-of president's claim to fame was to have run the first ever bath in the White House. The Sage of Baltimore would not be amused.

NICOLAS BATAILLE AND AKAKIA VIALA

*T*HE FRENCH THEATRE director Nicolas Bataille was famous for two things: directing and starring in the longest-running play at a single venue anywhere in the world, and 'discovering' the esteemed Romanian playwright Eugène Ionesco. Ionesco's play, *The Bald Prima Donna*, has been running for more than half a century at the Theatre de la Huchette in Paris and until shortly before his death in 2008 Bataille could be seen in the role of Mr Martin. It was in 1949, however, some years before that production made its debut, that Bataille accepted a work by the unknown immigrant dramatist Ionesco that would mark the beginning of the Romanian's stellar rise through the ranks of European drama. And if it hadn't been for reflected glory from bringing Ionesco to the world's attention, Bataille might never have shaken off the critical mud that stuck to him when he humiliated the Parisian cultural elite with a literary trick of a most daring sort.

Bataille was a rookie director who had teamed up with the actress and writer Akakia Viala (aka Marie-Antoinette Allévy), hoping to take the brave new world of avant-garde theatre by storm with their rehabilitation of late-nineteenth century literary symbolism. In 1948 their hard work and ingenuity paid off when their production of *Une Saison en Enfer*, based on Rimbaud's symbolist prose-poem of the same name, won them an award and a small measure of celebrity. While some applauded the efforts they were making to revolutionize the staid French theatrical tradition, other more vociferous critics were less impressed by their attempts at recapturing Rimbaud's idiom and, despite having won a prize, the two young dramatists found themselves pilloried from all sides by condescending Rimbaud scholars.

A few months later, still indignant and still convinced that they really did understand the rhythms of the nineteenth-century poet's style, Bataille and Viala hatched a plan to prove their detractors wrong. There had long been rumours of a great lost work by Arthur Rimbaud – rumours which stemmed from comments by the poet's ill-fated lover, Paul Verlaine. The work referred to by Verlaine was called *La Chasse Spirituelle* and was, he said, the greatest piece of writing Rimbaud had ever produced. Sadly, the manuscript disappeared during the two poets' stormy spell in London in 1872 and was never seen again. So when Bataille and Viala claimed to have found this very manuscript, and took it straight to the magazine *Combat*, the excitement in literary Paris was palpable.

Combat was the journal started by the French Resistance (and edited most famously by Camus) that continued to publish its left-wing cultural and political articles into the 1970s. The editor in 1949 was Maurice Nadeau, the famous historian of surrealism with a keen ear for French poetry and a commitment to modernism in all its forms. He was convinced that the verses were authentic, and so too were the editors of *Le Mercure de France*, a literary journal with several hundred years' pedigree as an opinion-forming cultural gazette. *Le Mercure* had been approached by the writer Pascal Pia (also a former *Combat* editor) who had been shown the verses and, believing them to be genuine, implored its editor to release the full text of the great lost manuscript for the edification of the reading public. The novelist Georges Duhamel was another famous name who had seen the text and was convinced of its authenticity, and so with all these discerning names behind it, *La Chasse* found its way into print with remarkable ease.

As soon as the two journals hit the news-stands, however, critics began to weigh in with words far harsher than those used to denigrate *Une Saison En Enfer*. By the spring of 1949 the comment pages of *Combat* and indeed most other Parisian journals were full of damning, not to say bitchy, opinions. The highly respected author and *Nouvelle Revue* editor Jean Paulhan wrote: 'The work is inconsistent, the metaphors are bombastic and garish, the ideas banal . . . modern poetry as country hicks imagine it to be.' Jean Cocteau asked: 'Is this text authentic? Is it apocryphal? As far as I am concerned it is laborious and soulless'; and the critic Rolland de Renéville said: 'I do not believe that one could seriously uphold the view that Rimbaud would have accepted to do in *La Chasse Spirituelle* what he never did elsewhere, namely mimic himself.' At best, then, it was seen as more Rimbaudy than Rimbaud. At worse, a cobbling together of various phrases and images from elsewhere in the poet's oeuvre by some bold *particheur*. Which is exactly what it was.

When Bastille and Viala admitted their hoax in the summer of 1949, there were still a few enthusiastic believers who were slow to admit they had been hoodwinked, although Maurice Nadeau's initial assertion that 'it is not enough to claim to be a forger, one must he able to prove it' was no doubt a rhetorical covering-up of his shame-facedness rather than a genuine statement of belief in the text.

Certainly, the two theatrical hoaxers who called literary Paris's bluff fell out of favour for a while with the critical establishment. But ultimately both went on to have illustrious careers in the French theatre and although neither was to perpetuate a hoax on that scale again, each must have looked back fondly on those few months in the late 1940s when no one could say they didn't know their Rimbaud.

JEAN SHEPHERD

O NE OF THE most inspired literary hoaxes of twentieth-century America is remarkable for having happened backwards. It was an idea born of a ground-breaking talk radio DJ called Jean Shepherd, who in the mid-1950s had just moved to New York and started a broadcasting career on WOR-AM which would go on to make him one of the best loved humorists of his generation. His style was subversive for his time because of its stream-of-consciousness tone and decidedly non-commercial brand of humour: he was a satirist before his time, picking apart the hypocrisies and vanities of East Coast media and culture at a time when the edgy social commentary of comedians like Lenny Bruce had barely been thought of.

Shepherd's shift was the night-time, and broadcasting his musings about life to insomniacs, night-workers, artists, nursing mothers, drunks, people who knew they'd feel dreadful when the alarm went at seven, he knew he was talking to the margins. It was in the course of one programme in 1956 that he came up with two things which would make history: the phrase 'night people' and the swashbuckling historical novel *I, Libertine*.

Both of these phenomena came out of a rambling disquisition on the notion that 'there's two kinds of people: the kind of guy who believes in the world of the office – he believes in filing cabinets and phone calls and lunches; that the time from eight a.m. to six in the evening is the time that he's alive and the time after that is dead time – tv, beer, sleep. That is a day person. But there's the other guy, whose world begins when he gets out of the office. He's a night person. And they're constantly battling but they don't know they are.'

Previously on that night's show, Shepherd had observed that one of the things he had noticed about New York as opposed to Philadelphia or Chicago or anywhere else, was that the whole city was obsessed with lists. The top forty records, the ten best-dressed people, the twenty bestselling books of the decade. 'It is,' he now observed, 'the day people who read lists – they are oriented to statistics.'

But these lists are of course completely bogus. He asked his listeners to ponder how they came about: an inexperienced journalist on a tight deadline is told to come up with the ten bestselling novels of the year so far. What does he do? He calls a few booksellers. The owner of one might be desperately trying to shift the 400 copies of something nobody wants to know about, so he tells the hack that that particular book is flying off the shelves. Sure enough, when it appears at number two in the list in Saturday's paper he can be sure of an influx of trendy shoppers asking him for that very title.

What if, Shepherd wondered out loud to his listeners, all of you went into a bookshop tomorrow and asked for a book that you knew did not exist. The first person to ask for it would be given the brush-off and told there's no record of any such book. The second person to come in that week asking for it would be told the book is on order. And by the third and fourth request for the book, the bookseller would be on the phone to his supplier, who would in turn consult his big list of all books scheduled to appear, and on not finding it there, start looking at where to find it. A buzz would be born. All book-buying New York would be talking about this hot new read.

As Shepherd continued to talk through this plan, his listeners began to ring in suggesting titles for the non-existent novel. And an author's name was invented: Frederick Ewing. Shepherd decided that Ewing ought to be an Englishman: a lieutenant in the British Army now a civil servant in Rhodesia with his wife Marjorie. Ewing's area of interest had long been eighteenth-century court affairs, and this first in a planned trilogy of novels on that subject was intended not for the common reader but for scholars and historians so, the story went, he was taken aback but not unpleasantly surprised by its run-away success amongst the general English reader on publication by an imprint of Cambridge University Press. The back-story now confirmed (and having a sense of the author's life was, he reminded his listeners, prerequisite in these days of celeb writers like Faulkner), a title had to be picked from the many suggestions that had been pouring in all night. *I, Libertine* was born. About to go off the air at 3.30 a.m., Shepherd encouraged his devoted listeners to write in over the coming weeks and tell him how their search for Ewing's masterpiece was going. And don't forget, he said, 'The day man is not listening to us – he thinks we're nuts.'

Neither Shepherd nor his band of followers could have foreseen the massive impact of his hoax. The next night he was able to report stories of New York's intellectually snobbish booksellers saying things like: 'Yes, it's about time the general public caught on to Ewing.' And when the more commercial shops told Ewing fans they had no record of the book in their lists, they were nonplussed to hear the customer say: 'Oh never mind, I'll go get it at Doubleday.'

A few days later one woman phoned in to say that she had mentioned the book at her bridge club, and four of her fellow players claimed to have read it, three of them liking it immensely. A college student sent in a graded essay he had produced on 'F. R. Ewing: Eclectic Historian': a nine-page paper with footnotes. His professor gave it a B+ and commended him on his excellent research.

Some of Shepherd's listeners were in fact writers and media people themselves, and true to their favourite DJ's injunction that they should pull out all the stops to make *I, Libertine* the most talked about book in town, one reviewer even got a piece published in one of the weekend literary supplements, and one PR man engineered it so that one of the city's leading gossip columnists, Earl Wilson, claimed to have had lunch with Freddie Ewing and his wife Marjorie who were passing through town on their way to India.

But the crunch came for Shepherd when a prominent Boston church had the book put on their list of proscribed books. He was starting to worry, he said later, that soon the president would be talking about it and then he wouldn't be able to believe in anything. Just as he was wondering how to out his listeners as the perpetrators of the hoax, one listener phoned in revealing himself to be a reporter for the *Wall Street Journal*. He had, he said, been following the prank from the outset and felt that a very important thing had been happening. Wasn't it time to reveal all in the newspaper? Shepherd, feeling that his prank was spiralling out of control, agreed that it was.

The story hit the news-stands at three p.m. the next day, and as Shepherd remembers it, three minutes later he had six countries on the phone seeking an interview. The foreign press had already picked up on the latest big novel to be wowing New York, so when they found out it was a hoax they were desperate to get a quote from the horse's mouth. British newspapers loved the story, being on the whole in agreement with Shepherd that popular culture in New York was a phoney and vain thing. Even the anti-American Russian newspaper *Pravda* took the story almost word-for-word from the pages of the *Wall Street Journal* – a highly unusual and probably unprecedented act on their part.

The New York press was not so delighted with the deception however, and mostly wrote up the story as one about a mean radio DJ having pulled one over on his listeners by telling them to go out and ask for a book that didn't exist.

It may not have existed then, but a few years later it would. In 1956 Shepherd's friend, the sci-fi author Ted Sturgeon, called him up and told him that there was a publisher trying to get his hands on the paperback rights to *I, Libertine*. This publisher was Ian Ballantine, and as soon as he realized the non-existent book could be put together quickly by the combined writing team of Sturgeon, Shepherd and Ballantine's wife Betty, and given a cleverly illustrated jacket by the sci-fi artist Frank Kelly Freas, he drew up a contract.

So, finally, the book became a reality. It did indeed sell enough copies to be called (legitimately, no doubt) a bestseller. Nowadays editions are prized amongst book collectors, and its cover art has achieved cult status itself: a gaudy scene from the eponymous rake's progress featuring the strap-line 'Gadzooks! quoth I, "but here's a saucy bawd!" ' over an image of a busty wench, a pub called the Fish & Staff whose sign references the two main authors' names, and Shepherd's well-known catchphrase 'Excelsior!' concealed in the ruff of the heroine's dress.

The proceeds of the real *I, Libertine* were donated to charity, as is the norm for the intellectual twentieth-century hoaxer, and although the whole affair is less well known now than others of its time and ilk, there can be no one to rival Shepherd, before or since, in encouraging ordinary people to beat the media at its own game. Soon after his grand hoax, WOR tried to sack him for not being sufficiently commercial. His protest was immediately to record an advertisement for a rival company (he was sacked but a public outcry brought him back). Shep, as he was better known to his thousands of devoted listeners, maintained his commitment to storytelling with a purpose, and his broadcasts on the days of Martin Luther King's rallying speech and the funeral of Kennedy will always be remembered by those who heard them. Although best known now for writing *The Christmas Story*, which became one of the favourite holiday movies of all time, there is a generation of New York radio fans who love him best for just one thing: pulling off the cheekiest hoax of the post-war period.

MIKE McGRADY

*I*F THE ERN Malley poems were aimed at sending up the avant-garde of Australian letters, the *Naked Came the Stranger* hoax was intended to ridicule an entire nation's literary mainstream. Advertising itself as a saucy erotic novel by a glamorous new author called Penelope Ashe, the work was in fact the brainchild of Mike McGrady, a well-known columnist for *Newsday* in America in the mid-1960s, and had nearly as many authors as the Bible. McGrady was hardly the stuffy reactionary that the Malley hoaxers were, but as a lover of literature and believer in the power of the great American novel, he found himself increasingly vexed at publishers' promotion of trashy authors like *Valley of* *the Dolls* writer Jacqueline Susann and Irving Wallace (whose *The Chapman Report* was a Kinsey-influenced look at female sexuality in suburbia) over better written but less saucy works.

So he hatched a plan to prove once and for all that as long as a novel had at least one sex scene per chapter, such conventional literary qualities as plot, character development and fluency of style could go out the window. Working for *Newsday*, of course, he had a host of versatile writers of all ages and descriptions at his fingertips, so he asked twenty-five of them to help him perpetrate what he hoped would be the literary hoax of the decade.

It would be a novel about a sexy married woman who resolves to avenge her cheating husband by receiving as many gentleman callers at their suburban home as possible and entertaining them in any number of ingeniously erotic ways. And in true porn-film style, each candidate would have his own clearly defined look and character: a boxer, a mobster, even a progressive rabbi and a gay man who fancies a bit of subversive straight sex. Throughout, she drinks, smokes and swears, and generally disports herself in a way that is carefree to say the least.

Each of the group was commissioned to write one chapter, and told to take special care to make the writing frightful. Although some contributors initially had their attempts returned by their demanding editor on the basis that they weren't bad enough, before long a manuscript heavy on soft-porn nonsense and light on good writing was ready to be submitted to New York's lucky publishing houses. It was sent off in late 1966 with a covering letter about Penelope Ashe, claiming she was a 'demure Long

Island housewife who thought she could write as well as J. Susann'.

The publishing house Stuart Lyle Inc. took the bait, and, as predicted by McGrady, threw a huge amount of money into promoting it prior to publication in August 1969. Interestingly, this was after McGrady had decided to come clean and confess to the director of the company that the book was a hoax title: obviously, the last thing he wanted was to be accused of fraud. Stuart Lyle was so keen on the idea, and so sure that the unusual nature of the book's authorship would not impact on its sales one jot and might in fact increase it, bringing the book to a wider audience than would normally buy his racy paperbacks, that he signed McGrady up without even having read the book.

In advance of publication in the summer of 1969, Lyle threw his publicity machine into overdrive. With risqué advertisements featuring some of the book's authors dressed up as characters from particular sex scenes *Naked* was big news even before anyone had bought it, with more than $50,000 spent on publicity for what promised to be the year's most outré title.

As soon as it hit the bookshops, copies flew off the shelves. Its success was due in part to the seductive figure of Mrs Ashe herself, who was played by McGrady's sister-in-law Billie Young at a number of personal appearances and signings, and gave sterling performances as the lusty housewife and outspoken commentator on the sexual liberation issues which were at the forefront of everyone's minds that summer in 1969. Almost immediately, two things became clear to the authors: their hoax had worked perfectly – sales figures were even better than imagined. And because of this, the perpetrators stood to make quite a lot of money. Keen to retain credibility as intellectual pranksters rather than get-rich-quick con-artists, and emboldened by their publisher's assertion that no one would mind if the book turned out to be a joke, they decided to come clean. Being journalists, they were well able to orchestrate a mass outing in the local New York and national press, and on 7 August 1969 the *New York Times, Newsweek* and the *Washington Post* were among the publications who ran stories on the real authors of the book everyone was talking about. Then one night on the *David Frost Show*, the host announced that his next guest would be the popular erotica writer Penelope Ashe, and out trouped the whole group of mostly male writers, led by McGrady.

As predicted, sales began to soar, the hoaxing aspect lending *Naked* an even more cultish identity – and, no doubt, enabling high-minded littérateurs and armchair critics legitimately to go out and buy a trashy book with a naked lady on the cover in the name of current affairs. By the middle of October that same year, 90,000 copies had been sold, according to *Publisher's Weekly*, and with almost constant print runs for months afterwards, this bold collaborative hoax quickly took its place on the bestseller lists. In the years that followed, it was translated into all the languages a 1970s porn-watcher might expect: Dutch, Danish, Norwegian, Italian, Spanish and French.

One happy consequence of the hoax was that it brought out the best in reviewers, both in America and the UK. Alan Coren remarked in *Punch* that 'the book fails all the tests of true pornography (there are sixty-nine). It is a victim of its own constant insistence on self-parody, and with pornography the last place the tongue should be is in the cheek.' And Miles Kington observed that 'the print is tolerably readable and all the pages in the last two chapters are correctly numbered'.

It is hard to imagine and may be hard to remember now just how sex-obsessed the publishers' lists were in the last few years of the 1960s. Apart from the slew of erotic bonkbusters about which McGrady was so disparaging, there was John Updike's *Couples*, Roth's *Portnoy's Complaint* and of course the classic *Everything You Always Wanted to Know About Sex But Were Afraid to Ask*.

And indeed the book itself went on to spawn many imitators in the field of collaborative, jokey fiction, the most famous of which is probably the 1996 comedy thriller *Naked Came the Manatee*, in which Carl Hiaasen and Elmore Leonard got together with eleven other mystery writers to produce a chapter each of a story about an environmentalist in Miami who gets a visit from a mysterious sea-creature called Booger. All proceeds went to charity.

Identical in aim if not title was 2005's *Atlanta Nights*, a book submitted by a group of sci-fi writers to the publishing house PublishAmerica. It was deliberately written as badly as possible, with two of its chapters actually generated by a computer program, and was in fact accepted for publication, but when the hoaxers revealed themselves prior to the presses rolling, the deal was scrapped and the hoaxers resorted to self-publishing under the pseudonym Travis Tea.

Recent years have also seen *Naked Came the Librarian*, a project undertaken by the staffers of the library at Augustana College, Illinois; a more serious multi-author novel masterminded by the Australian publisher Di Gribble, *The Stranger Inside*; and *Naked Came the Phoenix*, a more amateurish version of Hiaasen's. Another offering, *Naked Came the Plowman*, seems to have sunk without a trace; but the gory sci-fi fest that is *Naked Came the Sasquatch* has earned itself a devoted cult following.

Such has been the afterlife of the title alone that McGrady's original appropriation of it from a 1963 historical novel about the life of August Rodin was probably his smartest trick of all, and remains his most enduring gift to the Western canon of silliness.

ROMAIN GARY

*T*HE PRIX GONCOURT is more than just a literary prize. It is a French institution. The convention is that winners neither make an official acceptance of the honour, nor are allowed to turn it down, and it must never be given to the same person twice. But when, in 1975, the young Algerian author Émile Ajar was given the award for his second novel *La Vie Devant Soi* (*The Life Before Us*), the judges were unknowingly breaking one of their own cardinal rules. For Ajar had taken a Goncourt before, back in 1956 for *Les Racines du Ciel* (*The Roots of Heaven*), only that time it was under a different name, Romain Gary.

The extraordinary life of Romain Gary is one no post-war French novelist could make up, however hard they were trying to be experimental. And if it weren't for the efforts of his biographer (and former lover) Myriam Anissimov, we would have only his own highly unreliable version of events to go on, for his talent for fantasy extended very much to his autobiography as well as his many novels. He was born Roman Kacew in Lithuania in 1914 to Russian Jewish parents. Not, as he would go on to tell it, a Cossack and a famous film star. His father, Lebja, walked out on his wife and child when Roman was only ten, and his mother, the domineering, ambitious and desperately loving Nina, took her child to France to start a new life. Having spent some time in Warsaw before this, Roman – an incredibly quick-minded child – soon added French and English to his Polish, Yiddish and Russian, and while Nina took on any odd jobs she could find to pay for their two-room apartment in Nice, Roman concentrated on his studies.

Nina had the highest possible hopes for her son: not only that he would be a famous ambassador or politician, but that he would write great novels, be the next Victor Hugo, and have all the most beautiful women in the world 'dying at his feet'. Unbelievably, all these predictions came very close to coming true. It would be decades before Roman's breathtakingly beautiful film-star wife, Jean Seberg, would be found dead in the back of a car round the corner from their Paris home. But not long after graduating, he did indeed become a successful diplomat, ending up as the first secretary of the French delegation to the UN, a decorated war hero and a writer who knocked out prize-winning novels (both in French and English) at a rate of knots.

But first, Roman decided to change his name. As he later recalled:

> I sat day after day in my little room, waiting for inspiration to visit me, trying to invent a pseudonym that would express, in a combination of noble and striking sounds,

our dream of artistic achievement, a pen-name grand enough to compensate for my own feeling of insecurity and helplessness at the idea of everything my mother expected from me.

In 1935 he decided on the new spelling Romain, modifying it again while fighting for the Free French Air Force in England in 1940 to Roman Gary. After being awarded both the Croix de Guerre and the Légion d'Honneur, he returned to France, this time to Paris, to embark on his dual careers in the Foreign Service and literature.

Gary's first published work, *A European Education* (1945) was hailed by Jean-Paul Sartre as the best novel ever written about the Resistance. Its gripping investigation into man's potential for evil revolves around a young boy from Lithuania who is caught up in the ravages of war, and it set the agenda for the dozens of other books he would produce throughout his life. It also won the Prix de Critiques and soared to the top of the bestseller lists.

He continued to publish novels about war, cultural collisions, Jewishness, mothers and his own life, and although Nina had died aged fifty-nine without seeing him being awarded his first prize, her presence lingered in the form of an internalized 'witness' about which he would speak and write, in his classic account of their relationship *La Promesse de l'Aube* (*Promise at Dawn*) with fascination and wit.

But by the late 1960s Gary was living glamorously with beautiful wife number one as an in-demand celebrity and great lover of life but felt his writing was stuck in a rut. He had been trying to escape the confines of his earlier works, which were seen as traditional and predictable, but in so doing had produced writing too strange and tricksy to be successful. His *Genghis Cohn*, in which the ghost of a Jewish stand-up comedian inhabits the body of his Nazi persecutor, hardly registered on the critical radar and he was considered as good as finished by the arbiters of French literary taste.

Then he had an idea. In 1973, when he was the same age as his mother had been when she died (a marker in life which often makes people do bold things), he gave birth to Émile Ajar.

Ajar was a troubled young Algerian with a past he was already keen to forget. A newly qualified doctor, he had come to Paris to seek a better life than his homeland could offer, but after accidentally killing a woman in a botched abortion, found himself being chased by the police. On a whim, he fled to Brazil, and it was from here that his manuscripts were now being smuggled out by an anonymous associate. Gary took two people into his confidence to help him make the hoax seem genuine, a friend in Brazil who could assist with the posting of documents and his young cousin Paul Pavlowitch, who was to play the part of Ajar on the phone and at a few rare public appearances. Dark and handsome and with a knack for accents, Pavlowitch played the part with élan, and the job sparked in him a fascination with literature and hoaxers which resulted in his writing the fictional biography of Patricia Highsmith's famous faker-hero, Ripley. But Ajar's writing, of course, was all Gary's. And it was so good that as soon as *Gros-Câlin* came out in 1974 the plaudits were rolling in just as they had at the beginning of his career. This first novel (called *Cuddles* in English) was a domestic tragi-comedy about the love between a lonely office worker and his pet snake. Ajar – whose name comes from the Russian and Romanian words for 'embers' – was hailed as the freshest new voice in French literature and despite the retrospectively obvious clue of the skin-shedding python playing a major part in the story (one character comments that 'We all have identity problems. Sometimes you have to recycle yourself elsewhere'), no one, for a while at least, suspected the author of any duplicity.

Cuddles was an instant bestseller but the second Ajar novel, *The Life Before Us*, did even better. It was translated into twenty-two languages, made into a film and sold millions of copies all over the world. Its appeal was in its inimical narrator Mohammed, commonly known as Momo. Momo was a skinny orphan living in a deprived Paris suburb with the geriatric, morbidly obese Madame Rosa, a former prostitute and Holocaust survivor. Rosa had plied her trade all across Europe and North Africa after being liberated from Auschwitz, and now took in the unwanted children of other prostitutes and tried, feebly, to keep them on the straight and narrow. She spoke a mixture of Yiddish and Arabic to Momo, who, at fourteen, was exactly the same age as Gary had been when he arrived in France with his mother. Although a few critics picked up strains of anti-Semitism in the North African novelist's Rabelaisian anti-heroine, most reviewers were in awe at this remarkable new voice. In fact, the same writer who had opined in *Le Canard Enchaîné* that old Gary was now 'creatively impotent' dubbed his alter ego 'pure talent'.

Gary looked on at what his creation was achieving with a mixture of pride and despair. And when *The Life Before*

Us was awarded the Prix Goncourt, he knew his hoax had truly triumphed. He tried to turn it down, communicating through a lawyer that Ajar didn't need it, but of course that was not allowed, so he became the first and so far as we know the only illicit double-winner of that famous accolade.

Even before the award of the Goncourt in 1975, some academics and journalists had started to wonder whether this mysterious Algerian doctor-turned-novelist wasn't in fact someone more established writing incognito. But it was not until the publisher Lynda Noël reported seeing the a manuscript of Ajar's in Gary's apartment that the rumours started in earnest, and critics began to see similarities in theme and tone between Ajar and Gary. In an article in *Paris Match* by Laure Boulay the accusation was explicitly made, but a seemingly indignant Gary responded by accusing his alter ego of plagiarism.

No one ever managed to squeeze a confession out of Gary, at least not until he could do it exactly on his own terms. Terms which turned out to be posthumous. In the bedroom of his elegant Paris home on a wintry day in 1980 Gary, newly widowed after the suicide of Jean Seberg and tired of a life where the only literary credibility he could get was that ascribed to a younger, more exotic man than he, shot himself in the head. He left behind a note instructing his executors to publish his final confession, *The Life and Death of Émile Ajar*: a memoir in which he tells the full story of the hoax for the first and last time and which constitutes one of the longest and most engaging sucide notes in history. It is remarkably full of life and ends with the words: 'I've had a lot of fun. Thank you, and goodbye.'

One brilliant and unique writer was born in Vilnia in 1914 and in Paris on 2 December 1980, in the same instant, two were lost to the world.

ALAN SOKAL

*I*N 1996 AN eminent physicist from New York University called Alan Sokal submitted a paper called 'Transgressing the boundaries: towards a transformative hermeneutics of quantum theory' to the journal *Social Text*. This was a post-modern cultural studies publication produced co-operatively under the auspices of Duke University Press and edited by, amongst other, the controversial critic Andrew Ross.

The journal had been seeking papers for a special edition called 'Science Wars' which was to focus on the perceived battle between conventional scientists and those post-modernist sociologists who felt that scientific intellectual practice is marred by prejudicial attitudes to gender, race and class (social constructionists, in other words). These theorists, while writing about science, often boasted that they had no formal training in the field and even suggested that this would only hamper their thinking about the real issues at stake. They might have guessed that that sort of attitude would be a red rag to bullish scientists from America's traditional universities. But controversy was not something the *Social Text*-ers feared. On the contrary, it was their stock in trade: when Ross said, in the aftermath of what would be one of the most embarrassing literary hoaxes ever to hit American academia, 'I am glad to be rid of English departments. I hate literature, for one thing, and English departments tend to be full of people who love literature', no one was much surprised.

In the spring of 1996 Sokal turned out to be the only 'proper' scientist to have contributed to the 'Science Wars' edition. Not one of life's natural pranksters, he was nonetheless moved to commit his hoax after being inspired by a book he had recently read which collected together all the nonsense that was currently being spoken about science by non-scientists and exposed it for the vacuous and vain cant it was. The book was Paul Gross and Norman Levitt's *Higher Superstition: The Academic Left and Its Quarrels With Science* (Johns Hopkins University Press, 1994) and it had a profound effect on the physicist and others like him. He followed up the references provided by Gross and Levitt to various famous contemporary critics (known as the Academic Left because of their sensitivity to social issues like class) who, with little or no grounding in formal science, were attacking experienced practitioners like Sokal and, what's more, getting their findings published in famous journals.

Armed with this information, he came up with a plan to get these charlatans to hoist themselves by their own petard. And publicly. The paper he submitted was utter gibberish. He quoted all the trendy American and French theorists beloved by the editors of the journal, flattering *Social Text*'s general ideology but containing jokes, bloopers and non sequiturs that any scientist or mathematician would have spotted immediately. Some of his sentences contained absolutely no sense at all, being syntactically correct but completely devoid of meaning (afterwards, he confessed that 'I tried hard to produce [more of] them, but I found that, save for rare bursts of inspiration, I just didn't have the knack.'

The entire paper can be read online at the website of New York University physics department (http://www. physics.nyu.edu/faculty/sokal/transgress_v2/transgress_ v2_singlefile.html) and to anyone unfamiliar with the language of post-modernist scientific theory it reads about as absurdly as it ought to have done to an editorial panel of genuine sociologists.

Unfortunately for Ross and his colleagues, part of *Social Text*'s ethos of broad-mindedness was that it had no peer review process – that vital safety net that prevents most academic publications from being made fools of. The periodical had been set up in 1979 as a broadly Marxist collective, its editors believing that mainstream liberal thinking was redundant and that a new Chomskyan/ Lacanian/Foucaultian paradigm should be put in place to answer the crucial ideological questions of the day, it chose not to submit its contributors to the same editorial strictures that more conventional journals use.

So, despite a few misgivings about the style in which Sokal's paper was written, which were overlooked because the editors were glad to have the input of an experienced physicist, 'Science Wars' went to press in May 1996. The very same day of publication, Sokal confessed to what he'd done in another academic journal, *Lingua Franca*, and laid out his reasons for transgressing the bond of trust between academics.

The reason, he said, was not to defend science from the barbarian hordes of lit crit (we'll survive just fine, thank you) but to defend the Left from a trendy segment of itself.

He described what he had done as a necessary 'pastiche of left-wing cant, fawning references, grandiose quotations . . . structured around the silliest quotations I could find about mathemetics and physics', and expressed no remorse at having pulled one over on Ross and his fellows.

Of course, the editors of *Social Text* were angry with him, accusing him of having defrauded and humiliated them with his dishonest trickery. However, in an attempt to save face they also maintained that 'its status as parody does not alter substantially our interest in the piece itself as a symptomatic document'.

Sokal replied by saying his hoax article was 'an annotated bibliography of charlatanism and nonsense by dozens of prominent French and American intellectuals. This goes well beyond the narrow category of "postmodernism," and includes some of the most fashionable thinkers in "science studies," literary criticism, and cultural studies' and before long the scientific community had weighed in on both sides, with famous names such as Richard Dawkins lending his support to Sokal, who was seen as a crusader for honesty and truth in a scientific community beset by fantasy and hot air.

A couple of years after the hoax that lifted Sokal out of his relatively unglamorous corner of scientific endeavour and made him famous even outside the scientific community, he co-wrote a full-length study of the wrongs he had tried to expose with the French writer Jean Bricmont. *Fashionable Nonsense: Postmodern Intellectuals' Abuse of Science* (Picador USA, 1998) contains a long list of extracts of writings from well-known intellectuals containing what the authors characterize as blatant abuses of scientific terminology. The book received rave reviews from within and without the scientific community and now Sokal is a highly respected professor of mathematics at University College London as well as lecturing globally on the subject of pseudoscience. But it was the unfortunate editors of *Social Text* who came away from the affair with silverware. They may not have won many academic plaudits, but in 1996 they were the awarded the IgNobel Prize for Literature.

BEVIS HILLIER

*L*ITERARY LONDON AT the dawn of the twenty-first century is a fairly gentle place. So when a real live literary feud bubbles to the surface (especially one which involves swearing, low-down trickery and public humiliation) journalists, readers and even sometimes the feuders themselves tend to rub their hands in glee and wallow in the excitement of it all.

So it was in August 2006 when the *Sunday Times* revealed that one of the nation's best loved poets, John Betjeman, had become posthumously embroiled in a literary hoax which brought shame to one of his biographers and sheer delight to another.

The two biographers were A.N. Wilson, a London journalist and writer known for his sharp-tongue and scattering caricatures of his fellow literary players, and Bevis Hillier, the official biographer of Betjeman whose lifelong dedication to his subject has produced three volumes of well-received biography and landed him, in his retirement, in the very genteelly poor surroundings of the medieval almshouse of St Cross in Winchester. Hillier first approached Betjeman about writing his life in 1976. He was a young journalist who, after Oxford, had worked on *The Times* before becoming editor of the *Connoisseur* magazine but whose real loves were poetry, art and design. A colleague had introduced him to the aged poet in the mid-seventies and the two had got on well. Betjeman was happy to authorize this enthusiastic young man to write about him, but could not have anticipated the single-mindedness and passion with which the project would be pursued. For the next twenty-eight years Hillier would live and breathe his beloved subject, and in 1988, 2002 and 2004 his hard work was rewarded with ecstatic reviews as each volume was published. Professor John Carey in the *Sunday Times* referred to 'a model of biography', John Bayley called it 'brilliant . . . utterly utterly compelling' and the *Financial Times'* reviewer recommended volume three as a 'magnificent . . . cultural monument'. Others followed suit, but the exception to these encomia was one influential London magazine which poured scorn on the work from a great height: the *Spectator* gave volumes one and two blisteringly rotten reviews, and the two men who wrote them were A. N. Wilson and Richard Ingrams.

As soon as Hillier, in the bucolic surrounds of his Winchester almshouse, saw those articles calling his work 'a hopeless mish-mash' and 'undercooked', his hackles rose. He knew both men to be friends with Betjeman's daughter, Candida Lycett-Green, and he knew that she was no fan of his. (She disapproved of his take on her father's life and her daughter had even written a thinly disguised put-down of a man with 'no social graces . . . let's call him Bevis' in the *Oldie*, Richard Ingrams' magazine.) The

Wilson review particularly irked Hillier because he had long considered the man to be something of a bully and a snob and had been engaged in low-level feuding with him for some time. He therefore delighted in getting back at him by selecting Wilson's books *The Victorians* and *My Name Is Legion* as his 'non-books of the year' in the very magazine which had published the bad reviews. This act unleashed a brace of bitchy attacks on Hillier in Wilson's column in the *Telegraph*, referring to his rival as 'old, malignant and pathetic'.

If they were rivals then, they would become more so shortly after when, just as Hillier's final volume of Betjeman's biography – the crowning glory of his life's work, no less – was ready for publication Wilson announced that he, too, would be presenting a biography of the poet. Hillier's blood, quite understandably, began to boil when he heard this. Not only was his well-connected, high-profile enemy threatening to steal his fire in the very year of Betjeman's centenary, 2006, but he thought it unlikely that Wilson would have time to do much in the way of original research and so would draw heavily on his own three volumes of work, even though he had derided them in the books pages of the *Spectator*. Hillier decided, therefore, to orchestrate a grand literary hoax to show Wilson up as the careless and opportunistic writer he suspected him of being.

It was the work of moments to have some writing paper and visiting cards printed up bearing the name of an imaginary lady called Eve de Harben who lived in a flat in Roquebrune on the Côte d'Azur. He decided, correctly as it turned out, that although this name was unusual, Wilson would not immediately notice it is an anagram of 'Ever

Been Had', and he proceeded to concoct a false and saucy piece of evidence about Betjeman's love life which he felt sure would make it into Wilson's book.

The love-letter was from Betjeman to an Irishwoman called Honor Tracy during the war, and although the original had, according to Eve, been sold to an American autograph dealer, a copy had been passed down to her father, and she now enclosed that facsimile for Wilson's use. The letter reads as follows:

Darling Honor,

I loved yesterday. All day, I've thought of nothing else. No other love I've had means so much. Was it just an aberration on your part, or will you meet me at Mrs Holmes's again – say on Saturday. I won't be able to sleep until I have your answer.

Love has given me a miss for so long, and now this miracle has happened. Sex is a part of it, of course, but I have a Romaunt of the Rose feeling about it too. On Saturday we could have lunch at Fortt's, then go back to Mrs H's. Never mind if you can't make it then. I am free on Sunday too or Sunday week. Signal me tomorrow as to whether you can come.

Anthony Powell has written to me, and mentions you admiringly. Some of his comments about the Army are v funny. He's somebody I'd like to know better when the war is over. I find his letters funnier than his books.

Tinkerty-tonk, my darling. I pray I'll hear from you tomorrow.

If I don't I'll visit your office in a fake beard.

All love, JB

As well as not noticing the anagrammatic nature of his correspondent's name, Wilson had no reason to look closely at the first letters of each sentence in the body of the text and see that, taken as an acrostic, they spelled out 'A N WILSON IS A SHIT'.

(It is unknown how Hillier decided upon that phrase in particular, but he may well have been inspired by the diary entry of one of Wilson's more famous enemies, which described him in such terms after accusing him of the most ungentlemanly act an Englishman can commit – making public a private conversation between members of the royal family at a dinner party.)

Into Wilson's biography the letter went. And on the day of publication, as his friends were congratulating him on his timely and jolly book, an anxious sexagenarian in Winchester ran down from the Hospital of St Cross to the old bookshop behind the college to see if his ruse had worked. Barely able to breathe for fear that the letter would not have made it in or, worse, that Wilson would have abridged it somehow and ruined the all-important acrostic, he purchased a copy of his enemy's book. Out in the street he turned to the index. The entry for Honor referred him to page 154, and there it was in all its splendour.

Passers-by might have mistaken the jig-dancing, air-punching gentleman in the street for a lunatic, or a drunk waiting anxiously for the nearby Wykeham Arms to open. But for Hillier this was the greatest trick he had ever played in his life; he immediately felt the weight of Wilson's snobbism and unkindness lifting from his shoulders and dissolving in a delightful cloud of comic retribution.

Hillier is not alone in feeling that Wilson, although a talented and popular writer, has something of the naughty playground bully about him, so it is unsurprising that the English (and indeed American) press seized on this hoax with glee. The *Sunday Times* broke the story when somebody recognized the return address on Eve's letter to be the same as Hillier's sister's in the south of France. Gladly, Bevis Hillier admitted what he had done. And publicly, at least, Wilson took the hoax in good spirit. But of course he removed the offending item from the next edition of his book and declined the invitation to bury the hatchet at a ceremony to unveil a blue plaque outside Betjeman's childhood home, where the two rival biographers could have met and shaken hands. But how much more fun for both of them, and us, that this feud should continue into the second decade of the century.

And there is little doubt that Betjeman himself would have loved every minute of it.

WILLIAM BOYD

T HE GLITTERING PARTY in Manhattan was still in full swing as the clock struck midnight and the date rolled over to the first of April, 1998. The date on the invitation obviously had not deterred such cultural luminaries as Jay McInerney, Siri Hustvedt and Julian Schnabel, who had all turned up at the undeniably hot spot that is Jeff Koons' studio to celebrate the launch of the biography of Nat Tate, forgotten star of abstract expressionism and a martyr to the cause of artistic celebrity.

The book, *Nat Tate: An American Artist 1928–1960* was

by the celebrated English novelist William Boyd who had long been interested in the vibrant art world of New York in the 1950s and, while researching the potent mix of fame, money and intoxicants that propelled painters like Jackson Pollock on to the scene in the post-war period, had, he told interviewers, come upon the tragic life story and intriguing canvases of Tate. In 1960 Tate had killed himself by jumping off the Staten Island ferry after visiting Georges Braque and realizing he would never attain anything like the renown of the Frenchman. He was only thirty-one when he died, had destroyed most of his work in a fit of pique and left not a single known relative, his only family having been the mother who was run over by a bus when he was still a child. But in his short lifetime he had known Picasso, partied with Gore Vidal, made love to Peggy Guggenheim and created work which Boyd, for one, and David Bowie, for another (who happened to be a director of the company who published the biography) thought had real power. Some of his rare, remaining canvases were reproduced in the book, and at the launch party people cooed over the artist who, although admittedly marginal, was clearly a significant member of America's most turbulent school of painting. At one point in the evening David Bowie got up and read from the book, and afterwards more than one critic was heard to say they had known about Tate's work for years. Which was quite some achievement considering he was a figment of William Boyd's imagination.

Boyd, however, had not been motivated by the desire to expose *le tout* New York as celeb-hungry gulls, although that was an inevitable side-effect of the prank. He was, as he explained later in the *Sunday Telegraph*, attempting 'to make something entirely invented seem astonishingly real' in a writerly exercise of fictionalized biography. 'And the fundamental aim of the book,' he went on, 'was to destabilise, to challenge our notions of authenticity.'

Boyd had begun practising this art in his 1987 novel *The New Confessions* and finally perfected it in his brilliant journal of the (imaginary) minor cultural figure Logan Mountstuart, *Any Human Heart*. Indeed Mountstuart, who first appeared in a short story in 1995, appears, in his incarnation as a 1960s New York art dealer, as a key commentator in Tate's biography.

The story of how Boyd came to conceive the Tate hoax is fascinating in itself. Years before, he had been asked, along with twenty-five other writers, to contribute an entry to David Hockney's illustrated *Alphabet*, and came up with the non-existent Laotian philosopher Nguyen N, whose aphoristic jottings had been briefly popular in inter-war Paris. He referred to his seminal work, *Les Analects de Nguyen N*, and much to his amazement found himself talking to someone at the book's launch party who not only claimed to know *Les Analects*, but had recently heard of a wealthy book-buyer who was after a first edition. This gave Boyd pause for thought. He realized that it would be entirely possible to construct a plausible life through things like fake library records, old photographs, quotes from well-known writers and academic-style citations, and create an enjoyable book in the process.

A few years later, as an editorial board-member of the magazine *Modern Painters*, he found himself discussing ways in which the magazine might start publishing fiction as well as criticism and interviews. It suddenly occurred to him that he was looking at the ideal opportunity to perform his biographical magic trick. So, with the collusion not only of the magazine but with Picasso's biographer John Richardson and Gore Vidal (who both gave fake quotes about Tate for the book), David Bowie and the editors of the *Sunday Telegraph* (who agreed to run an extract), the hoax began to take shape.

21 Publishing, the firm who finally brought out the book in 1998, were perhaps even more excited than Boyd about seeing the effect this new lost celebrity would have on the current show-offs of the art world. As its director Karen Wright said: 'We were very amused that people kept saying "Yes, I've heard of him." There is a willingness not to appear foolish. Critics are too proud for that.'

As for the debunking of this gentle yet culturally significant hoax, Boyd said that he had hoped the truth would slowly dawn on readers as they picked up on the many 'covert and cryptic clues and hints as to its real, fictive status' he had planted in it. The subject's name alone should have rung bells for anyone familiar with the two most famous art galleries in Britain. As it was, a journalist from the *Independent* overheard two people who were in on the deception discussing it shortly before the London launch and forced a swift admission from Boyd after exposing him in print.

Although the fawning guests at the New York party might have been a little embarrassed about being duped, the fact that Boyd is that rare thing, an entirely serious but very well-liked and indeed fun writer (and that no one who was going to either earn or spend money on the book had been deceived) meant no one could complain seriously about the literary daedalics which turned out to be as equally edifying as diverting for all concerned. However, as he admitted recently in a *Guardian* article recalling those days in April 1998, even this most intellectual brand of hoaxing began to tax his conscience rather unpleasantly by the time of his unmasking:

> For any hoax to work there has to be a great deal of convincing mendacity. Things had got out of hand – it had all got too big and high profile. Angst had set in. Duplicity, pretence, obfuscation, covering tracks, ambiguities and evasions are all polite descriptions of 'telling lies'.